HOUSES OF LIFE

Jewish Cemeteries of Europe

JOACHIM
JACOBS

Contents

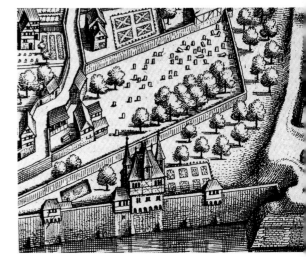

It gives me great pleasure to introduce to the British and American public this survey of 2000 years of Jewish cemeteries in Europe. In their enormous diversity, these cemeteries mirror the multiplicity and changing nature of Jewish societies in different eras, countries and cultures.

Surveying two millennia of 'Houses of Life', from the ruins of the catacombs of Rome to a new extension to a Berlin burial site designed by the author, I cannot help but feel pride in Jewish resilience and creativity. In the face of pogrom, deadly persecution and restriction, the Jewish peoples adhered to their way of life, even in death.

In its own way, this history of European cemeteries is a commemoration of Jewish struggle and a celebration of Jewish success through the millennia.

The *Shoah* is the great horror in this history, with most of those murdered not having found a place in a 'House of Life'. But New York's Museum of Jewish Heritage —A Living Memorial to the Holocaust —

with its Garden of Stones is a memorial to those whose ashes were dumped in the ponds of Auschwitz. The Garden of Stones also honours those who survived and who fought Nazism.

After the *Shoah* and the fall of the Iron Curtain, and notwithstanding present pressures, we see a Jewish renaissance in Europe today. This renaissance demonstrates how Jewish life flourishes as soon as freedom of thought, speech and religion become accepted rules of society.

Consequently, the book ends with cemeteries built in recent years by communities that hold in their hearts a strong sense of their local identity as well as the recognition of the importance of the state of Israel as a stronghold for Jews all over the world.

Robert M. Morgenthau has been the District Attorney for New York County since 1975. He is chairman of the Museum of Jewish Heritage in New York.

The Schmidl family vault at Budapest Kozma Utca cemetery by Béla Lajta, 1904.

Seventeenth-century tombstones at the Sephardic cemetery of Ouderkerk, Amsterdam, the Netherlands.

Introduction

Interior of the Katz-Lachmann family mausoleum (built 1910) in Weissensee, Berlin.

The Talmud,[1] the Jewish commentary on the Mishnah, describes how Adam and Eve learned the art of burial by watching how one raven buried the corpse of another in the sand. In the first Book of Moses (Genesis), after the flood and many generations later, Abraham, the father of the Hebrews, introduced the faith of his 'One and Only God' and thus becoming the founder of monotheism. When his wife Sarah died, Abraham, in order to bury her, acquired a field with a cave. The purchase of this field and Sarah's burial are described in depth, and it is here that the origins of Jewish burial culture and Jewish burial places are recorded, bound as they are into the traditions and customs of other Semitic peoples from the Near and Middle East. Over the course of centuries, they developed into what is now a specifically Jewish set of customs for dealing with death and the deceased, and these customs are still based on the very centre of Jewish life, the Torah, the Five Books of Moses, which Jews took with them wherever they went or were forced to go. It is the Torah which saved them and their identity as a people over the millennia, against all odds, in good and in bad times, during times of tolerance, through persecution and pogroms.

First, Abraham asks the leaders of the town now known as Hebron if he might purchase a family burial plot from them. They offer him the opportunity to bury Sarah in one of their finest graves. But Abraham declines. He insists on his own burial plot and, by so doing, founds the tradition of separate, solely Jewish burial sites.

'So the field of Ephron, which was in Machpelah, which was before Mamre, the field, and the cave which was therein, and all the trees that were in the field, that were in all the borders thereof or round about, were made sure unto Abraham for a possession in the presence of the children of Heth, before all that went in at the gate of his city.

And after this, Abraham buried Sarah his wife in the cave of the field of Machpelah before Mamre – the same is Hebron in the land of Canaan.

And the field, and the cave that is therein, were made sure unto Abraham for a possession of a burying-place by the children of Heth.'
(Gen. or First Book of Moses 23:17-20)

A few years after Sarah, Abraham died too.

'And Abraham expired, and died in a good old age, an old man, and full of years; and was gathered to his people.

And Isaac and Ishmael his sons buried him in the cave of Machpelah, in the field of Ephron the son of Zohar the Hittite, which is before Mamre.'
(Gen. 25:8-9)

During a long famine, Jacob, the son of Isaac, the son of Abraham, moved with his family to Egypt, where his son Joseph, who had been sold by his brothers into slavery, had become the second most powerful man after the pharaoh. When he reached a very old age, just before his death, he asked his sons to bury him in Canaan:

'I am to be gathered unto my people; bury me with my fathers in the cave that is in the field of Ephron the Hittite.

In the cave that is in the field of Machpelah, which is before Mamre, in the land of Canaan, which Abraham bought with the field from Ephron the Hittite for a possession of a burying-place.

There they buried Abraham and Sarah his wife;

there they buried Isaac and Rebecca his wife; and there I buried Leah.' (Gen. 49:29-31)

In the first Book of Moses, a lot of text is devoted to the description of the burial places of the patriarchs. For the nomadic family of Abraham, the burial place in Hebron was a place of return and permanence; it was the only land they had bought in their lives, and this at a high cost. The Bible relates almost nothing about the dwelling places or tents of the sons and daughters of Abraham; they prayed in the open countryside, in the places where they roamed as nomads and where God appeared to them. The opening chapters of the Bible therefore describe all the elements that in later centuries would define the lives of the Hebrews, the Israelites and the Jews: an inconstancy in terms of living places — mostly involuntary — and a constancy in the locations in which the dead are laid to rest. Just like Abraham, Isaac and Jacob, Sarah, Rebecca , Rachel and Leah, the Jews of later generations were able to pray everywhere: in small rooms and chambers, in the temple in Jerusalem or in synagogues. For prayer, it is not the place, but rather the time that is important: morning, midday and evening, and special periods during festivals.

The burial place, the cemetery, on the other hand, was always a specific, definite place in the lives of the Jews. As it was for Abraham, the purchase of a piece of land to establish a cemetery was always the first step in the process of establishing a link to a new location. It was not - and still is not - a synagogue that a group of Jews settling in a new location would establish first, but rather they would create a cemetery as soon as the first member of the community died. Prayers would be held in the smallest *stibln* (small rooms), often rented from non-Jews, it being felt that the beauty of synagogues was a distraction to concentration during prayer. The burial ground had, if possible, to be bought through a commercial transaction. Often, however, Jews were not allowed to buy land, so they at least attempted to lease the plot for centuries, in the hope that they would later be able to purchase it. These sites are intended to be the resting place of the dead until the coming of the Messiah and the subsequent resurrection of the dead. This is why

Jewish cemeteries are also known as *beth olam*, or 'house of eternity'. The euphemism *beth hachaim*, or 'house of life', is also used, however, probably because Jews love life this side of the grave and are sceptical about life beyond it, long harbouring doubts over the existence and nature of the afterlife. Perhaps the most sobering name for a Jewish cemetery is *beit kevarot* (Neh. 2:3), or the 'house of graves'.

Over the centuries, since the cave of Machpelah was purchased around 1,800 years BCE, the appearance and design of Jewish burial places have changed repeatedly. Determined as they were by the society of the time, the natural geographic and topographic situation and people's changing ideas, Jewish burial places have never been the same at different times or in different places — and they will surely continue to change in centuries to come.

This book charts this process of change in Europe. Starting with the catacombs in Ancient Rome – the first major settlement of Jews in Europe – then proceeds it through the cemeteries of the Middle Ages on the Rhine, in Venice, Prague and England, moving across those of the Renaissance and the Baroque periods, of the Sephardim and the Ashkenazim in London, Amsterdam, Berlin, Krakow and Istanbul, and on to the cemeteries of the period of emancipation in Paris, Budapest, St Petersburg and Berlin, before returning back to Rome. But the Jews not only lived in big cities, but also in smaller towns and villages such as Venosa, Fürth, Endingen, Meinsdorf, Faro and the countless villages, or *shtetls*, of Eastern Europe. Hence the Galician cemeteries are also part of the Jewish legacy that was destroyed during the *Shoah*. After 1945, Jewish life tentatively began to re-emerge in many parts of Europe, but how is this returning life reflected in the continent's post-war cemeteries?

In the tradition of a history spanning two millennia, cemeteries will be described primarily from the point of view of their spatial, functional and aesthetic design. What did these burial places look like? How were their perimeters determined? What buildings did they incorporate? How were the graves arranged? Were there paths, tree-lined alleys and other features to make the cemeteries aesthetically pleasing? And what relationship did the cemeteries have with the Jews' places of residence? Cemeteries always reflect the Jews' specific living conditions in various locations at different times. The 'houses of life' reflect the houses of the living – an aspect that will be explored in detail later in this book. This study is hence a history of Jewish cemeteries, and so will focus less fully on the developmental history of Jewish gravestones, or sepulchral culture.[2]

Before starting this journey through two millennia of the 'houses of life', we will look at the religious background, how Jews deal with death and dying, and the rituals that accompany a Jew's final journey to the grave.

Life after death – eternity in Jewish belief

In the five Books of Moses, nowhere is the resurrection of the dead mentioned. There is no word of an afterworld, *olam haba*, to which people go after death. All that is said is that the dead 'return to their people'. Prophets such as Isaiah revere life, since only the living can serve and praise God:

'Behold, for peace I had great bitterness;
But thou hast in love to my soul delivered it from
the pit of corruption,
For thou hast cast all my sins behind thy back.
For the grave cannot praise thee,
Death cannot celebrate thee;
They that go down into the pit cannot hope for
thy truth.
The living, the living, he shall praise thee,
As I do this day.'
(Isa. 38:17-19)

The first references to resurrection appear only with the Book of Job:

'Lo, all these things worketh God
Oftentimes with man,
To bring back his soul from the pit,
To be enlightened with the light of the living.'
(Job 33:29-30)

In Ezekiel's vision, the process of resurrection is dramatically described:

'The hand of the Lord was upon me, and carried me out in the spirit of the Lord, and set me down in the midst of the valley which was full of bones. …

And he said to me, 'Son of man, can these bones live?' …

So I prophesied as I was commanded; and as I prophesied, there was a noise, and behold a shaking; and the bones came together, bone to his bone.

And when I beheld, lo, the sinews and the flesh came upon them, and the skin covered them above … and the breath came into them, and they lived, and stood upon their feet, an exceeding great army. …

Thus saith the Lord God: "Behold, O my people, I will open your graves, and cause you to come up out of your graves, and bring you into the land of Israel… ."

And [I] shall put my spirit in you, and ye shall live, and I shall place you in your own land.'
(Ezek. 37:1-14)

In Daniel, a vision of eternal life is finally developed in full, and is already intertwined with the distinction between good and evil:

'And many of them that sleep in the dust of the earth shall awake, some to everlasting life, and some to shame and everlasting contempt.
And they that be wise shall shine as the brightness of the firmament;
and they that turn many to righteousness
as the stars for ever and ever.'
(Daniel 12:2-3)

With Ezekiel, the idea of physical resurrection becomes the fundamental doctrine of Jewish belief. The rabbis of the post-Biblical period, drawing on the exodus from Israel, ultimately associate resurrection with the end of the period of exile. 'All of Israel has a share in the world to come, as it is said (Isa. 60:21). And the people who have a claim to it, in the end they will inherit the earth. And he who says that there is no

resurrection of the dead will forfeit his share in the world to come.' (Mishnah, Sanhedrin 10:1)

Care for body and soul – Jewish burial rituals

This doctrine of physical, and not just spiritual, resurrection has far-reaching consequences for the development of burial rituals in Judaism. Since both the body and soul of the dead will be resurrected, the corpse must also remain intact until it decays naturally. It must be afforded great respect, care and attention, whereas, in the Christian faith, the resurrection relates more to the soul than the body, whose handling is accorded less attention after death. 'This element may well be responsible for the original differences in the relation of Christian and Jewish living to their dead and, by extension, for the separation of Jewish and Christian burial grounds.'[3] The early consolidation of the doctrine of physical resurrection led to the forms of Jewish burial rituals becoming largely complete even by Talmudic times, i.e. 500 CE. 'A Christian burial of the Middle Ages – or even of the eighteenth century – can be clearly distinguished from a present-day burial, yet Jewish practices, by contrast, seem to have remained largely unchanged. From the time of the Mishnah and the Tannaim, the basic elements resting on the idea of individual and corporeal resurrection have led to a ritualization that seems to have evolved without fundamental modification. These elements, bound to conceptions of the relation between the living and the dead body, have remained the same.'[4]

So it is no surprise that the classic and normative text on burial rituals is found in the Talmudic treatise of Evel Rabbati, written in around 300. The treatise in question is euphemistically entitled *semachot* (rejoicings) and contains the most important instructions and laws governing the process of dying, death, burial and mourning. Although some of these conditions have been abandoned or amended over the centuries in accordance with local, varying customs (*minhagim*), the core elements have always been passed on. These include the laws that affect the *Cohanim*, the descendents of the *Cohen Gadol*, the high priest Aaron, brother of Moses. Since *Cohanim* performed their office in the temple, they had to be ritually pure. This included the stipulation that they must not contaminate themselves by coming into contact with the deceased. They were only permitted to enter grave-yards to bury parents and siblings. But to enable them at least to take part in burials by watching, separate forecourts or windows were created in the cemetery walls, as is the case in Worms, or special funeral paths were created, as in the Schönhauser Allee in Berlin. Special burial grounds were also reserved for the *Cohanim* near the entrances. A few of these rules have been relaxed today, and most *Cohanim* now enter cemeteries if certain rules are observed. An example of this is the Scholzplatz cemetery in Berlin, which has an extended area built in 2000.

Burial societies

The duty to look after the sick and dying and to take care of the burial of the dead has been one of the most profound commandments (*mitzvot*) of Judaism since Biblical times. The care of the dead and their burial in particular is regarded as especially commendable, since no thanks can be expected from the recipients in this world. Following the principle that nobody shall benefit from another's death, honorary burial societies known as the *Chevra Kaddisha Gomel Chassadim* (religious society of those who carry out charitable deeds) were established from the end of the thirteenth century, initially in Spain. Their organizational structures, with binding statutes, the power to impose sanctions and the obligation to provide assistance, may have been based on models taken from Christian guilds and associations. Probably with the expulsion of the Jews in 1492, they then spread to Central and Eastern Europe,[5] notably to Prague where a *chevra kaddisha* was founded in 1564 by Rabbi Eliezer Aschkenazi, and which since that time has been in charge of maintaining the city's cemeteries. Their strict rules and regulations, compiled in 1692 into a book of statutes entitled the *Pinkas ha-takanot*, became the model for many of the other burial

societies founded later across Europe, which tended cemeteries until the nineteenth century. The members of the *chevra* had to be elderly, married and pious men who had the necessary knowledge and skills to provide the sick and dying with practical, religious and emotional support. A *chevra* always had to have eighteen members; numbers are depicted in Hebrew script with letters, with the word for 'eighteen', when read, meaning 'alive'. Membership of a *chevra* was regarded as an exceptional honour and so only the most respected men of the community were included. Since the washing and dressing of female corpses must be taken care of by women, there were – and still are – sisterhoods to carry out this task.

The activities of burial societies were financed by pious gifts (*tsedaka*), which is why the collection of donations (*tsedaka* boxes) is often shown in historical depictions of burials. The donated money was used for welfare programmes and to bury impoverished Jews, but also to fund the hospitals and orphanages run by the *chevra*. The burial societies therefore served both rich and poor, literally from cradle to grave.

Thanks to their strong position – they had their own direct income and often owned the cemeteries – the burial societies evolved 'into a powerful, de facto autonomous interim structure'.[6] This led in the nineteenth century to more and more conflicts with community leaders, who were trying to 'take the burial societies more under their wing'.[7]

The Prague Paintings

Around 1772, the Prague burial society commissioned paintings that depicted the various stages from the sick- and death-bed to burial in the cemetery. The paintings clearly show various actions and rites associated with a Jew's final journey. It is an exemplary snapshot of the evolution of a ritual, parts of which have changed repeatedly, in accordance with local conditions and the ideas of various ethnic groups within the Jewish faith. There are differences, for example, between the Sephardim, who walk around the coffin seven times (*hakafot*) in the house of mourning, and the Ashkenazim, who don't perform this ritual at all. The basic structure of the sequence, as shown in the paintings, however, has always been retained.

At the same time, there are similarities with Christian mourning customs, such as the opening of a window in the room where death has occurred or the covering of mirrors. These also include the idea of a 'death in a social setting' – of being surrounded by family and fellow believers in one's final hours. Jewish and Christian worlds have often influenced each other in this respect.

1. The sick-bed

In the bedroom of an affluent house a very sick man lies in bed. Beside the bed sits a physician, taking the patient's pulse and dispensing medicine. The wife and son of the sick man stand at the foot of the bed, with a visitor at the head. The visitor is fulfilling an important commandment or *mitzvah*: visiting the sick, or *bikur holim*, which has a crucial place in Judaism. It does so for three reasons: the visitor may learn how to cure other sick people; he can help the patient in his suffering and also help his soul through prayer.

2. The death-bed

Now, the angel of death (*malach hamaveth*) approaches. Gathered around the man's bed are the members of the *chevra kaddisha*, joining each other in prayer. They hold candles, since the human soul is associated with light ('The spirit of man is the candle of the Lord', Prov. 20:27). The weeping mother is leading the young son from the room. If possible, a dying man should confess his sins (*vidui*) and his last words should be those of 'Shema Israel', which reveres the uniqueness of God.

The sick-bed, from the Prague Cycle, around 1772.

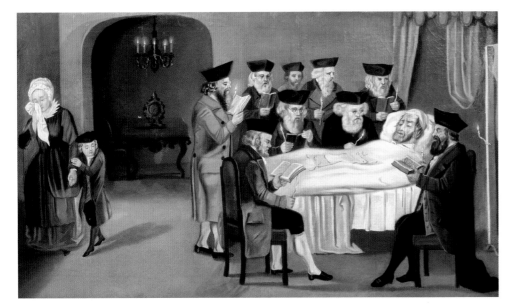

TOP: The death-bed.
BOTTOM: After death.
Both from the Prague Cycle,
around 1772

3. After death

The windows are opened and the mirror covered, so the soul may leave the room. The painting shows the deceased being carefully shrouded in linen by the *chevra kaddisha* and laid on the floor. In the background, a man prays and a candle is held up. (As all this went on, relatives not shown in the picture would have been tearing parts of their clothes as a sign of grief.)

4. The bearing of the body

The body is carried from the house of mourning, and it is customary to give alms en route to the cemetery. Where possible, the deceased is buried on the same or next day, unless it is the *Shabbat* or a holiday. So swift a burial method led in the late eighteenth and nine-teenth centuries to serious fears that comatose people were being buried alive. This concern was also discussed at length in the context of the *Haskala*, the Jewish Enlightenment. In various places, local leaders therefore introduced longer periods between death and burial, despite resistance from orthodox communities.

5. The making of the coffin

The members of the *chevra kaddisha* make the simple, plain coffin in the cemetery, while …

6. The making of the burial clothes

… also in the cemetery, a tailor, an assistant and two women make the burial clothes.

7. The digging of the grave

The grave is dug, and …

8. The journey to the cemetery

…the deceased is carried through a gate into the ceme-tery. The gate and the other constructions are adorned with blessings, and in the background we see the water basin for ritual handwashing, as well as an alms box.

9. *Tahara*

The body is carried to the house of purification – *beth tahara*. *Tahara* houses appeared in increasing number from the seventeenth century, for example in Worms. In earlier centuries, the preparation of bodies appears mostly to have taken place outside the ceme-teries, in living quarters. The cleansing of the body is a complex ritual, with details varying greatly from place to place.

While prayers are read, the body is washed with warm water, starting from the head and working down to the feet. An egg is often mixed with the water as a symbol of life. Nails are cleaned and the hair combed. The body is then sprinkled with wine and wrapped in the prepared burial clothes made from pure, white linen (*tachrichim*). These clothes comprise shirt, undershirt, smock, ruff and belt, stockings and cap. The deceased, thus clad, is placed in the coffin. Men are also buried with the prayer

TOP: The bearing
of the body.
MIDDLE: The making
of the coffin.
BOTTOM: The making
of the burial clothes.
All from the Prague Cycle,
around 1772

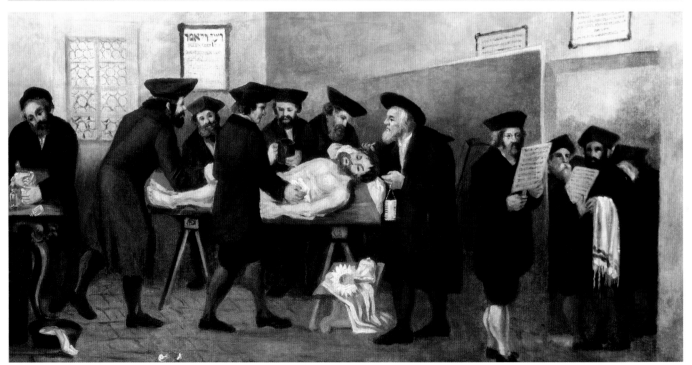

TOP: The digging of
the grave.
MIDDLE: The journey to
the cemetery.
BOTTOM: *Tahara.*
All from the Prague Cycle,
around 1772.

shawl (*tallit*) they wore in the synagogue, with the
fringes (*tzitzit*) removed. A prayer book is placed in
the coffin with the body. Since it is the wish of pious
Jews to be buried in 'Erez Israel', it is customary to
put a small bag of earth from the Holy Land under
the deceased's head. In some regions, pieces of broken
pottery are also placed over the eyes.

10. The funeral speech

The dead man, covered by his *tallit*, is carried from the
beth tahara and a rabbi delivers a funeral speech from
a pulpit.

11. Carrying the coffin to the grave

The deceased is then carried to the grave in the funeral procession. The director of the *chevra kaddisha*, the
rabbi and then the other male mourners follow the
coffin. Walking to the grave, the *hazan*, or cantor,
recites Psalm 91, which affirms the belief in God's care
of the individual, seven times.

12. The burial

At the prepared grave, the coffin is closed and
lowered into the ground. A prayer is said in which the
name of the deceased is read out. Each mourner
throws three shovelfuls of earth onto the coffin. Then,
either at the coffin or in a house of mourning, the
kaddish prayer is recited by the son or another male
relative of the deceased (or by a female relative if no
male kin are present). The mourners express their
sympathy to the bereaved.

13. Leaving the cemetery

When leaving the cemetery, all the mourners wash
their hands in a well by the exit, since cemeteries are
ritually unclean places. In many places, it is also
customary for mourners to throw tufts of grass behind
them on departure.

ABOVE: The funeral speech.
BELOW: Carrying the coffin
to the grave.
Both from the Prague Cycle,
around 1772.

Introduction

Friends and neighbours invite the bereaved to a meal of condolence after the burial. Then begins a seven-day period of mourning for the bereaved, during which they can neither work nor leave the house. They pray and sit only on low stools to do so (hence the expression 'sitting shiva', *shiva* being Hebrew for seven). During these seven days, the bereaved are supposed to be visited assiduously by friends and relatives. After this, a thirty-day, less strict period of

TOP: The burial.
MIDDLE: Leaving the cemetery.
BOTTOM: *Yahrzeit.*
All from the Prague Cycle,
around 1772.

mourning begins, known as the *shloshim* (thirty). Over the remaining eleven months, the 'orphan's *kaddish*' is recited every day for the deceased in the synagogue, as well as on the *yahrzeit*, the anniversary of the death.

14. *Yahrzeit*

Until the first *yahrzeit*, a headstone (*matzevah*) or sign (*ziyyun*) is erected at the head of the grave. Inscribed on these gravestones, which were often also made from

wood in the Middle Ages, is the name of the deceased, along with the name of the father, the Hebrew date of death (which counts from the creation of the world according to the Biblical calendar) and often the profession, honorary titles or descriptions of his or her achievements. The formulation of the headstone texts has varied over the centuries and indeed varies greatly from region to region. The appearance of the grave-stone has also changed constantly. Since they were

BELOW: Members of the *chevra*, from the Prague Cycle, around 1772.

The *chevra's* annual banquet, from the Prague Cycle, around 1772.

usually hewn by non-Jewish stonemasons, their design strongly reflects the stylistic trends of contemporary society. The journey from the small, simple nameplates of the ancient Roman catacombs and the heavy, rectangular and unadorned gravestones of the Middle Ages to the temple-like, monumental family burial plots of the nineteenth century, complete with photographs and lifelike busts of the deceased, has been a considerable one.

15 & 16. The members of the *chevra* and their annual banquet

The paintings illustrated here are by an unknown artist, and were commissioned by the then directors of the *chevra kaddisha* and were intended to grace its meeting room. So unique a project must be understood in the context of the period's historical background: 'The commissioning of the paintings was clearly inspired by an attempt to demonstrate, in the light of the new ideas of the Enlightenment, the importance of the role that the Burial Society had played in the Jewish community for centuries. It was through these paintings that the spirit of the emancipation first found its way into the Ghetto.'[8] The members of the *chevra kaddisha* pose proudly for a group portrait. The third figure from the left holds two *tsedaka* boxes in his hands, and it is striking that some are sporting fashionable styles of beard. Once a year, on the day of the new moon in the month of Tammus, the *chevra* would hold a banquet in its meeting room. They ate and drank – sharing a special cup – luxuriously and happily, thereby creating a balance with the solemn and sad duties they carried out during the rest of the year.

Pax Romana
From Hebron to Rome

In Erez Israel, as already described, it has been the norm since the time of the patriarchs to bury the dead in caves, as in Hebron, with the result that the majority of families buried their dead in their own, separate vaults. True cemeteries as communal burial places are found only in the post-Biblical period, although the Bible does mention 'the graves of the common people' in the Kidron Valley in Jerusalem (II Kings 23:6), and their creation reflects a process of increasing population density and urbanization. The dead from cities and larger villages could no longer be laid to rest in individual graves or in caves scattered across the landscape. The growing number of dead and the ever-dwindling amount of space available ultimately led to the merging of subterranean single graves in specially constructed, again subterranean cemeteries: the catacombs. Burial in caves and catacombs remained the most common Jewish method of burial during the entire period of Antiquity. The term 'catacomb' is derived from catacomba, a compound of the Greek kata and the Latin comba, meaning 'near the sepulchres'. Originally it designated a specific place on the Via Appia near Rome, but since the ninth century it has been applied to all subterranean burial places in Italy as well as in other countries. Unlike caves, which were usually only intended to accommodate individuals or families, the catacombs offered purpose-built, collective burial sites which probably developed from the communal graves intended for members of the Sanhedrin, the most senior advisory and legislative council.[1]

Beth Shea'rim in Galilee in Erez Israel became a central burial place for the Jews of Palestine and the diaspora from the second century CE. The extensive catacombs found there were created so that they could be sold for burying dead persons who also came from outside Beth Shea'rim. With entrance gates, forecourts and rooms for setting up sarcophagi, these cata-

combs, which were used until the fourth century, are among the best-preserved examples of catacombs from the Roman period outside Europe, and their typology is similar to that of the catacombs in Rome, which were built around the same time. In Beth Shea'rim, the evolution from a separate family grave to a communal burial ground was completed so that the catacomb had become a subterranean cemetery, not just for the dead from local and surrounding areas but for bodies from further afield. 'Beth Shea'rim ...also contains bodies from other countries, such as Antioch, Tyrus, Sidon, Beirut, Byblos, Palmyra, Messene and Southern Arabia. Beth Shea'rim is therefore both a communal burial ground and a necropolis for the dead of the diaspora.'[2]

Since the 3rd century BCE, long before Titus destroyed Jerusalem and dissolved the kingdom of Israel, Jewish merchants and traders were settling in cities all around the Mediterranean. The most famous and important settlements were in Alexandria, Cyrene and Antioch.[3] To begin with, Rome was not one of the centres of Jewish life. Even when the Roman Republic's supremacy had been confirmed after the war with Carthage, only a few Jews moved to the city and it was not until Rome gradually became a commercial metropolis in the following decades that more and more Jews moved there, creating large synagogue communities from imperial times onwards.

Despite the destruction of Jerusalem in 70 CE, the living conditions of Jews in the Roman Empire were such that, often with the same legal status as Roman citizens, they enjoyed the same rights to religious worship and were able to go about their daily business. The system of polytheism gave the Jews enough scope to establish themselves as a tolerated minority within Roman culture.

The dead were laid to rest in catacombs, in accordance with the tradition brought from Israel and in line with local topographical conditions. While these catacombs were situated on the metropolis's arterial roads, in the empire's smaller cities too, such as Venosa and Syracuse, and also on Malta, the Jews buried their dead in catacombs. This burial practice was adopted by the Christians, many of whom were initially Jewish, in contrast to non-Jews and non-Christians who buried their dead mostly in the ground or in monuments above the ground. 'In point of fact, the mode of burial followed in catacombs is undoubtedly of Jewish origin.'[4] Although some modern authors[5] see the origins of the Roman catacombs also as a result of lack of space above ground, scholars like Eric Meirs point out the Jewish origins of the catacombs. And Künzle notes: 'The catacomb at Monteverde (Porta Portese) was already built in the 1st century B.C.E. ... Therefore the Jewish catacombs predate the Christian ones ... and anyway, the concept of subterranean burial places the Christians took from the Jews.'[6]

The synagogue of the port of Ostia near Rome, second century. Two columns frame a flight of stairs leading up to what was once the shrine with the Torah scrolls. The beam resting on the left column shows a menorah.

Rome/Catacombs of the Vigna Randanini on the Via Appia

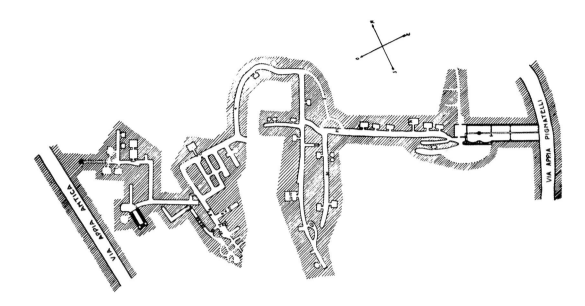

Plan of the catacomb of Vigna Randanini. The forecourt with the entrance from the road to Rome is on the right side. The plan shows the main walkway with the burial chambers going off it.

The forecourt of the catacomb looking towards the entry into the subterranean area.

In the reign of Augustus, 40–50,000 Jews lived in Rome, the majority on the right bank of the Tiber, in the district now known as Trastevere. We know the names of no fewer than eleven synagogues or communities and there may have been even more, although, to date, no physical remains of these synagogues have been discovered. A few of their names, however, have survived on nameplate inscriptions in the catacombs. Modern-day Trastevere bears no visible traces of this previous Jewish settlement, and it is worth travelling to Ostia, where remnants of the *insulae* (tenements), and extensive remains of a large synagogue have survived. These *insulae* are strongly reminiscent of modern-day apartment blocks, with staircases and self-contained flats on several floors. Here it is possible to picture the lives of the Roman Jews, the majority of whom consisted of poor tradesmen, workers and beggars. If they had a home it was usually only a tiny room next to a workshop. But there were also wealthier Jews living in *insulae* and even villas. These different living conditions are clearly reflected in the catacombs.

It was Roman practice to cremate their dead and inter the ash caskets in tombs above the ground. The Jews of Rome, on the other hand, had brought with them from Erez Israel the custom of burying their dead in caves; but in the countryside surrounding Rome, they found none of the above-ground rock formations required for this, and burials within the city walls were forbidden by the authorities for reasons of hygiene. The volcanic tufa that lay under the ground in the expansive fields around the city offered the perfect solution, ideal for creating subterranean burial chambers, being easy to cut, but also strong enough to support subterranean vaults. The earliest Roman Jewish burial sites found so far are catacombs dating from the second century CE. As communal cemeteries, they reflect the cheek-by-jowl living conditions of Roman residential districts: 'The Jews of Rome, living crowded together in the slum quarters of the great city and possessing no private estates outside the city proper, found it necessary to develop community cemeteries.[1]

Walkway with grave niches.

Burial chamber with frescoes in the red-green linear style.

To date, we know of six such Jewish catacombs in Rome. All lie within a radius of one to three kilometres around the ancient city walls, always near an arterial road such as the Via Appia, a location which bears a surprising similarity to the large Jewish cemeteries of the nineteenth and twentieth centuries since, for ease of access, these also lie on major roads. At the time of the Roman Empire, Rome was a modern city even by today's standards, with more than a million inhabitants, a highly-developed infrastructure and a bureaucratic system controlling every aspect of life. Not surprisingly, this modernity was also reflected in the locations of the cemeteries, which were probably maintained by individual synagogue communities, outside the city walls, mostly on streets that led to the synagogues. The main Jewish cemetery, the catacombs of Porta Portese, lay very close to Trastevere's Agrippan synagogue, which was under imperial patronage. Here, over four or five centuries, the dead of six different synagogue communities were buried, so the site is regarded as one of the earliest examples of a Jewish community cemetery.[2]

Vigna Randanini

One of the best-preserved Jewish catacombs in Rome is that of the Vigna Randanini on the Via Appia Antica. This catacomb is newer than that at the Porta

Detail from a fresco.

Marble epitaph with a menorah.

Portese and is situated further outside the city. Burials were carried out here from the start of the second century to the third century CE. Visitors reach it from the Via Appia Pignatelli by descending six steps into a forecourt which is open to the sky like an atrium. The other five Jewish catacombs in Rome all appear to have had a similar forecourt. The outer walls are built from brick, known as *opus reticulatum*. Arched niches, sometimes painted blue, are set into the walls for structural support. Although these niches were not originally intended for this purpose, by the end of the second century CE they were being occupied by sarcophagi. It is likely that particularly important members of the community were buried here. The forecourt has a rectangular base area measuring roughly 27 by 5.7 metres and the floor was painstakingly laid with a black and white mosaic in the second half of the second century. A dividing wall, which is set into a passageway, splits the atrium into a western and eastern courtyard. The eastern courtyard is in turn divided along the centre by a longitudinal wall. Two doorways are set into the forecourt's western wall.

The right-hand doorway leads through a narrow passageway into a room which housed a well which can no longer be seen. It is possible that this room previously functioned as a *tahara* space, or simply for ritual handwashing after leaving the catacombs. The left-hand doorway leads to an antechamber linked to the well room. It is through this antechamber that the catacombs proper are accessed. From the function of this antechamber and in particular the forecourt, with its two divided sections, Toynbee suggests that this was the place where burial ceremonies were held (whereas nowadays they are held directly at the graveside), the catacombs being too dark and narrow for such purposes. It is also possible that eulogies were given here and psalms recited, just as they are in the modern-day house of mourning. 'Most likely the appropriate ceremony was performed in the large antechamber before the body was borne down the dark passages to be placed within the grave niche, which lay open and ready.'[3]

From the antechamber next to the well room, several steps lead into the catacombs which, unlike Christian catacombs, extend only along one level. The layout of the passageway system is irregular and therefore does not appear to follow an original plan. The reason for this appears to be that catacombs were often created in passageways produced through the commercial use of tufa as a building material. (A few – non-Jewish – building companies left their guild trademarks in the catacombs. One such logo, in the shape of a hammer, is also found in the Vigna Randanini.) These passageways can stretch for several hundred metres. Only in two places, known as *luminaria*, does natural light dispel the darkness, so additional lighting was provided by oil lamps left in nooks.

On both sides of the corridor, there are grave niches or *loculi* set into the tufa, running lengthways along the passages. In most cases, four niches are arranged in tiers, but there are also Jewish catacombs in which up to eight niches are stacked. The size of the niche varies, depending on whether the deceased was a child or adult. Next to the *loculi*, although more rare, are grave niches that the Mishnah refers to as *kokim*, hewn into the tufa at right angles to the passageway. These represent the prevailing type of grave at this time in Israel. In later centuries scarcely any of these types of graves were built, nor are they found in Christian catacombs.

Openings to the grave niches were walled up. While in many cases their fronts are not marked by an epitaph, sometimes there are also plaques painted (*dipinto*) or etched into the plasterwork (*graffito*) with a few rarer examples made of marble. Surrounding the name of the deceased on the plaque there is often a picture of a *menorah*, a *lulav* symbolising the Feast of Succoth, a citrus or *etrog*, and a ram's horn or *shofar*.

Next to the corridors, home to the *loculi* and *kokim*, are burial chambers known as *cubicula*, into whose walls are set further *loculi*. These separate burial chambers appear to correspond to modern-day family burial plots and were reserved for wealthy families. In the catacombs on the Via Appia, two such burial chambers, featuring vaulted ceilings, have been preserved, illustrated with frescoes that imitate the decorative style of contemporary houses. Paintings in burial chambers have also been preserved in other Jewish catacombs. They often show floral motifs, animals and even representations from heathen mysticism such as putti. Alongside there are also the Jewish motifs already mentioned, augmented, for example, by the palm as a symbol of righteousness. On the post at the entrance to one of the burial chambers, which is adorned with pictures of palms, is the picture of a *mesusah*, a vessel containing a parchment on which an excerpt from the Bible is written and which, in accordance with one of the commandments, must be hung on the doorway of the home.

The difference between the burial chambers for the wealthy and the *loculi* or *kokim*, stacked one on top of the other, of the less well-off, reflects the conditions in which Jews of the time lived. The rich occupied separate, sumptuously decorated homes, while the others lived in *insulae*, as in Ostia. Since not many Jews were wealthy enough to be buried in sarcophagi, only a few Jewish sarcophagi have been preserved.

Tenement house or *insula* at Ostia, the port of ancient Rome.

Venosa / A Roman Town in Southern Italy

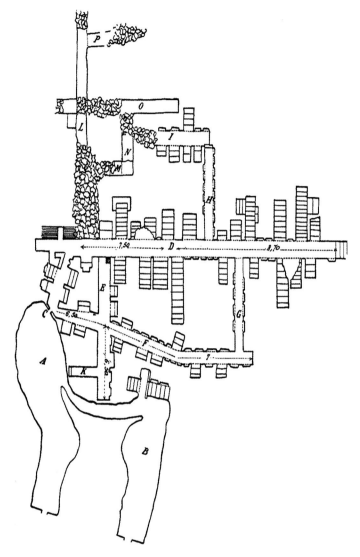

Plan of the Venosa catacomb with the main walkway and several smaller walkways leading to burial chambers.

Fresco with a *menorah* from the Venosa catacomb.

OPPOSITE PAGE: Detail of a map of Frankfurt showing the Jewish cemetery, Matthäus Merian, 1628.

The small southern Italian town of Venosa (Roman Venusia), situated in the Basilicata in southern Italy, was founded as a Roman colony in 291 BCE. Five hundred years later, before the third century CE, a group of Jews settled in the town and the earliest grave inscriptions in Venosa date from this time. Recent investigations (2003) appear to confirm that in 70 C.E., Titus brought 5,000 prisoners to Basilicata after the destruction of the second temple in Jerusalem, and many of these captives then moved to Venosa and its surroundings, bringing with them their burial customs.

The Jews of Venosa buried their dead, like the Jews of Rome, in catacombs. Recent excavations have uncovered an arch with a multi-coloured fresco, showing a *menorah* surrounded by a *shofar*, an *etrog*

and a *lulav*. The catacombs, situated outside the gates of the ancient city, were investigated in 1853 (and described by François Lenorman and Nicolas Müller) and again in 1935. Dug into the volcanic tufa, they were found to be open and empty. From two parallel-running galleries, shorter passageways lead off at right-angles, with the galleries being two metres wider than those in Rome. The *arcosolia* (round niches) are on the top with a column of burial niches underneath dating from the fourth to the eighth centuries.

It is not known how large the community was that buried its dead here. The grave inscriptions in the catacomb, however, provide detailed information showing that Venosa had a well-organized community with various religious functionaries: there were *rebbites* (rabbis) and *apostuli* (delegates of the Palestinian patriarchy or the Babylonian exilarchs), while a few members are listed as *maiores* and *patres civitatis* (elected officials of the city). One grave inscription remembers a *pateressa* – presumed to be a type of honorary chairwoman of the local synagogue, similar to the *Mater Synagoga* of a contemporary Roman synagogue community.

Some fifty-four catacomb epitaphs have been found so far. The inscriptions, dating from the third to the sixth centuries, are written in Greek and Latin, with only a few Hebrew words. One states: 'May God grant his soul peace, together with the just of Heaven, until He carries them into his sanctuary, and may he sit together with all those dedicated to a life in Jerusalem.' The inscriptions suggest that the Jews of Venosa were well integrated into the city's political and administrative life and had largely assimilated. In Venosa too, this mostly peaceful existence under the *Pax Romana* came to an end only when the Western Roman Empire fell in the fifth century.

Jewish funeral procession in front of a cemetery with trees visible over the wall. Italy, end of fifteenth century. Princeton University Library.

catacombs to the cemetery probably occurred in the early Middle Ages.[1] The same happened in Rome, where above the Porta Portese catacomb in the early Middle Ages a cemetery was created, whose gravestones were found in the nineteenth century. Both in Rome and Venosa the transition from the ancient catacomb burials to above-ground cemeteries can be studied.

Absence of cemeteries in the early Middle Ages

No cemeteries have survived, however, from the eigth to the eleventh centuries – only a few isolated gravestones. This led Sylvie-Anne Goldberg to conclude that: 'Ordinary Jews were buried – not at the dump, as Gérard Nahon ironically puts it – in funerary spaces shared by others and doubtless without the benefit of headstones, as was customary in the *extra muros* cemeteries of the late Middle Ages.'[2] This presumption that Jews buried their dead alongside Christians in multi-faith cemeteries outside the areas where they lived – probably in separate sections – is a plausible explanation for the lack of Jewish cemeteries during the early Middle Ages. The Jewish parts of the cemeteries were then ransacked and destroyed together with the Christian graves over the course of subsequent centuries. The small number of preserved gravestones can also be explained by the fact that, up until the eleventh century, either they were made from wood, which decays comparatively quickly, or no headstone marked the grave at all. This practice reflects the pronouncement by Maimonides (1135–1204) instructing that no gravestones should be erected at the heads of the pious.

With the gradual decline and collapse of the Roman Empire in the fourth and fifth centuries, the Jews' social and economic positions suffered too, especially after Emperor Theodosius (379–95) finally elevated Christianity to the status of state religion.

In southern Italy, small communities survived in a few towns such as Venosa and initially, the catacombs there, as described earlier, appear to have continued in use. But some twenty-three known gravestones from the ninth century do not come from there, but from a nearby cemetery discovered shortly after the catacombs: 'The dead were first buried in the catacombs and then, probably no later than the ninth century, in a cemetery, meaning that the transition from the

Between the ninth and eleventh centuries, a trend developed of performing Christian burials close to churches or actually inside them. This practice was of course not acceptable to the Jews and from the eleventh century the first separate Jewish cemeteries, such as those in Speyer and Worms, began to reappear. The creation of the Jewish cemetery of the late Middle Ages, as can still be seen in Worms today, is thus the result of religious segregation.

From the eleventh century, with the re-emergence of major cities and safer trading routes, architectural traces of Jewish life begin to reappear in Europe. Thriving Jewish communities grew up in the major cities along the trading routes of the Rhineland, as well as in Spain, England, France and Italy. The Jews established synagogues and ritual baths (*mikweh*), which were often built by the same architects as the large romanesque and later gothic cathedrals that also sprang up around the same time. The cemeteries of this period are almost the only remaining witnesses to communities that became the victims of murderous pogroms during the crusades (from the eleventh century onwards) and of major plague epidemics (especially in the fourteenth century). On the other hand, the cemeteries of the Iberian peninsula, which the Jews built until they were finally driven out in the late fifteenth century, have all been lost, at least superficially. Today, gravestones from this period are found in museums and the famous Montjuich in Barcelona, a former Jewish cemetery which is now a park close to the buildings from the World Fair of 1929. Since most of the cemeteries in Spain and Portugal were built outside towns and villages, some have been retained as meadows, fields or parks. The gravestones have gone, but the graves are often still there, as is the case in the Basque town of Vittoria, where the Jewish cemetery has survived through the centuries as an expanse of green.

The remains of later cemeteries in Frankfurt, Venice and Prague exhibit many structural similarities in terms of their design: they were originally situated outside or on the outskirts of the city, were surrounded by walls and appear not to have had any *tahara* houses – the *tahara* ritual being performed in homes or community halls. The cemeteries were filled in chronological order, with particularly law-abiding people, such as rabbis, being buried separately from sinners, who were generally interred along the cemetery walls. The graves were laid at the prescribed distance from one another, mostly in irregular rows without any walkway areas. It was rare for the Jews to be given extension areas for their cemeteries and then only with many strings attached, which resulted in cemeteries being very densely populated. This reflects the cramped living conditions of the overpopulated Jewish quarters which were also rarely expanded. If space became short and the cemetery could not be extended, soil was laid over the existing graves and new graves dug without disturbing those underneath.

The nature of the generally walled, but always demarcated, Jewish cemetery outside the gates of residential areas[3] remained unchanged until the late eighteenth century. Then, with the Enlightenment and French Revolution, rulers – like the Roman emperors of their day – decreed that for hygiene reasons all cemeteries had to be moved beyond the city gates. The pre-twelfth century pattern of shared Christian-Jewish burial sites resumed in 1804 in Napoleon's Paris, where the new multi-faith cemetery of Père-Lachaise provided the Jews with a separate section.

Rome/Cemeteries of Trastevere

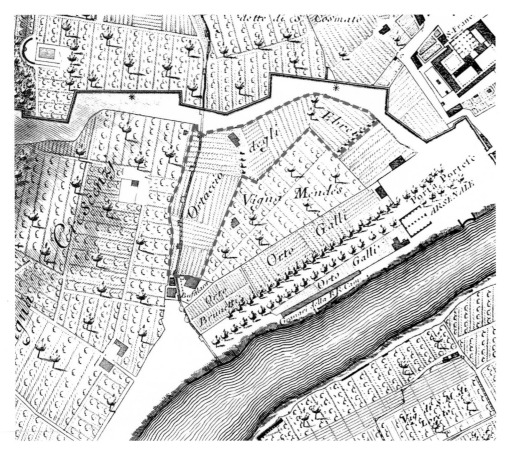

Map of Rome with the Jewish cemetery at Porta Portese. Giovanni Battista Nolli, 1748. The cemetery lies outside the city walls (top of the plan, the river Tiber at the bottom) and is surrounded by gardens and vineyards.

With the fall of the western half of the Roman Empire, the bishop of Rome, the Pope, became the ruling power in the former imperial capital. People began to desert Rome in droves from the fifth century, and for a time, a city previously of a million people had fewer than 40,000 inhabitants. The number of Jews also fell dramatically, and many of the synagogues, if they had not already been gutted, fell into disrepair. Life in medieval Rome was eked out among grandiose ruins. Jews who remained at first continued to live in Trastevere, but over the following centuries they moved to the left bank of the Tiber, where later the ghetto was created. The well-being of this small community of Roman Jews depended on the goodwill of the city's political and religious leaders: 'Hence, over

a period of some 1,400 years, the history of the Jews in Rome is in great part a reflection of papal politics toward the Jews.'[1] This is reflected in their cemeteries as well.

The burial sites at the Porta Portese

By the early Middle Ages the outlying catacombs were gradually abandoned and the dead buried in the ground in cemeteries close to the ancient city walls. As a result, the cemetery created by the Roman community in the Middle Ages lay on the right-hand bank of the Tiber, near the Trastevere residential area. Positioned just before the Porta Portese (Portuense), the main Jewish catacomb was rediscovered in 1602, and in 1884 it was re-explored shortly before it finally collapsed. Above the catacomb, in the open air, a more recent burial place was discovered. 'This connection of the catacombs with a cemetery on top was also seen in Beth Shea'rim and occurs in Venosa, in the south of Italy.'[2] The necropolis on the Porta Portese, which is dated by grave inscriptions to the period of late Antiquity, when combined with the cemetery in Venosa, represents an important link between the subterranean cemeteries of Antiquity and the above-ground cemeteries of the Middle Ages.

In 1267 a catastrophe occurred when a mob vandalized and desecrated the cemetery. (Shortly afterwards Rabbi Binyamin ben Avraham Anav wrote a poem about it that is still recited by Roman Jews.) Historical sources[3] report that the walled cemetery lay on a Colle Rosato 'in the middle of the rosebeds'.[4] Listed on historical maps as 'Ortaccio', the cemetery was surrounded by the vineyards of Vigna Mendes and Vigna Crescenzi, with the entrance facing the city walls. A map of 1748 by Giovanni Battista Nolli, made 103 years after the cemetery closed, shows a long

building alongside, possibly a medieval *tahara* house.

In 1587, the church stripped the cemetery from the *Ghemilut Chassadim*, the *chevra kaddisha* founded only a short time earlier and based on the Prague model. Pope Urban VIII decreed that the cemetery was again to be surrounded by a wall made from broken gravestones, so that it could spread no further. But it was not until 1645 that the site was finally closed and its levelling ordered. 'To render the withdrawal from the old cemetery definitive, the pope required that the *Ghemilut Chassadim* level the terrain "giving them permission to take clay from the old walls and thus ruin and destroy the old city walls of Rome".'[5] But it was not, as Nolli's plan from 1748 shows, until the end of the eighteenth century that the cemetery was finally levelled.

So far, no trace has been found of this medieval cemetery. The ground used for the Porta Portese cemetery has now been built over, with roads and houses, so that only a few later gravestones survive. Of particular note in this context are those made from the capitals of ancient pillars and on which the inscription has been chiselled into the top of the capital.

The building of the medieval synagogue in Vicolo dell'Atleta at Trastevere.

Map of Worms with the
Jewish cemetery, 186c.
The Jewish quarter with
the Judengasse is shown in
the top right corner, next to
the city wall. The cemetery
is outside the walls on the
bottom left side, not far
from the cathedral.

SCHUM - The three linked sites of Speyer, Worms, Mainz

The names of the three Rhine cities of Speyer, Worms and Mainz together create the name **SCHUM**. **Sch** stands for **Sch**pirah — Speyer; Uvormaisah / Vermaisah — Worms; **M**agenza — Mainz. Since the first quarter of the eleventh century, the three cities formed the most important centres of Jewish learning in Ashkenaz, the home territory of Jews living in Central and Eastern Europe. The name SCHUM became synonymous with one of the most glittering eras of Ashkenazi Jewry, a period in which the rabbis laid the foundations for the *halakha* legal code of forthcoming centuries, and not just for the Ashkenazim.

The Jewish communities in these cities are often believed to have originated in Roman times, but the first written source for Mainz, for example, does not appear until the early tenth century. Shortly after come Worms and Speyer, so that by the end of the eleventh century, all three cities had established and thriving Jewish communities, thanks to trading routes

along the Rhineland's roads and waterways. Their prosperity was, however, cruelly interrupted again and again and was finally ended through pogroms and massacres carried out as a result of crusades and plagues, for which the Jews were blamed. Entire communities evaded baptism through acts of *kiddush hashem* – sanctification of God's name through suicide. In Mainz alone, 6,000 Jews perished in the flames of their homes and synagogues in 1394.

In the early days, from 1000 CE onwards, the Jews of the SCHUM often lived side by side with Christians, but from around 1200 they formed their own communities in parts of the city close to the markets. These Jewish quarters were home to community institutions such as synagogue, *mikweh*, bakery and dance hall, and although distinct, they were not initially closed off at certain times, like ghettos, a practice which generally began in the fifteenth century. Cemeteries lay outside the city walls; this satisfied *halakhic* rules, but the then municipal authorities would not have sacrificed valuable land inside the city walls for Jewish cemeteries anyway. Of the SCHUM's original cemeteries, only that in Worms survives; the Speyer and Mainz sites were destroyed. Some Speyer gravestones are preserved in museums, while scattered stone survivals have been regrouped on the old site in Mainz.

Jews in Worms

The first written references to a Jewish community in Worms date from the end of the tenth century. The community prospered so greatly that, in 1074, Emperor Heinrich IV mentioned them in a document relating to the city of Worms ahead of the other inhabitants. The Jews of Worms had freedom to trade and travel; they could work as money-changers, employ Christians as workers and servants, and acquire property. Christians were forbidden to convert Jews, and converted Jews even lost their birthright freedoms. During this period, a number of leading scholars lived and worked in the city: Judah ben Baruch, a famous *halakhic* authority and poet of *piyyutim*, Meir ben Isaac, Jacob ben Yakar and Isaac ben Eleazar. The latter two taught one of the

The Judengasse in Worms.

most important scholars of the Middle Ages, Salomon ben Isaac (1040–1105), known as Rashi, during his stay in Worms.

Periods of prosperity were brutally interrupted by massacres following the crusades and a plague pogrom. Over the ensuing centuries, the Worms Jewry never fully recovered from such bloody persecution and never again reached the level of importance it had previously enjoyed.

The Jews of Worms lived in a north-eastern district beside the city wall. The heart of the district was the Judengasse, running parallel to the city wall. When the Jewish quarter was declared a ghetto in the fifteenth century, the city council built upper and lower Jews'

TOP: The cemetery forecourt with *tahara* house, hand washbasin and inner gate.

BOTTOM: The new entrance buildings, 1913.

RIGHT: View through a *Cohanim* window into the cemetery.

FAR RIGHT: Fourteenth- and fifteenth-century gravestones.

gates (*Obere* and *Untere Judentor*) to the rest of the city. These gates were locked at night and on Christian holidays, and by the mid-fifteenth century some 300 people were crammed into just forty-two houses. The key religious and civil buildings of Worms Jewry were also located in the centre of the Jewish quarter: the synagogue, *mikweh* ritual bath house, school, dance hall and wedding house, hospital, slaughterhouse and flour store, thus providing all the institutions that a functioning community needed to live. The tally omits only the cemetery, which was built at the opposite end of the city.

The cemetery

The cemetery must have been created almost together with the pre-crusade synagogue, since the first remaining gravestone of Jacob Ha-bachur dates from 1076. This makes the site, known as the 'Holy Sands', the

oldest preserved medieval Jewish cemetery in Europe. It was built just outside the walls of the inner city, and in choosing such a site – or by being ordered to do so by the city council – the Jews were following the rules of *halakha*. The piece of ground set aside for the cemetery was an elongated, equilateral triangle on the western side of the current Andreasring. To create the land, the former wall moat had to be filled in. Legend has it that sand from the Holy Land was used for the purpose, hence the cemetery's name.

The present-day cemetery comprises older and newer sections. The older, lower-lying part was created at the start of the eleventh century from the site's southern corner, known as the *Rabbinental*, and built in a south-north direction. Burials began in the adjoining western section only in the eighteenth century. In 1250, around 200 years after the cemetery was founded, boundary railings were replaced by a strong wall. A gravestone from 1287 states that the father of Jochebed bat Jechiel ben Ephraim, who died in that year, donated a large sum to help pay for the cemetery's wall. Over the following centuries, the cemetery was successively laid out from south to north while, unusually, the gravestones all faced north, in the approximate direction of the synagogue, and not east as was customary elsewhere. Only the particularly pious Jacob Moses Moellin the Maharil, who died in 1427, chose the conventional direction. No consecutive rows are distinguishable in the layout of the graves, but grave inscriptions give kinship clues, for members of the same family were often buried close together.[1] In the fourteenth century, Worms was finally surrounded by a new wall which bypassed the cemetery on the west side and thereby enclosed it. This put the cemetery in a dangerous position between the inner and outer walls with their Andreas gates, and was in jeopardy many times from planned and even executed entrenchment and fortification works.

After 1615 a rich member of the community, David Oppenheim (d. 1642), instituted rebuilding and repairs to the cemetery. The almost 400-year-old wall was restored. A redesigned entrance area (*chozer*), still to be seen, included a separate forecourt. The external entrance gate was built facing the street, with a gate-keeper's house alongside which was replaced by a new building in 1911. Towards the inside of the cemetery, Oppenheim built the 'inner gate'. The purpose and function of the demarcation of this forecourt to the cemetery follows *halakha* rules for the *Cohanim* who must not enter a cemetery, since they would be ritually contaminated by the proximity of bodies. By separating the forecourt from the actual cemetery, the *Cohanim* were able at least to watch burial ceremonies once the procession and the body left the forecourt. To this end, windows were cut in the cemetery walls, from which the *Cohanim* could see the graves without actually having to enter the cemetery. When the wall and gate were rebuilt in 1911, *Cohanim* windows were again integrated into it.

Oppenheim had a stone tablet inscribed with the *kaddish*, or prayer for the dead, inserted into the inner wall next to the internal entrance, and a small *tahara* house was built. For the living, he had a free-standing basin built for handwashing. By so doing, he created an early seventeenth-century entrance area in a Jewish cemetery which is now by far the finest and best-preserved example in any German-speaking region. The building has remained, even though the initial period of peace ended in 1661 when Juspa Schamesch, in his twelfth saga, reports that Christians again razed parts of the cemetery wall.

At the start of the eighteenth century, a new, more elevated section of the cemetery was created, to the west of the older part, along the former city wall.

The gravestones of Rabbi Meir ben Baruch of Rothenburg (d. 1293) and Alexander ben Salomo Wimpfen (d. 1307).

This new section is accessed from the old via a set of steps. Burials took place here until the 1911 consecration of a new cemetery on the Hochheimer Höhe, where an elaborate Art Nouveau design offers a completely different interpretation of Jewish cemetery culture. Ultimately, however, it reflects the tradition of intense concern for the aesthetic characteristics of a cemetery, as interpreted by David Oppenheim almost three centuries earlier.

Individual graves

Some 3,000 gravestones dating from the eleventh to the twentieth centuries have been preserved on the Holy Sands – with eight from the eleventh century and almost fifty from the twelfth. These earliest gravestones are generally sandstone squares, narrowing towards the base and with letters incised on the face. The inscriptions have horizontal ruled lines above the rows of letters, a characteristic absent from 1100 onwards. The historical significance of these gravestones is tremendous, since they are rare relics of Romanesque gravestone culture; the majority of Christian gravestones from the Middle Ages have been destroyed, with the graves generally reused after a few years and the old stones removed and used for other purposes.

Two key examples include that of Sagira bat Samuel (d. 1100), one of the twelve oldest in the cemetery and previously celebrated, due to incorrect dating to the year 900, as being the oldest German gravestone. The other is a pair of graves marking the burial of Rabbi Meir ben Baruch of Rothenburg and Alexander ben Salomo Wimpfen who gained significant fame and are still visited today by Jews from all over the world. Rabbi Meir, also known as Mahram, remains a leading *halakhic* authority through his writings. His last office was that of rabbi in Mainz. On 19 June 1286, Rabbi Meir, blamed for spurring a wave of Jewish emigration to Israel, was imprisoned by Emperor Rudolf of Habsburg concerned about loss of revenue from *his* Jews in the event of a mass exodus. In accordance with Jewish law stating that hostages must be redeemed, German Jews repeatedly offered the enormous sum of 23,000 marks for his release – but in vain. Rudolf even tried to ransom the scholar's corpse. It was only in 1307 that the Frankfurt merchant Alexander Wimpfen managed, with his entire wealth, to secure the release of Rabbi Meir's body and carry out the dead man's wish to be buried in the cemetery at Worms. In reward for redeeming the body, Wimpfen asked only to be buried beside him. He died shortly afterwards, on Yom Kippur in 1308, and was interred next to the esteemed scholar.

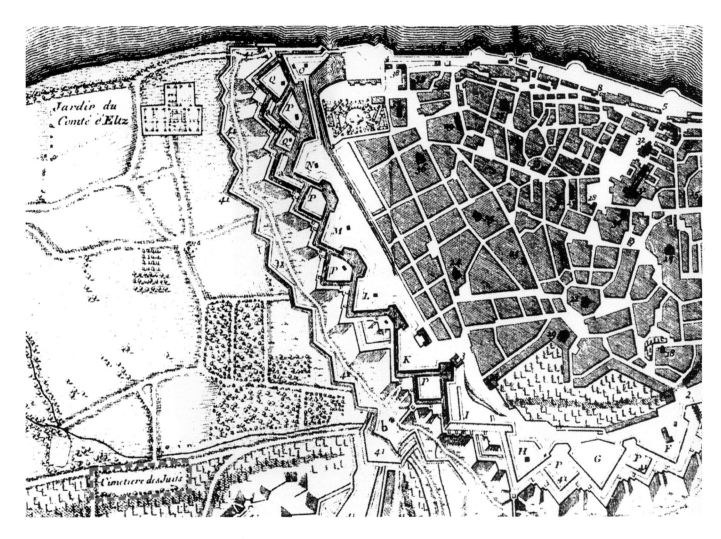

The first written confirmation of a Jewish presence in Mainz is an ecclesiastical decree from the year 906. In the following centuries, the Jews were repeatedly expelled from the city or were the victims of terrible pogroms, yet they kept being brought back to the city where they were urgently needed as traders. The community's cemetery, known as the 'Judensand', was situated outside the city on a slope above an old Roman arterial road, the modern-day Mombacher Strasse, just like the cemeteries in Rome and other Roman cities in the Rhineland. This position is often regarded as an indication that Jews had settled in

Mainz even in Roman times and that the cemetery had thus been in use since then. Bernd Vest points out that it was mostly only the Jewish rather than the Christian communities that kept their old burial places since they did not want to abandon the practice of burial next to the graves of their ancestors (*kvarot ha'avot*).[1]

There is a written indication, dating from 1013, that two benefactors, a married couple, bought a cemetery plot for the community, which was possibly the site of the cemetery of the ancient Jewish community on which burials had continued to take place. In any case, there has been a Jewish cemetery in Mainz since

Map of Mainz, late eighteenth century. The cemetery lies outside the city's eighteenth-century walls, next to an old Roman road.

View into the site of the
medieval cemetery with
the re-erected gravestones.

A thirteenth-century
gravestone.

around the turn of the first millennium and it
remained in use up until 1438. In that year, the cemetery was destroyed and the gravestones reused all over
the city as construction material. The cemetery land
was converted into a vineyard, and Jews were only
permitted to be buried there in exceptional cases.

The tombstone memorial

Since 1825, more and more Jewish gravestones were
unearthed in the city as a result of construction work
and by 1922, their number had reached 188. The liberal
community rabbi Sali Levi (1883–1941) established a
tombstone memorial on the site of the medieval Jewish
cemetery, in 1926, with the preserved gravestones
distributed more or less at random across the site, since
they could no longer be allocated to individual grave
sites; to indicate this, they were not positioned pointing
eastwards. In 1936, eight further gravestones that had
been unearthed as a result of building work were
secretly resited here. A catalogue of the tombstone
memorials put together in 1977[2] includes 157 dating
from the period between 1049 and 1421.

The gravestones are mostly made from local shell
limestone, but there are some made from sandstone
and even one made from black lava tufa. They are
either rectangular blocks or have rounded upper
sections, a feature common to later stones. The
inscriptions are at first mostly engraved in a runic
style, and it is only later that these inscriptions are
made in inset frames.

Mainz's monument cemetery is a rare example of
a medieval Jewish cemetery that has been restored as a
tombstone memorial. Apart from its collection of
gravestones, it is also an important monument to
contemporary history and the era of the Weimar
Republic. A few years before the National-Socialist period began, and with it the renewed annihilation of Mainz
Jewry, it was possible once again to display the Jewish
cemetery as a monument. Furthermore, since the Nazis
did not remove the cemetery, the Mainz community,
proud of its glittering, almost thousand-year history, is
still able to resurrect the witnesses to its medieval past
as a monument to the dead and a reminder to the living.

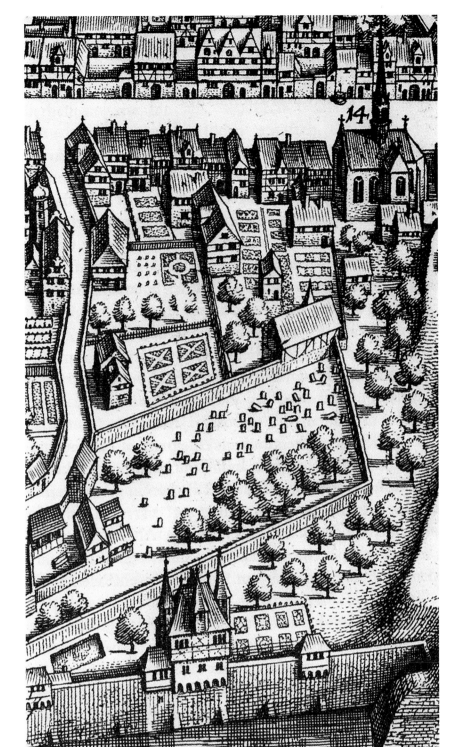

Although it is assumed that Jews lived in Frankfurt from the Carolingian period of the eighth and ninth centuries, not until the second half of the twelfth century, in a work by Rabbi Elieser ben Nathan, is there mention of an established Jewish settlement. A first Jewish cemetery is mentioned in an entry dating from 1180 in the 'Bartholomew Book' in Frankfurt's city archives, with reference to a 'tax for a garden outside the gates where one finds the Jewish cemetery'. It is generally thought that in 1270 the Jews created the second cemetery, still standing today, in accordance with *halakhic* rules, on garden and pasture land outside the fortifications, to the east of the city. The city was expanded in 1333, and since this time the cemetery has lain within the fortified zone, a development similar to that of Worms. This remained the burial place for Frankfurt's Jews for more than 500 years but between the fourteenth and sixteenth centuries, it also accommodated Jews from neighbouring towns and cities. In 1460 Frankfurt city council ruled that the Jews had to move to a separate quarter, the Judengasse, and together with the residential quarters, a new dance hall, hospital, synagogue, *mikweh*, community hall and two guest houses were built – generally with the Jews' own money. By 1612, there were 195 houses ranged along the 275-metre length of the Judengasse in which around 3,000 Jews were crammed, so it was

Detail of a map of Frankfurt by Matthäus Merian, 1628. The cemetery is surrounded by houses and gardens. The entrance with Jewish hospital, *tahara* house and stables is visible on the cemetery's left side.

The old Jewish hospital with the entrance to the cemetery, 1870.

small wonder this crowded and unhealthy area came to be called 'New Egypt'. Houses bore names such as 'Churn', 'Monkey', 'Wolf', 'Box Tree', 'Elephant', 'Swan' or 'Dove'. The ghetto was closed off from the city by three gates, with the cemetery being closely connected to the ghetto via a market. Such proximity to the Jews' living quarters, through the forced creation of the ghetto, is fairly rare in medieval Europe, Prague being one of the few examples where the cemetery is also located virtually in the centre of the Jewish quarter.

The cemetery wall with the names of thousands of Frankfurt's *Shoah* victims written on small square blocks.

View into the cemetery.

The cemetery

Covering 1.18 hectares, and enclosed around 1270, the cemetery grounds formed a rough rectangle with a curved, irregular profile to the western side. Initially the perimeter was 'merely marked out with sunken posts'[1] but a siege plan of 1552 shows a wall. There were several points of access: 'To the east, the cemetery connected directly to the city's fortifications, and there was a small gate here. The quickest route to it led via the cemetery, which the Christians often used as a short cut. The western gate was the one the Jews used to access their cemetery. To reach the graveyard, one had to go left around the hospital, known as the *Hekdesch*.'[2]

The site held two unacquired buildings, one of which was used for producing powder until the late sixteenth century. Following the plague epidemic of 1585, the Jewish community also bought this former powder mill and turned it into a *Blatternhaus*, or pox house. At the same time, the converted building also served as a *tahara* and a *kippeschdub* – a gathering-place for the two burial societies founded in 1575 – and a coffin workshop. The Frankfurt *tahara* house was one of the earliest of its type.

By 1570, gravediggers were in charge of preparing the bodies and carrying out the burials. They lived in their own gravediggers' house. The two burial societies then took over these tasks. There was a clear division of labour. Members of the *chevra kaddisha dekavranim*, the 'Holy Brotherhood of Gravediggers', chose and dug graves, while the *chevra kaddish degomle chassadim*, the 'Holy Brotherhood that Carries Out Pious Works', washed bodies, made coffins and visited the sick.

Following another plague epidemic in 1632, a separate *tahara* house was erected to the right of the cemetery entrance on the south side, with a special *tahara* for female bodies noted by 1689. Together these buildings created a separate forecourt, known as a *chozer*, which the actual graveyard, the *kvores*, adjoined from the east. As well as the *tahara* houses, the site also had a well for drawing water to wash bodies and for ritual handwashing for mourners

leaving the cemetery. One peculiarity of the Frankfurt courtyard is the presence of a stable, known as a *bechorimstall*, built into the western wall, for first-born male animals. 'The *bechorim* were not slaughtered in Frankfurt, in accordance with *halakha* and thus spent their lives in the cemetery in Frankfurt.'[3]

The cemetery was never extended. It has been estimated[4] that the cemetery saw 26,000 burials over five centuries and that, given the 6,500 gravestones still present in 1900, many of the dead never had their own gravestones. This may be particularly true for the many children who died prematurely, buried together on a hill called *Kinderberg*. Dead from the Jewish hospital, the *hekdesch*, were also buried in a separate area known as the *Hekdeschplatz*. Suicides, criminals, bankrupts, 'amoral women' and *mamserim* (bastard children) were buried on a separate *Schandfeld*, or 'field of shame'. The *chevra kaddisha* normally chose the location of the grave following the person's death. Generally, relatives were buried next to each other wherever possible, but there were also areas for special graves: those who had died for their faith were interred as martyrs, or *kedoshim*, on the *Hügel der Heiligen*, or 'Hill of the Blessed'; rabbis were buried on the *Rabbanimplatz*.

In 1828 the old *Judenmarkt* cemetery was closed and progressively abandoned, as a new site opened on the Rat-Beil-Strasse. The Börneplatz synagogue was built in 1882 on the site of the old Jewish hospital and cemetery entrance, but it was burned to the ground in 1938 during *Kristallnacht*. Shortly before that, gravestones had been sorted by community leaders according to historical and aesthetic criteria, with 175 stones being moved to the Jewish cemetery on the Rat-Beil-Strasse. In the wake of *Kristallnacht* the Nazis began breaking up remaining gravestones using a specially built stone mill on the site of the cemetery. Subsequent bombing raids, however, put a sudden end to these activities and a third of the original 6,000 gravestones were saved. After the war, the displaced gravestones were returned and, since their original locations were no longer known, erected along the cemetery wall.

Detail of an eighteenth-century gravestone. Like harts, windmills and many other symbols, this head of a 'Moor' indicates that the person buried here lived in a specially named house. In this case it was the 'House of the Moor'.

London / A Cemetery for a Country

Jews may have lived in London even in Roman times, when the city known as Londinium was a key colonial trading centre, but the first official record of a Jewish presence in England does not occur until Norman times. The medieval community of London lived around one road, which still bears the name 'Old Jewry', where the 'Great Synagogue' was located until destruction in 1290 during the expulsion of England's Jews.

By 1177, the cemetery in London was the central burial place for all the Jews in England. It was situated beside the north-west corner of the city wall, which stood on Roman foundations, near the church of St Giles Cripplegate. Sources[1] from 1218 onwards refer to it under names such as the 'cemetery of the Jews' or 'the cemetery of the entire community of the Jews of England' or, from 1277 onwards, the 'Jews' garden'. It is not known when the Jews acquired the land, but one source from 1268–9 reports an extension to it: 'The entire Jewry of England' acquired the new land from one Jacob of Oxford for five marks. The Jews were to have the land forever and even those sentenced to death were allowed burial there. In the years that followed, and even in 1289, the eve of expulsion, the 'Jews of London and the entire community of the Jews of England' acquired extra land. In its final extent the area covered one hectare.

Surrounded by gardens and houses, the cemetery was enclosed by a wall. There was a short frontage and entrance gate on Red Cross Street, while a second, side entrance was located on the west side of Aldersgate. On the southern and south-eastern side, the Jewish cemetery adjoined the churchyard of St Giles Cripplegate and the moat of the city's fortifications.

As the central burial place for all the Jews of England, the costs of maintaining the London cemetery were spread across the country.[2] Corpses had to be

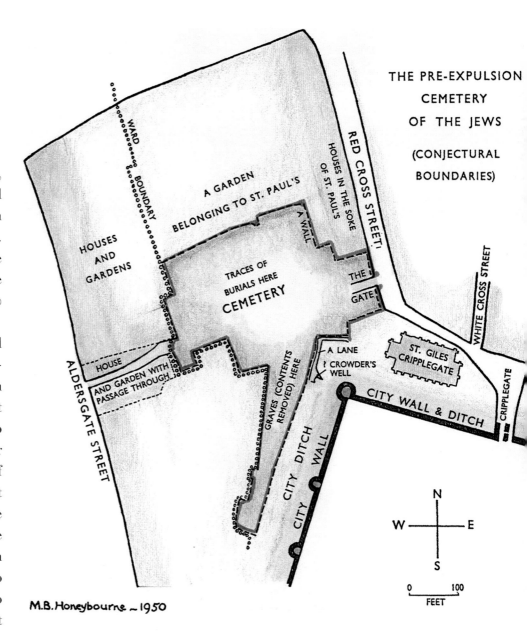

THE PRE-EXPULSION CEMETERY OF THE JEWS (CONJECTURAL BOUNDARIES)

M.B. Honeybourne – 1950

Map of the area of St Giles Cripplegate with the site of the Jewish cemetery. Map by M. Honeybourne, 1950.

carried by wagon to the capital from places as far afield as Exeter, Norwich and York. Cecil Roth describes these journeys vividly: 'The toll-lists specified the charge to be made for a dead Jew; and we read gruesome accounts of how the dogs would bay after the corpse on the road.'[3] With a growing population density, such long-distance transportation of the deceased became impractical. In 1177, local Jewish communities were granted permission to build their own cemeteries outside their city walls. Over the years, ten Jewish cemeteries were to be built in England, of which only three have so far been documented archaeologically. Besides the seven graves in London, ten have come to light in Winchester and as many as 482 in Jewbury in York.[4]

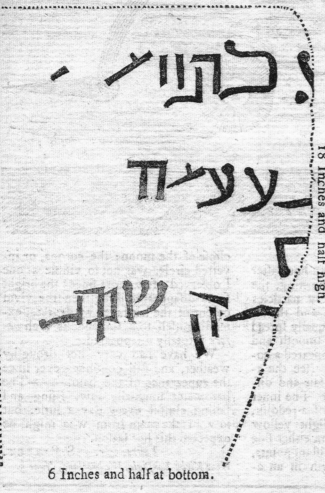

Of an antique Stone in London Wall.

To Dr *Rawlinson*, and the other Gentlemen, Governors of *Bethlem* Hospital *Some Notes concerning the* Stone *found in* London Wall, *on the Backside of* Bethle in their Apothecary, Mr Weaver's, Apartments, in July 1753.

11 Inches and a half.

18 Inches and half high.

6 Inches and half at bottom.

LONDON WALL said to have b built about the year *Christ* 306, by *Hele* the mother of *Conſt tine*, (See Simon Durham) according others, 434. (See *St* in many of books) It was deſtro by the *Danes* about year 839, reſtored repaired by K. *Alſi Anno* 886. In 994, citizens defended th walls againſt the *Dar* in ſupport of K. *Eth red*. The *Danes* rep ſed from *London* wa by the *Londoners*, *A* 1016. Earl *God* with his navy aſſaul the walls 1052. *Fitz Stephen*, in time of *Henry* II. theſe words : ' T ' wall is high and gr ' and well towered ' the North ſide, w ' due diſtances betw ' the towers. On ' South ſide alſo the ' tie was walled ' towered ; but the fi ' ful river of *Than* ' with his ebbings

' ſiowing, hath long ſince ſubverted them. The wall on the North ſide is like ' bow ; and the South like the ſtring of it.' *Stow* ſays, ' I read that in the year 1215, the 17th day of *May*, being *Suna* ' the Barons came to *London*, and entred thro' *Aldgate*, in the ſervice time, wh ' they took ſuch as they knew favoured the king, and ſpoiled their goods : Th ' brake into the houſes of the *Jewes*, and ſerched their coffers, to ſtuff their o ' purſes that had been long empty.' After this, *Robert Fitzwalter*, and *Geffery* ' *Mandevil*, E. of *Eſſex*, and the E. of *Gloucefter*, cheif leaders in the army, ' plied all diligence to repair the walls of the city with the ſtones of the *Je*

Print of a medieval gravestone from the London city wall. Gentleman's Magazine, 1753.

The site of the pre-expulsion cemetery. today the Barbican.

Following expulsion in 1290, the cemetery was closed and divided among new owners. Some parts were built on, while others remained as farmland and gardens. During the Second World War, the City of London was badly bombed, with St Paul's Cathedral surviving amid a sea of rubble. The very first bombs of the Blitz fell around St Giles, and by 1945 the densely-developed site of the old cemetery was reduced to a wasteland. In the 1960s after the debris of war had finally been cleared away and before the building of the Barbican Centre, archaeological excavations were carried out in this area. A cluster of seven graves was unearthed between the former Well Street and St Giles cemetery, but all seven were empty, leading archaeologist W.F. Grimes to surmise: 'There could be no doubt that the graves had been deliberately carefully emptied and backfilled with made or garden soil. In one of the graves, above the floor, was the skeleton of a small dog. The dog might be due to desecration by Gentiles.'[75]

According to sources from 1290 onwards, the cemetery was described as a Jews' garden with dovecot and pond. Honeybourne concludes 'there can be little doubt that the dovecot was the old cemetery building, and the pond had been used for the Jewish burial.'[76] While it is possible that a former and very early *tahara* house had been converted into a dovecot, the pond water on the other hand could scarcely have been used to wash bodies because of its impurity. 'Crowder's Well', mentioned in many texts amd situated on the south-eastern side of the cemetery, was most probably used for this purpose. No gravestones were found in the area of the cemetery itself, but fragments were unearthed in the surrounding area on several occasions over the course of the centuries.

The city of York in the north of England had a flourishing Jewish community from the mid-twelfth century. Led by well-known figures such as Benedict Josce and the Tosafist Yom Tov of Joigny, the Jews of York became very wealthy and thus highly vulnerable. Horrific scenes on 16 and 17 March 1190 (shabbat hagadol) ended this development in very bloody circumstances. Fleeing a mob, the Jews barricaded themselves in the royal castle and committed kiddush hashem – mass suicide – to escape enforced baptism. Although a new Jewish presence formed from the start of the thirteenth century, it was a shadow of the community destroyed a century earlier and was ended by the expulsion of all Jews from England in 1290. York's cemetery was just outside the city walls,

between Monkgate and Bakergate, on the banks of the River Foss. It lay in an area of gardens and pasture, split into strips and bordered by ditches and hedges. Although the Crown had allowed the building of local cemeteries only from 1177, it is thought 'more likely that the Jews dying in York would have been buried informally, possibly on the Jewbury site, before formal recognition'.[1] In the absence of more precise sources, it is assumed that the cemetery was built between the mid-twelfth century and 1230. The land acquired by the Jews was not built upon and satisfied the religious rule of being at least fifty ells (i.e. over fifty metres) from the nearest dwelling – like all the other Jewish cemeteries in England located so far.

Map of York with the Jewbury area, 1766. The cemetery is outside the city walls.

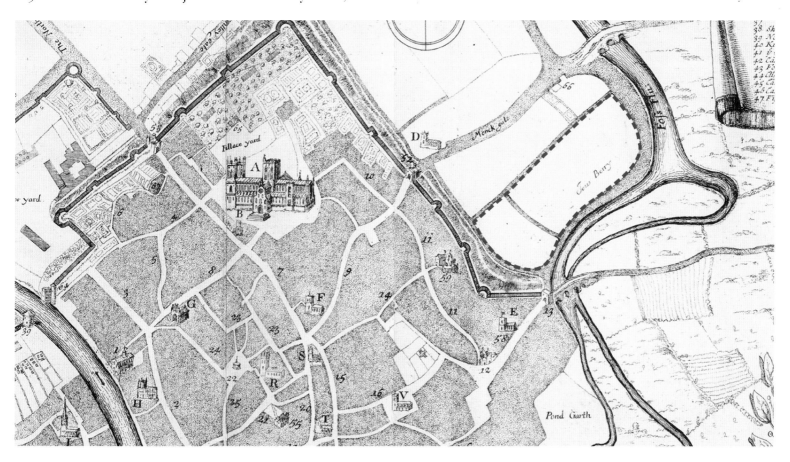

The archaeological excavations

During the centuries after expulsion of the Jews from England, the people of York forgot that the city had ever held a Jewish cemetery, though the name Jewbury remained. In 1980, plans emerged to develop the cemetery area, to that point free of buildings. After exploratory archaeological digs, the Chief Rabbi, Lord Jakobovits, doubted whether the site had contained a Jewish cemetery, since no gravestones were found and the dead were not buried in the traditional east-west position. Later, large-scale excavations dispelled such doubt and proved that this was indeed a halakhic Jewish cemetery. At this point, a supermarket car park was mooted for the old cemetery site – and then approved in a planning process which never considered whether such hallowed ground should be left alone. Mortal remains uncovered in an emergency excavation were to be re-interred in an untouched area and marked with a commemorative plaque.

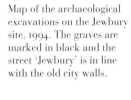

Map of the archaeological excavations on the Jewbury site, 1994. The graves are marked in black and the street 'Jewbury' is in line with the old city walls.

Archaeological investigation of the graves revealed interesting information about health and medical care among York's medieval Jewry, as well as proof that they were buried in accordance with halakhic rules still observed today. Excavation also confirmed the enclosure of a cemetery of 0.18 hectares by embankments and stone walls. The graves were arranged in irregular rows and the generally uniform distance between the 900 to 1,060 graves was so small that there was no space for pathways. Care was taken to ensure that no new grave encroached on an existing one, which would have disturbed the deceased's eternal rest. Overlapping appears to have occurred in only eight places, most likely by accident.[2] Rabbis appear to have been buried in a discrete area, following an often-observed custom of burial that they 'will face their communities on the day of resurrection'. Children of more than a month old were also buried in a special section, but men and women were not interred separately. Most intriguingly, the dead, laid to rest facing from west to east in Winchester and London, lay in a

north-south arrangement in York, with their heads at the southern end of the grave.

Although no gravestones were found – these had all probably been removed for construction material after 1290 – some of the graves bore special markings. At one grave there were stake holes, 'which could have "fenced" off the grave'.[3] Other graves retained collections of stones, which may have been used to secure wooden grave perimeters or markers. Boarded coffins were held together by up to 107 iron nails. Some had iron brackets and fittings, making it possible for a coffin to be reconstructed despite the long-since rotted wood, which was pine or oak. According to tradition, the dead were mostly buried with their arms stretched out alongside the body. Although the cemetery grounds lacked paths, there are indications that tree plantations may have enhanced the appearance of the graveyard, as described in medieval text (Shulchan aruch) and picture sources (see page 32).

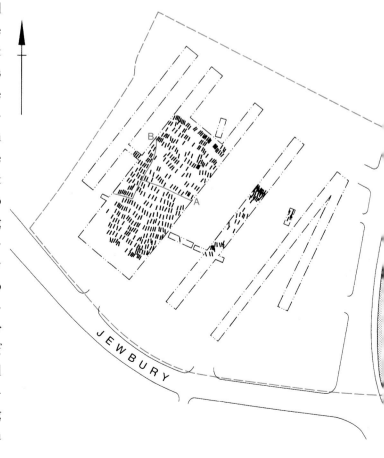

JEWBURY

The beginnings of Jewish settlement in Prague are steeped in legend and it is impossible to pinpoint an exact date. The first written mention however is dated 970 and in 1160 Prague's Jews found a permanent settlement in the so-called Old Town. This Jewish district ran along the river Vltava which, until protection in the nineteenth century, was frequently flooded. On the other hand, it was well positioned near the Charles Bridge linking the Lesser Quarter with its Hradcany Palace, and the economic centre based on the large square of the old town market. Prague's Jewish quarter was unusually large for the period and it was separated from Christian areas by five gates referred to as the *Portae Judaeorum* or 'Jewish gates'. At the ends of major streets, one of which led to the Vltava, the gates were closed at night. Within this gated Jewish quarter, a complete Jewish infrastructure quickly developed so that ultimately there would be nine synagogues, called *schul* in the Ashkenazi dialect, ritual and ordinary bath houses, butchers, bakers, many offices, businesses and workshops and, from 1541, the community's own town hall.

In the 1430s a piece of land on the western side of the Jewish quarter was acquired by the community for a new cemetery, an older one having been closed before. A source from 1440 states that 'the Jewish wardens acquired a house with garden next to the *hampas* [brothel], that lies next to the Jews' Garden where burials are at present carried out.'[1] In 1526, this plot was extended when 'the Jewish administrators bought a garden to bury the dead that lies next to their first garden where they have graves.'[2] Around the same time, an independent, walled-in graveyard was created on the eastern side near the Pinkas synagogue. In 1573, 'the administrators of the Jewish schools and hospitals'[3] acquired a house with a garden on the banks of the Vltava that 'clearly became

the foundation for a further independent cemetery. Primas Mordecai Maisel bought a house with garden in 1598 that extended the middle section of the existing cemetery to the west. In 1630, the cemetery was again extended to link the two main sections.'[4]

It was only at the end of the seventeenth century that the community succeeded in linking the eastern section with the main western one and surrounding the entire site with a wall also serving as a flood barrier. A final extension took place in 1768, a few years before the cemetery was closed.

The cemetery grounds came to encompass buildings such as the Pinkas and Klausen synagogues. To east and north lay Jewish residential areas; to the west, down to the banks of the Vltava, there was scant

Map of the ghetto with the Jewish cemetery, 1690. The cemetery is marked in green, almost surrounded on all sides by buildings. The river Vltava is visible as a green line to the left of the cemetery.

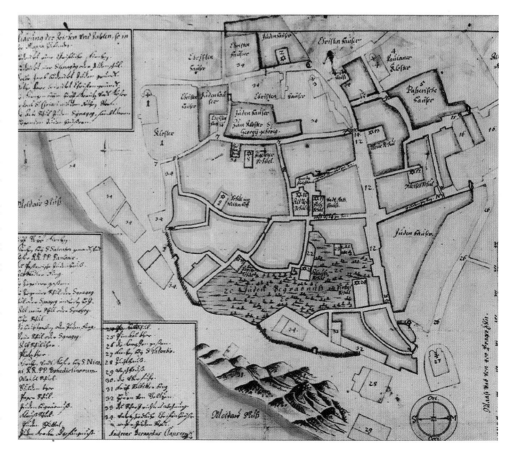

Painting of the entrance
building to the cemetery.
Anonymous, *circa* 1800.

development in the Middle Ages due to threat of flooding. The area was used, among other things, for storing driftwood. As noted already, such proximity to residential areas and the position within the city walls, is unusual for a medieval Jewish cemetery and flouts the *halakha* rules. The explanation is almost certainly the crowded living conditions in medieval Prague. Possibly the long-undeveloped area beside the Vltava allowed the cemetery at least partly to satisfy the formal criterion of being situated outside the city.

There was an entrance, with an impressive gate-house, which was situated next to the Klausen synagogue in the Hampas Gasse. The gatehouse had an orator's pulpit on the side facing the cemetery from which eulogies could be addressed to the mourners. After the building was torn down in 1906, a similar pulpit was integrated into the neo-Romanesque replacement by architects Gerstel and Gabriel. The new building provided rooms for the *chevra kaddisha*, whose old base next to the Pinkas synagogue had been taken down earlier. The new building is now a part of the Prague Jewish Museum with exhibits including the burial society's celebrated cycle of pictures.

The cemetery as a reflection of the Jewish quarter

Modern-day visitors enter the cemetery from the Pinkas synagogue. From its forecourt, steps ascend to the cemetery, at the top of which a small gate gives a breathtaking view of an almost 600-year-old site in a beautiful state of preservation. Some 12,000 gravestones stand packed together in apparent chaos beneath a closely woven canopy of trees and between narrow, winding paths. In rising and falling waves, the stones can be several metres higher than surrounding roads and squares. Although the cemetery has been extended several times, it was often necessary to make space for new graves on the existing land, which was achieved by laying at least six handbreadths of soil on existing graves, as required by Talmudic commandments, thereby creating adequate distance between the old and new plots. Old gravestones were reinstated after the infill of soil in original spots – only higher. Over time the cemetery ground became ever more elevated, with as many as ten layers created in some parts. Historical plans clearly show the cemetery's hilly topography.

The narrowness and concentration of the cemetery, with multiple layers of overlapping graves, reflects the living conditions of Prague's Jews. Since scarcely any extensions to the Jewish quarter were permitted for centuries and despite pogroms, expulsions, epidemics and fire, the number of inhabitants was steadily rising, land became densely developed and houses rose ever upwards, like those of the Venetian ghetto. At the same time, houses and apartments were further divided to create extra, smaller living quarters. By the start of the seventeenth century around 7,000 people were packed into the Jewish quarter.

Langweil's famous model of Prague from 1837 shows a deceptively idyllic Jewish quarter, as it appeared before radical redevelopment around 1900. A district then

The cemetery with the old building of the burial society. Engraving by Vincenc Morstadt, 1840.

known as the Josefov displayed an extremely complex, urban structure with a high density of population in which a diversity of social relationships flourished. The flipside to this was often terrible unhygienic conditions that led to epidemics and premature death. The link between the house-of-life cemetery and the houses of the living is particularly evident on the Nefele Hill next to the Klausen synagogue, where children and stillborn babies (*nefele* is Hebrew for miscarriage) were buried. The hill is almost three metres higher than the Hampas Gasse and is accessed from the cemetery via separate steps, having attained this height due to the high level of infant mortality over the centuries.

At the end of the eighteenth century a cemetery of 1.3 hectares covered more than an eighth of the total area of the Jewish quarter. Since the Middle Ages, the cemetery and residential area had formed so compact a unit that it is no wonder many gravestones bear a quote from Jeremiah (9:21): 'Death is come up into our windows.'

The 'stone archive'

The cemetery's 12,000 preserved gravestones form a unique 'stone archive' of the inhabitants of the Jewish quarter between the fifteenth century and the end of the eighteenth century, although thousands of other

View into the
cemetery.

The entrance
to the cemetery
at Pinkas
synagogue.

graves have been lost or cannot be seen. As a result,
many gravestones were not 'raised' when additional
layers of earth were filled in for new graves, but were
instead laid flat – for their own protection – on top of
the old graves and then covered with earth. Many
grave markers for poorer Jews were made from wood
which subsequently rotted away.

The oldest preserved gravestone is that of Avigdor
Kara (d. 1439), the rabbi and poet, who wrote many
synagogue songs and the famous *selicha 'Et Kol
ha-Tela'ah'* lament for the victims of the Easter
pogrom of 1389 in which most of Prague's Jews
perished.[5] The unadorned and upright stone with its
rectangular, wide frame and inset inscription block is
typical of medieval Ashkenazi gravestones. Other
significant gravestones of this type include those of
Ahron Meschulam (d. 1545) and Menachem ben
Moshe (d. 1529). Menachem's gravestone has a Star of
David in the bottom line of the inscription which is
probably the first time that the Star of David was used
explicitly in Europe as a symbol of Jews and Judaism.
From 1580 onwards, a Renaissance influence begins to
appear in the design of the gravestones, such as gables
adorned with volutes, and tympana with inscriptions.
The script blocks are often divided into several
sections and framed with pilasters. The early
seventeenth-century gravestones of Yitzhak ben
Schlomo, Schemuel ben Juda Kohen and Yehuda
known as the Lion – this latter showing a coat of arms
with the twin-tailed Bohemian lion – are good examples of this type of monument.

From 1600, graves were built in the form of tombs
or sarcophagi that are known as *ohel* (Hebrew for hut)
or, more popularly, as *hojsl* (little house). The four-
walled tombs with two high ends strongly resemble
Sephardic graves, although it is not known whether
their occurrence is due to the influence of the
Sephardim. There are a total of twenty-one such

Two sixteenth-century gravestones.

The gravestone of Schemaia ben Eberl Geronim (d. 1616), Pesl bat Schemaia (d 1602) and Pesl bat Zalman Eberl (d. 1642).

sarcophagus-style graves in the cemetery, one of which belongs to Yehuda ben Bezalel, known as Rabbi Loew (1512–1610) and his wife Perl. Rabbi Loew was one of the Jewish quarter's most innovative thinkers and influential chief rabbis. The author of numerous religious tracts, his name is also associated with many legends, including that of the golem – a man-made creature whose wicked deeds can only be ended by speaking the name of God.

One of the most ornate and exquisite tombs in the entire cemetery is for Hendl Bashevi (d. 1628), wife of the wealthy and influential leader of the Prague community, Jacob Bashevi. Bashevi served three emperors as chief financial adviser and was the first Jew to be ennobled with the title of Treuenberg; when his wife died, he was at the peak of his power. Lions holding Bashevi's noble coat of arms sit at either ends of the dead woman's memorial. But graves of lower-ranking women are also remarkable. Some, especially those of the young and unmarried, show unusual illustrations of female figures, at times roughly outlined but more often detailed. In one case, the image portrays the woman's profession: she spins *tzitzits* (tassels for the prayer shawl).

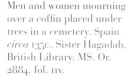

Men and women mourning over a coffin placed under trees in a cemetery. Spain *circa* 1350. Sister Hagadah. British Library, MS. Or. 2884. fol. 11v.

Interior of a synagogue in Spain, *circa* 1350. Sister Hagadah. fol. 17v. London. British Museum.

Jews probably lived on the Iberian peninsula from the second century CE. From the chaos following the collapse of the western half of the Roman Empire, the Goths ruled Iberia from 506 and created a Christian realm with harsh anti-Jewish policies. When the Goths were defeated by the Arabs in 711, the Jews welcomed the Muslims as liberators. 'The Jews enjoyed an untroubled situation under the Muslims compared with what they had suffered under the Gothic monarchy, although they were also subject to certain restrictions.'[1] Slowly, there was a process of arabization of the Jewish minority. 'Language, poetry, good taste, and culture in general, all became arabized under the Muslim rule.'[2] At the same time there developed a synthesis of Arabic, Muslim and Jewish cultures which led to what is now termed 'Sephardic culture'. 'Within the continuity of the religious tradition, it would eventually become something very different from the rest of the Jewish communities.'[3] As a result the cities of Muslim Spain, or *al-Andalus*, became flourishing centres for the then Jewish diaspora. This golden age came to an abrupt end when, at the end of the eleventh century, Muslim zealot Berbers, the Almoravides from northern Africa, arrived in Spain and conquered the small Muslim kingdoms of Andalusia.

When the Islamic invasion of Spain began in the eighth century, a few outposts in the north of the country remained in the hands of Christians, who refused to bow to Muslim hegemony. With time, these pockets of resistance grew to form a new geopolitical structure comprising the three kingdoms of Castilla-León, Navarre and Aragón. Many Andalusian Jews had fled in the eleventh century into these Christian kingdoms to escape the Berbers. For the most part, the Jews benefited – until, in 1492, with the reconquest complete, the Jews were no longer needed and were chased out of the country.

During the prosperous era of Jewish-Christian coexistence in many places and Jewish-Muslim coexistence in Arab-ruled territories, co-operation between followers of the three 'religions of the book' led to tremendous economic and cultural advances. Powerful families ruled Jewish communities as oligarchs, and held high office in the courts of kings and caliphs. Men such as Joseph ibn Selomo ibn Sosan, Cag de la Maleha and Yehuda de la Caballeria were indispensable tax collectors, finance ministers and even military leaders for Christian kings such as Alfons VIII and Peter III. Despite this period of far-reaching integration into their surrounding societies, Jews still lived mostly in their own residential quarters, the *Juderia*. Such separate living arrangements were often enforced, but there were also benefits to Jewish communities: it was easier to defend themselves against a Christian mob, use the shared infrastructure of synagogues, schools, baths, bakers and slaughterhouses, and enjoy the communal life that strengthened their identity in the face of a dominant external society.

The cemeteries

The cemeteries of the *Juderias* were situated, as names such as *Castro de los judios* and *Montjuich* indicate, on hills outside the city, in accordance with the *halakha* and within easy reach of residential districts. Usually of little value, this land was officially signed over to the Jews, while Christians buried their dead beside or in their parish churches. Occasionally, Jewish cemeteries were also situated within city walls. In 1326, King James II gave the Jews of Burianas, in the province of Castellón, a piece of land to build a cemetery inside the town, to spare them the long journey to a neighbouring city.

Cemeteries were walled and had one or more sets of gates. The *tahara* was carried out in the *Juderia* and the dead then carried to the burial site. Some cities still have *Puentes de los judios* ('Jews' bridges') recalling the processions that crossed over them en route to medieval cemeteries. Some 110 Jewish cemeteries have been located in Spain, which 'is considerably lower than the true number and is a provisional figure'.[4] Some of the known sites not built on, and where only the gravestones are missing, have been investigated by archaeologists. Digs have shown that the dead were generally interred in rows, but in Valencia a mass grave was found containing victims of the plague massacre of 1348. Normally, the dead were laid with heads pointing

west and feet pointing east, towards Jerusalem. Again, however, there are a few exceptions: in Valencia, the dead were found laid in a north-south direction, facing the main synagogue, as in Worms. Graves uncovered so far date from the tenth century. Intriguingly, a few cemeteries appear to have been in use into the sixteenth century, after the expulsion of the Jews.

At the end of the thirteenth century, burial societies appeared in Spain for the first time. Until 1492, these societies tended the cemeteries and oversaw burials, *tahara* and transportation of the dead to the cemetery. In rare cases, the dead were interred wrapped simply in linen, but the general rule, as revealed by archaeologists, appears to have been coffins. In contrast to Ashkenazi custom, many of the Sephardic dead wore jewellery. 'Some were buried with rings on every finger, in keeping with the fashion of the time. Many women were buried wearing hairdress adorned with various accessories, including pins and even gold hairnets.'[5]

Gravestone of Mar Selomó ben Mar David b. Parnaj (d. 1097) from the cemetery of León).

Gravestones further reflect the trend that was common in other religious and cultural areas of adopting the customs of Christian and Muslim neighbours. 'The different types of burial roughly correspond to the customs of the other religions practised in Spain. The brick gravemarker now housed in the Museo Sefardi is typically Muslim. Among the oldest tombs are the anthropomorphic type that are hewn out of a

rock; they resemble Christian graves in both form and date.[6] Generally, horizontally laid plaques are based on Islamic-Moorish *mqabriya* (Islamic funeral steles), while vertical stones reflect Christian traditions.[7]

Not all Jewish gravestones are modest in terms of size or shape. As Christians began to use large slabs arranged like gable roofs, so too did the Jews, as shown by the thirteenth century gravestone of Abraham Satibi. More and more Jewish gravestones, or fragments, are now coming to light that were bricked into house walls or reused as foundations or doorsteps after the cemeteries had been destroyed. In Barcelona alone, eighty-nine inscribed stone relics have been found so far.[8]

One of the best-preserved and oldest gravestones in Europe is that of Mar Selomo ben Mar David ben Parnaj, who died on 15 July 1097 in León. While Jewish cemeteries on the Iberian peninsula largely suffered destruction, defamation and grave-robbing after 1492, in some towns the 'Jews' hills' remained after removal of the gravestones, turning into pasture, meadow or woodland. Since the graves remained, these sites are still regarded as cemeteries under Jewish religious law, although some have been excavated by archaeologists, mostly without the permission of Jewish authorities. Historical and religious interests collide in such cases.

Montjuich in Barcelona is one of the most well-researched Jewish cemeteries in Spain having been partly excavated. Here, where the World Fair was held in 1927, was one of the largest Jewish cemeteries in Europe. Montjuich was in use from the ninth to the fourteenth century housing thousands of graves of which 500 were discovered during building works in 2001. Since then the present Jewish community of Barcelona has been fighting to protect the site from further plans for new buildings, such as toilets and bars to serve the nearby Olympic stadium.[9] So far without success they have also asked for a memorial to point out the significance of the site and the fact that it is still a cemetery.

The cemetery of the Basque Vittoria

The Jewish cemetery of the Basque town of Vittoria experienced a unique fate. On Judemendi Hill, east of the city, the Jewish community ceded its cemetery to the town shortly before being expelled under the edict issued by the Catholic monarchs Ferdinand and Isabella. They made one condition, however, that the cemetery grounds, situated near the ghetto, should never be built upon; in other words, the site would remain a cemetery even with all the gravestones removed. The reason the city fathers accepted this condition was more practical: at the time, the city was suffering a raging epidemic and help was desperately needed from the few Jewish physicians remaining in the city. Even after 1492, the condition continued to be observed. One royal decree concerning Vittoria states: 'We command that the ground and soil of the said cemetery of the Jews be excluded (from development) and that it shall remain a local pasture for the said town of Vittoria.'[10] The city obeyed the command until 1952 when a plan arose to build a school on what had become a park. The authorities consulted the Jewish community of the French town of Bayonne, where the majority of Vittoria's Jews had fled in 1492, requesting approval for the plans. Rather surprisingly, the community agreed, with the proviso that a monument be erected to the cemetery. The school, however, was never built and the park remained undeveloped. On 10 December 2004, a 'Peaceful Cohabitation' monument by artist Yael Artsi was unveiled on the site.

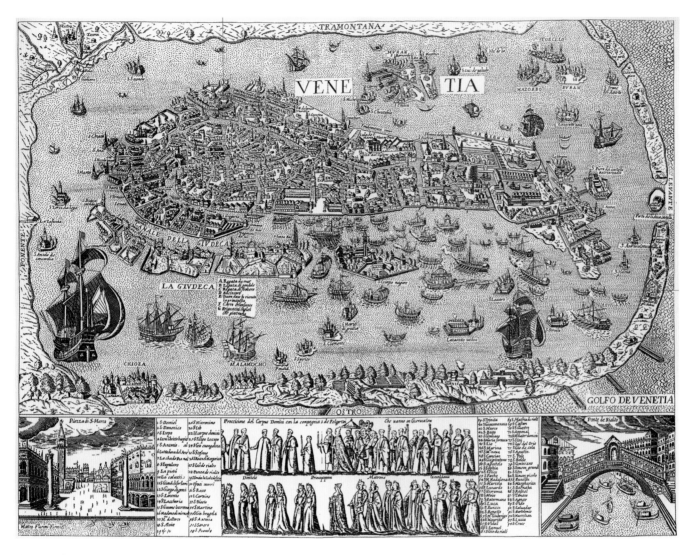

Map of Venice with the
Ghetto and the cemetery
on the Lido (marked with
the red lines). Bernardo
Salvioni. *circa* 1597.
State Archive, Venice.

The Ghetto

While evidence shows that Jews had lived in Venice since 1290,[1] it was only in 1382 that a group of Jewish refugees from Verona, Treviso and Mestre gained permission to settle permanently in the city. The government of the republic of Venice, which called itself 'La Serenissima', issued a *condotta*, a kind of residence permit, which had to be renewed every few years.

The Ghetto of Venice, after which all districts in which European Jews were forced to live are named, was located on an island in the district of Cannareggio. It was originally used by foundry workers, whose activities gave the place its name; the island location was intended to prevent fire from spreading to neighbouring residential areas. In 1516 it was allotted to the Jews. The Ghetto boasted a comprehensive Jewish infrastructure with bakers, butchers and a wide range of traders selling every kind of daily necessity. Above all,

synagogues were built, usually on one of the floors of the tenements. Each group of Jews, who migrated to Venice from various places over the centuries, established its own synagogue, or *Schul*.

The cemetery

On 25 September 1386, a mere four years after the granting of the first *condotta*, a special authority of the republic, the 'Magistrato del Piovego', allotted to the Jews a piece of land near the monastery of San Nicolo on the Lido.[2] The Lido, a narrow island one kilometre in length, still forms the border between the lagoon and the Adriatic, protecting Venice from maritime storms. In the fourteenth century the island was near-deserted, apart from the Benedictine monastery of San Nicolo, whose monks took immediate but unsuccessful legal action against their new Jewish neighbours. After the first *condotta*, this was a further significant step

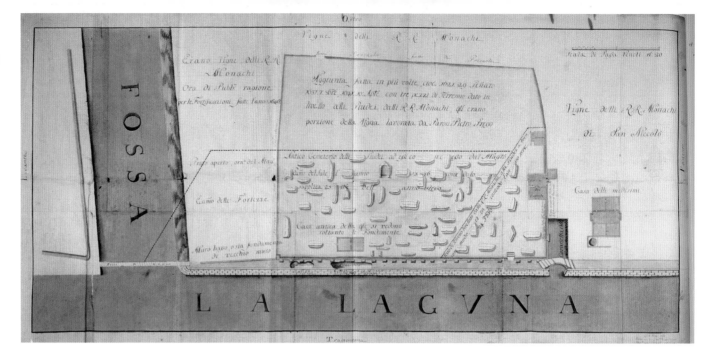

Plan of the cemetery with
the little harbour and the
warden's house. 1768.

towards consolidating and confirming the Jewish presence in the city, long before the Jews were allotted the Ghetto as a permanent residence. The land granted to the Jews lay on the side of the Lido facing the lagoon and was about two kilometres away from the city. Roberta Curiel graphically describes the funeral processions from the Ghetto to the Lido: 'It is traditional for the hearse to make a complete circle round the Ghetto Nuovo, as a symbol of farewell to this narrow strip of land. Funerals would [next] go by gondola down the Rio di Cannareggio, along the northern boundary of the city, and then would set out across the lagoon for the northern side of the Lido. It seems that in the second half of the seventeenth century funerals avoided passing under the bridge of S. Pietro di Castello, then the seat of the Patriarch, in order to avoid hostility, sometimes expressed in the throwing of rubbish and filth.'[3]

The cemetery grounds were measured carefully and its boundaries determined with precision. The site was oblong in form and about 0.5 hectares in size. A narrow path, leading to the monastery of San Nicolo, extended between the shore of the lagoon and the cemetery; a branch canal spanned by a bridge ran along its western edge. Much of this canal was later filled in, with only a portion near the lagoon remaining; a small dock thus developed at this spot. The boats carrying the dead were moored here and a boathouse, or *cavana*, was erected. In 1593 conflict again arose with the neighbouring monks over this boathouse and the adjacent strip of land. The historical documents detailing this dispute are of particular significance, as the Jewish

representatives in this case were all members of the *Fraterna della misericordia*, the local *chevra kaddisha*, which shows how well established the Ghetto community was at this point. A house for the cemetery keeper, the *casa del custode*, the cemetery gardens and perimeter wall were all constructed at the same time. No building for the ritual cleansing of bodies existed, as the *tahara* was carried out in the Ghetto. Although the *condotta* for the Jews was revoked in 1397, funerals continued to be held in the cemetery.

A young man named Shemuel Ben Shimshon, who died on 30 November 1389, was the first resident of the ghetto to be laid to rest in the new cemetery, which then remained in constant use during the subsequent centuries, being enlarged and structurally altered, but never abandoned, until modern times. The first extension was made as early as 1578, and the second in 1630, at the time of a serious plague. Two boundary stones, preserved to this day, and inscribed with 'Ebrei 1631', indicate the new boundary line. This was the last enlargement of the cemetery, which had thus attained the not inconsiderable size of one hectare. In 1646 and in the course of the early eighteenth century portions of the cemetery were repeatedly annexed for defensive purposes, but were for the most part returned shortly afterwards, or the loss made good by allotting new areas to the cemetery. In 1763, the Jewish community finally acquired a further piece of land from the aristocrat Zuanne Grimani, which became the nucleus of the New Cemetery separate from the old. Funerals take place here to this day.

Around 1880, the old cemetery was in a state of

general decay. Many of the gravestones were half-buried or had fallen over, the wall was destroyed, as were the other buildings, and the entire grounds were choked with rank growth. Commissioned by the *Fraterna della Misericordia* and the *Fraterna Generale* of the Jewish communities, in 1882 Graziano Ravà wrote a report on the lamentable condition of the cemeteries on the Lido. He suggested edging the cemetery with a hedge in place of the destroyed wall, and erecting a five-metre high marble obelisk at its centre. The foundation of the cemetery in 1389 and those buried there were to be commemorated in Hebrew and Latin on this monument. The gravestones recently uncovered during construction of a shooting range were to be placed around it. The obelisk was indeed soon erected and the cemetery enclosed by a new wall with, on the Lido side, a classical-style gate set into the wall. The branch canal with the *cavana* had already ceased to exist by this point. The grounds bordered by the wall were, however, at a mere 0.4 hectares, significantly smaller than the original cemetery, large parts of which had disappeared under the grounds of the shooting range. In 1929, the road on the lagoon side was widened at the expense of the cemetery and the gate and wall moved to a new position. This revealed a large number of gravestones, all of which

were placed in the remaining grounds of the cemetery. Utterly exposed to the elements and vegetation, these rapidly began to weather. The Jewish community of Venice and the Committee for the Historic Jewish Centre repeatedly called for restoration work to be carried out, for instance on the wall, which had been threatening to collapse since the 1960s. Restoration finally began in 1998, and was completed in 1999.

All the gravestones in the old cemetery are made of Istrian limestone, a very hard stone from which, apart from brick, almost all of Venice is built. Around 1600, the state issued an edict prohibiting upright gravestones so that from then on all new gravestones had to lie flat. They were made in the form of sarcophagi, though the dead were not buried in these, but deeper under the ground. Most of the older upright gravestones feature stylized ashlar masonry at the base recalling the *Cotel*, the western wall of the Temple in Jerusalem. A further distinctive feature are circular holes on the lower halves of the gravestones, which are normally hidden below the ground for which there are several explanations. Some have suggested that they were used to transport the stones while another school of thought holds that girders were inserted into them to hold the stones in place underground. The most pleasing explanation, however, is that the souls of the dead

A gondola taking a coffin from the Ghetto to the cemetery on the Lido. Etching by Giovanni de Pian, 1784. A less than friendly crowd is gathering on the bridge watching the 'spectacle'.

View through the cemetery gate towards Venice.

The centre of the cemetery with the nineteenth-century obelisk and a gravestone featuring stylized ashlar masonry recalling *Cotel*.

can leave the earth through these openings, facing in the direction of Jerusalem, on the day of resurrection.

As in the Sephardic cemetery in Amsterdam, some of the gravestones feature depictions of people, contravening Jewish tradition. One remarkable gravestone depicts the spies sent to reconnoitre the land of Canaan on Moses' behalf. Both figures – apart from their hats – are naked. Alongside the usual Jewish symbols such as hands raised in benediction (*Cohanim*) and pitchers (*Leviim*), the gravestones are often adorned with coats of arms and other heraldic symbols of the dead's Hispanic origin.

Eighteenth-century gravestone depicting two men carrying a giant bunch of grapes, coming back from spying in Canaan (Fourth Book of Moses 13:23).

The cemetery wall with late eighteenth-century gravestones in the shape of columns.

Retaining Tradition

After their victory over Granada, the last 'Moorish kingdom' in Spain, in 1492, the Catholic monarchs Ferdinand and Isabella promulgated the 'edict of expulsion': Jews had to leave their homeland, known to them as Sepharad, within four months. However, many Jews had left the Iberian peninsula for havens abroad long before the fall of Granada, some going to North Africa, particularly Morocco, and a large number fleeing to Istanbul, which had been taken by the Ottoman Turks in 1453, where they were warmly welcomed by the sultan.

More and more *Maranos*, baptized Jews, left the Iberian peninsula in terror of their lives, to spread across the globe. They went to England, the Netherlands, Germany and Italy, where – in one of history's great ironies – they settled in the Papal States and in particular in Rome. Soon Sephardim lived in both the Old and New Worlds. In 1654, some moved to what is now New York from Brazil, and built their first cemetery two years later. In many places they met Ashkenazi Jews, with tensions often arising. In some locations, Ashkenazim and Sephardim established parallel communities with separate synagogues, as in Venice and Istanbul, and – more rarely – their own cemeteries, as in Amsterdam and London. Often, however, the dead were buried in shared sites as in Berlin, Krakow and Rome.

Despite the open anti-Semitism of Protestant reformers such as Martin Luther, life improved considerably for seventeeth-century Jews in non-Catholic countries, as well as in the Ottoman empire. In Amsterdam *Maranos* who had re-embraced Judaism in hordes, following flight from the Inquisition, were as well treated as in Istanbul, London and Venice. While the reasons for this were primarily economic and political, Protestant powers such as the Netherlands and England, and later Prussia, proved increasingly tolerant on matters of religious practice.

In Prague's Olsany cemetery, a new trend developed from the end of the eighteenth century. For the 800 years in which separate Jewish cemeteries had been situated outside residential areas they were built in accordance with the rules of *halakha*, but with little regard to aesthetic appearance. From 1784, however, Prague's Olsany cemetery featured the designs of contemporary English landscape gardens, aiming to counter sombre thoughts with beauty. This process of beautifying the Jewish cemetery is a key developmental strand, and the park cemetery of Prague's Olsany is therefore an important bridge between the traditional Jewish cemetery and the cemeteries of the time of emancipation.

The early 18th century gravestone of Moses de Mordechai Senior (d. 1730), from the Sephardic cemetery in Amsterdam. This detail depicts Moses holding the tablets with the Ten Commandments, flanked by King David playing the harp (left) and Abraham looking to heaven (right).

Amsterdam/Sephardic
Cemetery on the Amstel
66

'The Jewish Cemetery.'
Oil painting by Jacob Isaaks
van Ruisdael. 1654–55.
Detroit Institute of Arts.

Around 1655, Jacob van Ruisdael painted the Sephardic Bet Haim cemetery, which had by that point been in existence for some forty years, in Ouderkerk on the Amstel. In the foreground are bright marble gravestones, while in the background, the ruins of a medieval church form the second focal point of the picture. A dramatic, stormy sky covers the scene. This painting is often interpreted as a meditation on transience, with a world of bleakness and hopelessness relieved by a fleeting and powerfully symbolic rainbow, a reminder of God's promise after the flood: 'I have set my rainbow in the clouds, and it will be the sign of the covenant between me and the earth. Whenever I bring clouds over the earth and the rainbow appears in the clouds, I will remember my covenant between me and you and all living creatures of every kind. Never again will the waters become a flood to destroy all life.' (Gen. 9:13-15)

With the rainbow looming behind the gravestones and church ruins, van Ruisdael therefore sees a fitting image for the Jews' faith in God, a faith set in stone in the cemetery on the Amstel. At the same time, the setting also testifies to a particular obsession with the issue of life after death: 'More than any other Jewish community in Europe at the time, the Sephardim of Amsterdam took great interest in what happened to a person after death. They were especially concerned with the fate of the soul.'[1] This is one key reason why the community lavished such care on the building of its cemetery. Today, the cemetery in Ouderkerk, together with that in Hamburg-Altona, can lay claim to being the most important Sephardic cemetery in Europe.

Sephardim in Amsterdam

The history of the Jews in the Netherlands begins relatively late, at the end of the sixteenth century, inseparably linked as it is with the fate of Sephardic Jews driven from the Iberian peninsula. With their newly acquired religious freedom, which the Netherlands granted from 1579, the desire of the *Maranos* grew to renounce officially the Christianity lately forced upon them and return to Judaism as *Conversos*. With public services of worship not yet

permitted, James Lopes da Costa set up a synagogue in his own home and around this time the Sephardim made their first attempts to open a cemetery.

Between the seventeenth and early nineteenth centuries most Sephardim lived in the centre of Amsterdam. Together with the Ashkenazim, who arrived later, and other immigrants, they settled chiefly in a newly-created part of the city known as the Vlooijenburg in the present-day Waterlooplein. The Vlooijenburg was a rectangular district surrounded on all sides by canals and divided into four residential quarters by two intersecting streets, with bridges

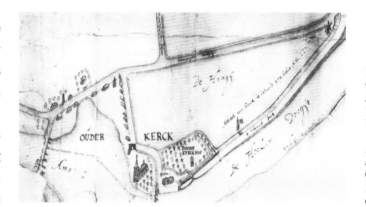

Detail of a map of Ouderkerk with the Jewish cemetery called 'Joodse Kerckhof'. C. Dankersz. 1636

A boat with a coffin arriving at the cemetery at Ouderkerk. Etching by Romeyn de Hooghe, eighteenth century.

View of the cemetery from the Bullewijk river with gate and *tahara* house. Copperplate by Abraham Rademaker, 1791.

One of thirty-four maps of the cemetery at Ouderkerk. Henriques de Castro, 1883.

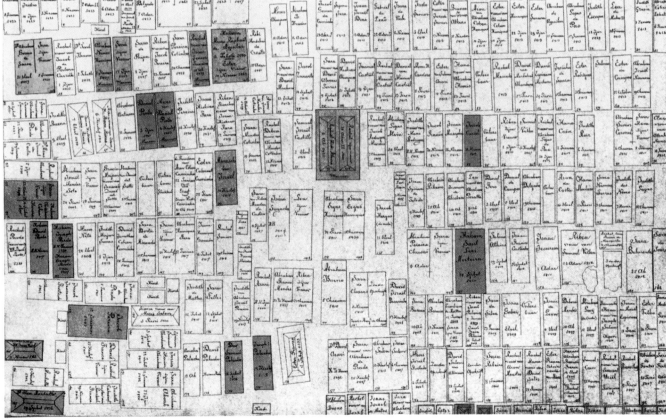

leading to this 'island'. Despite such separation, Amsterdam saw no ghetto along Venetian lines and Jews lived freely in the city until the Nazi invasion. Life in the Vlooijenburg was largely shaped by its Jewish residents, but non-Jews were also present. While Rembrandt spent too much money buying a house here in 1639, his interest in themes of the Jewish Bible intensified with close proximity to the Sephardim, and he found among them many models for the portrayal of biblical figures.

On the then *Houtmarkt* (wood market), today's *Mr Visserplein*, the Sephardim of Amsterdam built their imposing synagogue designed in 1675 by Elias Bouman (1636–86), the *Esnoga*. Opposite, the Ashkenazim had built their synagogue, the *Grote Sjoel* (Great School), by 1671. Over the centuries, this area of worship grew into a group of four buildings – the only ensemble of its kind in Europe, visible from far and wide on the city's skyline. These synagogues formed the centre of Amsterdam's Jewish quarter.

In 1614, the Sephardic communities bought a piece of land in Ouderkerk on the Amstel for 2,700 florins from a lawyer called Jacob Backer. The first burial took place that same year: Joseph Senior, infant son of a community leader, received a small gravestone inscribed with a Hebrew poem in which the child explains he is the first to be buried in the cemetery. All the dead were to be transported by barge on canals and rivers from the city of Amsterdam and the neighbouring towns in which the Sephardim lived, very often over considerable distances.

In 1616 the cemetery on the Amstel was officially inaugurated and the date was proudly marked on a gate situated on the Bullewijk landing jetty. A map of 1636 clearly shows the first piece of cemetery land in the south-west corner of an almost triangular field surrounded by two roads and the Bullewijk river. During the following years the cemetery was repeatedly enlarged.

The first *metaher (tahara)* house, shown on the 1636 map, was replaced by a new building on an eastward extension in 1705. Restored in 1966, this is now one of the oldest and best-preserved *tahara* houses in Europe. Here occurred ritual washing of the body and subsequent mourning ceremonies which gave the building its second name as the *rodeamentos* — the house of circuits, or *hakafot*, in which mourners processed round the coffin ritually. The cemetery was not surrounded by a wall, but rather by fences and hedges. A 1791 copper engraving by Abraham Rademaker shows the border with the Bullewijk, and a narrow path runs between a bank and a high hedge in which two gates have been cut. The entrance in the foreground was used by the *Cohanim*, in order to enter the *tahara* house while maintaining a suitable distance

from the graves. The house had a carefully separated extension from which the *Cohanim* could follow the *hakafot* through a window, without being under the same roof as the dead person. Close to the *tahara* house was a separate area for *Cohanim* burials. They were able to see the graves of their relatives without getting too close by means of a special path. This complex spatial and functional system of separate paths, spaces and graves for the *Cohanim* is still in use, giving us a fine example of the very specific rules to be followed in a Jewish cemetery. The old part of the cemetery was so densely populated that no paths have

The seven circular walks (*hakafot*) around the bier in the *tahara* house. Etching by Bernard Picard from *Cérémonies et coutumes religieuses de tous les peoples du monde*, 1723.

A burial at Ouderkerk. Etching by Bernard Picard from *Cérémonies et coutumes religieuses de tous les peoples du monde*, 1723.

Les ACAFOTH ou les sept tours, autour du CERCUEÏL.

Les ASSISTANS jettent de la terre sur le CORPS.

The *tahara* house with
a wooden extension for
the *Cohanim*.

The interior of the
tahara house.

been retained: those in existence are 'trampled walk-ways' and were not designed as proper pathways. In newer sections, on the other hand, there are planned paths and the graves are often enclosed by hedges.

A small hill occupies the centre of the old section. Here, until the early seventeenth century, there was a house, the *Huys ten Amstel*, next to the site of a castle owned by the Count of Amstel and destroyed in the thirteenth century. This hill was also the focus for Jacob van Ruisdael's painting (see p.66), which shows some of the cemetery's oldest gravestones still visible today. Ischac Uzeil's 1622 marble gravestone is in the centre of the picture, along with the pagoda-shaped gravestone of Ishak Franco Medeyros and that of Eliahu Motalto both from 1616. Often, these early stones are adorned with ostentatious family crests, since the *Maranos* had adopted the names and coats of arms of their Christian godfathers. Following their return to Judaism, they retained these symbols, as did their descendants. Alongside gravestones which, like those of medieval Spain, bear only Hebrew inscriptions, Ouderkerk also features some with text in Spanish or Portuguese (often mingling with Hebrew) such as that found on the grave of Miguel de Spinoza (1654), the father of the philosopher Baruch Spinoza. The grave of Rabbi Menasseh ben Israel (1657), who petitioned Oliver Cromwell and made it possible for Jews to resettle in England, is one of the simpler gravestones inscribed in Hebrew alone.

Towards the end of the seventeenth century, gravestones become more elaborate, and it is striking that they very frequently show detailed representations of people, thus flouting the Biblical ban on human imagery. Very often the particular pictures on these graves were requested by the people later buried beneath them. All this outraged the strict Ashkenazim who were also horrified by the many symbols of death common to Christian belief (skulls, sickles, hourglasses, putti, crying children). 'The liberal use of such general symbols can most likely be explained by the fact that Sephardic Jews had lived as Christians for around a hundred years and had during this time come into contact with Christian art.'[2]

View over the cemetery
with two gravestones in
the foreground.

Detail of the gravestone of
Moses de Mordechai Senior
(d. 1730) with a scene from
the book of Esther depicting
Mordechai on his horse.

The entrance of the Bevis Marks synagogue, built in 1701 by a Quaker builder.

Although the Jews were expelled from England in 1290, individuals and small groups still settled there, particularly in London which, since the fourteenth century, was increasingly renowned as an international city of trade. Following expulsion from Spain in 1492, *Maranos* drifted to England, and especially to the capital. However it was not before 1656 and after petitions by Rabbi Menasseh ben Israel that Oliver Cromwell, the Lord Protector, permitted religious services and the influx of further *Maranos*, as well as allowing Jews to trade on the stock exchange and acquire a cemetery. This typical piece of pragmatism from a state without a written constitution would ultimately allow the readmission of Jews into England. Following the restoration of the monarch in 1660, Charles II, largely indifferent to matters of religion, was not only disinclined to repeal this agreement but actually reaffirmed it, again via the circuitous route of allowing Jews to trade. In 1699, a plot of land was acquired on a street named Bevis Marks, and Joseph Avis — as a Quaker, another religious and social outsider — was commissioned to execute a design based on the Sephardic example in Amsterdam. Barely changed over the centuries, the first synagogue on English soil since 1290 still survives today having emerged unscathed from the Blitz that destroyed the nearby Great Synagogue.

The residential district and the old cemetery

During the 18th century, the area around Bevis Marks became an increasingly Jewish residential district. By 1800, most of London's Jews lived between Moorgate and Brick Lane, while the wealthy preferred nearby Finsbury Square and Finsbury Circus. Poorer Jews lived in the streets around Christ Church, Spitalfields.

Here, along Brick Lane, they increasingly moved into the houses of the Huguenots — and also their churches. The present-day mosque on Brick Lane was originally a Huguenot church that later became a mission institution for Jews and then a synagogue.

A main road, Mile End, led from the part of the City of London in which Bevis Marks is situated (known in the eighteenth century as the 'Synagogue District',[1]) and passed Brick Lane heading eastwards, serving as the main arterial road along the Thames and into Essex. Sparsely populated in those days, the surrounding area had space to build a cemetery.

In 1656, the year of Cromwell's dispensation, Antonio Carvajal leased a 1.5-hectare plot of land for 900 years for the Sephardic community, lying a little way back from Mile End and known as the 'Soldier's Tenement'.[2] Mrs Isaac de Brito was the first to be interred there in 1657. The fact that the elders of nearby St Katharine Cree allowed the church bells to ring during the burial, illustrates the unusually friendly rapport between Jews and Christians in seventeenth-century London.

By 1660, a few plague victims had been interred, and the high number of children's graves, known as *angelito*, complete with their small gravestones, bears witness to the dreadful infant mortality rates of the time. It was not until 1684 that the cemetery was surrounded by a wall, the occasion being marked by a plaque. A *chevra kaddisha* was established in 1665, to ensure that *halakhic* rules were observed. In 1684 special administrator David Israel Nunez held the key to the cemetery, overseeing all proceedings, keeping a burial register and ensuring that the gravestones did not exceed specific dimensions – for, in death, all are equal. From sunset until 5 a.m., the cemetery was protected by a watchman. His task was 'to watch for the safety of our bodies. The guard was for the dual purpose of preventing desecration and foiling body snatching.'[3] He also kept an eye on the alms box. The duties of the cemetery administrator were clearly defined. He was forbidden to bury an uncircumcized man or his family without the prior permission of the *mahamad* and the eldest member of the *chevra kaddisha*.

Plan of London with the *Velho*, the Sephardic cemetery, Mile End, 1850.

The original cemetery quickly filled, as did an extension on a neighbouring piece of land. In 1733 the Sephardim acquired another 2.6 hectares of land a few hundred metres to the east known as Cherry Tree. Like the old cemetery, or *velho*, the new cemetery (*novo*) was surrounded by a wall and a *tahara* house was built which survived until 1922: only the dedication stone remains today. The entire grounds of the new cemetery cost £2,000, a fortune for the time, comparable in size to the cost of the Bevis Marks synagogue built in 1701 for £2,650. A third cemetery was opened in 1853.

In 1790, the community of Sephardic Jews in London built a hospital, a *beth holim*, on the side of the cemetery facing Mile End. The cemetery thus also served as a hospital garden and in 1916 Basil Holmes, a Victorian researcher, noted: 'These [cemeteries] are neatly kept, the former [*Velho*] being actually turned into a sort of garden for the patients in the hospital, with trees in it, paths and seats.'[4] With the construction of cottages for the elderly on one side in 1913, the site's unusual character as a place of recovery was accentuated further (a position echoed in the cemeteries in Fürth and Frankfurt, and on Berlin's Grosse Hamburger Strasse and Schönhauser Allee). Although the former hospital and cottages for the elderly are now used by nearby Queen Mary College, the cemetery still looks as it did at the time of Holmes's visit.

View into the *Velho*.

The gravestone of Haham David Nieto. Nieto is best known for two treatises, one of which was based on a sermon he gave at Bevis Marks (1704). Accused of Spinozian beliefs, the accusations were later refuted. Visitors frequently leave stones and memorial candles on the gravestone.

Dense rows of flat, mostly severely weathered, gravestones stand amid a few sarcophagi and an edging of displaced stones. There are no paths, and trees are slowly uprooting the gravestones. Surrounding terraced houses seem to peer over the cemetery wall.

The majority of gravestones are now difficult or impossible to read. Erosion has blurred the name of Antonio Carvajal, who leased the cemetery for the community and was buried there two years later, or the memorial to Simon de Caceres (d. 1704), a merchant advising Cromwell on the defence of Jamaica and possible conquest of Chile. The grave of Don Isaac Lindo (1636–1717), first Jewish broker on the London Stock Exchange and an ancestor of Disraeli, is particularly poignant.

Present-day visitors access the cemetery through a new gate on the eastern side. Until the 1970s access was obtained through a courtyard passage originating in Mile End. This concealed entry is in stark contrast to the grand entrance to Amsterdam's Ouderkerk cemetery. This illustrates the lack of confidence among the returning Jews of England, unlike their fellow believers in the Netherlands. Whereas the Amsterdam synagogues were clearly visible, the Bevis Marks synagogue was hidden in a courtyard and surrounded by buildings, like the cemetery in Mile End.

Following the expulsions from Spain in 1492 and Portugal in 1497, a new life began for thousands of Jewish refugees in the Ottoman Empire. In 1453, the Turks had conquered Constantinople, renamed it Istanbul, and made it their new capital. The city, which had largely been deserted by this point, was rebuilt and thousands of the inhabitants under the old empire were moved back in. For the Jews of Constantinople, there dawned a new era of significantly improved living conditions. 'Mohammed (Mehmet) the Conqueror (1451–81), on entering the capital, granted to the Jews equal rights with all his non-Mussulman subjects, assigning to their chief rabbi a seat in the divan next to the spiritual chief of the Greek Church.'[1] While the legal position of the Jews in the Ottoman Empire differed over the centuries from region to region, generally it is true 'that the Ottoman's attitude towards non-Muslim subjects was relatively tolerant.'[2] Since the invitation to the Sephardim fleeing from Spain and Portugal by Sultan Bayezid II (1481–1512), the Jews were free to travel, conduct business and form settlements so that by the early sixteenth century, many of them held key economic and political positions within the empire. The number of *Maranos* who settled in Constantinople up to 1574 amounted to 10,000 and the whole Jewish population numbered 30,000.[3] They were organized in many different communities or *kehilot*, according to the places where they came from. Jews who had lived here since Byzantine times called themselves *Romaniotes*. Many Jews occupied lofty positions at the court of the sultan, with the post of chief physician or chief apothecary traditionally being held by Jews right up until the eighteenth century, conducting their practice in a tower-like construction within the Topkapi Palace complex, the sultan's seat of government.

Following the Ottoman victory, no fewer than three centres of Jewish settlement formed, alongside which there were also a few other quarters less densely populated by Jews. During the Golden Age of the sixteenth century, many successful Jewish merchants, bankers and court officials were able to build grand homes, some of which were situated on the popular banks of the Golden Horn. Hasköy district was the most popular centre of Jewish life in Istanbul.

From 1453 onwards, Sultan Mehmet II also encouraged the *Romaniotes*, arriving from the old imperial territories, to settle in Hasköy. This district lay on the north bank of the Golden Horn, i.e. opposite the Balat district of the old town. In the seventeenth century, there were around 11,000 Jews living in Hasköy, accounting for the majority of the area's residents. 'The history of Hasköy is in fact the story of the Golden Age of Istanbul Jewry ... No neighbourhood was more blessed than Hasköy with Jewish educational and cultural facilities. In view of this tradition, it is not surprising that the first Hebrew press in Istanbul

Street scene from the Jewish quarter of Balat.

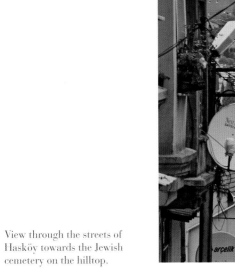

View through the streets of Hasköy towards the Jewish cemetery on the hilltop.

OPPOSITE PAGE, TOP: Detail of a map of Istanbul by George Hoegnagel (1572–1617). The old city with its ancient city walls is on the left, facing the waters of the Golden Horn. Opposite lies the newer city quarter of Pera (Galata). Above Pera is the area of Hasköy with two harbouring boats and the Jewish cemetery.

OPPOSITE PAGE, BOTTOM: Scene from the cemetery at Hasköy. Lithograph by A. Preziosi, *circa* 1841.

was established in Hasköy.'[4] If you visit Hasköy today, traces still remain of the district's earlier Jewish inhabitants[5] such as the rabbinic synagogue and the Karaites' synagogue, still in use today, although the Ezgher synagogue on the banks of the Golden Horn has been converted into a restaurant. Given this strong Jewish presence, it is no great surprise that the biggest and most important cemetery in the Ottoman period was also built here. 'Hasköy-based Jewish institutions such as synagogues, schools, hospitals and a cemetery, served the entire Jewish community of the capital.'[6]

Kasim Pasa and Hasköy

The Jews of Istanbul built their first cemetery of the new Ottoman era on the banks of the Golden Horn in Kasim Pasa, between Galata/Pera and Hasköy. 'At the end of the sixteenth century, the Jews of Istanbul claimed that the cemetery in Kasim Pasa had been given to them by Mehmet the Conqueror [in the

fifteenth century].'[7] It contained large and impressive gravestones, which were later plundered by Muslim neighbours. In the nineteenth century, the cemetery was destroyed completely when the government built shipyards here for the sultan's navy.

The district of Hasköy, near Pera, sweeps up from the banks of the Golden Horn, where the shipyards have been located since the sixteenth century, towards the chain of hills that adjoin the district to the north. On one hill, towards Galata, is the Muslim cemetery and, separated from it by a valley that is now developed, is the Jewish cemetery. Following the plundering of the cemetery of Kasim Pasa, the elders of the Jewish community negotiated with the *vakif*, the representative of the Sultan Bayezid Han, over the purchase of new cemetery grounds. An official edict from the court, dated 3 November 1582, confirmed the final agreement: 'Above the garden of the late Piri Pasa, near the nether part of the public thoroughfare known as Karlik Harman, up the Yorgi vineyard, to the public thoroughfare in the wadi overlooking the garden of the Mustafa Aga, to the canal on western side – all the uninhabited land thenceforward is available.'[8] This description makes it clear that, at the end of the sixteenth century, Hasköy and its environs were not particularly densely populated. Vineyards, forests, meadows and fields adjoined the open country from which, despite the enclosure, wild animals would enter the cemetery and dig up fresh graves.

Numerous town plans from the sixteenth century, such as that compiled by Vavassores in 1520, Johann Baptist Homann and the famous 'Civitas Orbis Terrarum' by George Hoegnagel (1572–1617) show with rare clarity the 'Sepulture de Giudei', i.e. the Jews' cemetery. Adjoined in places by roads, the cemetery is demarcated from neighbouring fields by a fence or wall, and on all of the plans, a two-storey building is shown at the northern perimeter of the cemetery which has a separate, walled-off yard, distinct from the cemetery proper. This may have been a very early *tahara* house or a warden's house. The entrance to the cemetery was on the south-east side of the burial site, towards Hasköy, unlike today, where the entrance is located on the opposite side. Vavassores and

Hoegnagel indicate the actual cemetery grounds symbolically with rectangular gravestone insignias, while Homann shows six schematic areas with rod insignias which certainly do not indicate any real field dividers and should only be understood as symbols.

After several extensions in 1814, 1836 and 1953, the cemetery covered a total area of 24.5 hectares, but in the 1970s, large parts were destroyed by the construction of a six-lane motorway and it was divided up into four parts. Graves from the nineteenth century in particular fell foul of the motorway, some of which were resited, but many were cleared and dumped on another part of the cemetery. The oldest part of the cemetery, with its valuable gravestones, fortunately remained untouched. It is surrounded on all sides by a wall of varying age. The present cemetery grounds are in turn divided by a wall into the cemetery of the rabbinical community and that of the Karaites. The term 'rabbinical community' refers to the majority community of Istanbul, which was traditionally based on rabbinical teachings; the Karaites are a Jewish sect which does not follow Talmudic traditions, and often is not even recognized as Jewish by mainstream Jewry.

The current entrances to the two cemeteries are situated on the northern side, along the motorway that cuts deep into the landscape. A few years ago, as the cemetery is still used for burials, new and elaborate buildings for the *tahara*, mourning room and modern functions were built at the entrance to the cemetery of the rabbinical community, from which an old connecting pathway runs between Hasköy and Okmeydani to the south, towards the Golden Horn. On both sides lie the graves, located on terrain that falls steeply away to the east and south. Subsidence of the land and earthquakes, but also vandalism and frequent robbery, led to repeated slippage and many of the gravestones lie at odd angles, as if scattered randomly. Given the irregularity of the terrain, the graves were not arranged in rows or in any recognizable order right up until the nineteenth century, but instead followed the topography of the hilly landscape. This higgledy-piggledy layout is one of the reasons for the chaotic impression that visitors get, an impression that the cemetery has given since the sixteenth century. 'A grid-like network

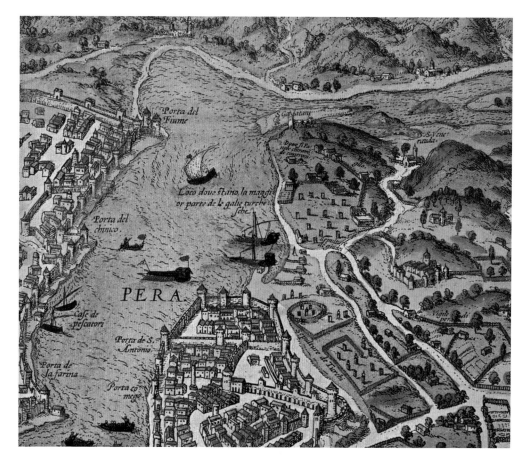

View over the Jewish cemetery at Hasköy and the waters of the Golden Horn towards the centre of Istanbul with its Imperial mosques. Monochrome ink wash, English 1830.

The same view in 2007.

and all of the burial societies of the *kehilot*, one in each quarter and collectively known as the *Hevrat Qevarim*,[10] exercised their authority on the cemetery. Each *chevra* was responsible for an individual part of the cemetery, resulting in almost separate community cemeteries,[11] where they buried the dead of their respective communities.[12] Although not discernible in the landscape now, the cemetery thus also reflects the significant fragmentation of the Jews of Istanbul into 'sovereignties'.

The graves

Burials have taken place in Hasköy since 1582, with the result that the cemetery, with its 22,000 preserved graves, represents a unique document of a European Jewish community living under Muslim rule. A survey[13] of the gravestones in 1990 yielded valuable information on the development of Istanbul Jewry. An analysis of the types of stone used demonstrated that the earliest gravestones were all made from soft chalk, but by the end of the sixteenth century this chalk had been replaced by travertine, and from the first half of the seventeenth century onwards, the often Jewish stone-masons made the majority of gravestones out of marble. This change of material shows the growing wealth of the city's Jews and the improvements in transportation within the Ottoman Empire.

The majority of gravestones lie horizontally, in keeping with Sephardic tradition.[14] However, there are vertical ones, which generally indicate, as would be expected from their tradition, the graves of *Romaniotes* and Ashkenazim. Rozen, an Israeli scholar on Sephardic culture, postulates the theory that the vertical Jewish gravestone migrated in the form of a grave plaque leaned against grave pits and catacombs in Erez Israel and the Near East to Italy, France, Germany and from there again to Istanbul.

The horizontal gravestones of the Sephardim are in fact a fascinating expression of adaptation to surrounding Ottoman-Muslim culture. At the head end, where the inscription is, the majority exhibit a cambered ogive in the form of a *mihrab*, a niche that marks the direction of Mecca in every mosque. The elaborate *mihrabs* of the mosques of Istanbul 'were

of paths'[9] is however superimposed on the irregular arrangements and while it is difficult to discern nowadays, they lead to the graves of particularly wealthy and significant families and individuals, about which more will be said later. The cemetery's access structure thus reflects the social hierarchy of Istanbul's Jews.

The cemetery is further based on structures that are not at first obvious from a spatial perspective. Its creation was due to the negotiating skills of the representatives of the entire Jewish community in Istanbul, clearly the source of inspiration of the Jewish stone cutters'.[15] There are also horizontal gravestones with the *mihrab* motif set into the flat gravestone in the form of a Muslim-Turkish prayer mat, known as a *seccade*.[16] Frequently, the gravestones' *mihrabs* are filled with lines of text that give the impression of an illuminated Muslim manuscript, but these *mihrabs* do not serve to indicate the direction of Mecca – in fact, they are not even laid facing Mecca, but instead to the south, to Jerusalem.[17] At the same time, despite all the integration of and adaptation to Muslim surroundings, they also exhibit something new, since the use of the *mihrab* and prayer mat on a gravestone, for example, is a Jewish invention not found in Muslim cemeteries.

Further proof of this is found on the horizontal gravestones. At their top and base, many of these gravestones, apart from the *mihrab*, have a depression on each side that was intended as a receptacle for memorial candles or oil. This is one of the oldest deco-

rative motifs in Hasköy and stems from the quotation, "The soul is the lamp of God" (Proverbs, 20:27). It is found only in the Jewish cemeteries of Istanbul. The custom of lighting candles at the heads of the dead in the funeral house, but not in the cemetery, was found in Prague (see chapter 1), London, Jerusalem and Krakow. Apparently, the lighting of candles in the funeral home stems from the belief that it banished evil spirits, whereas illuminated candles in the cemetery were intended to highlight the bond between the soul and *olam haba*, or the kingdom of eternity. The Istanbul candle niches also appear to have been adopted from the Ottoman surroundings and transformed, since the similar depressions on Muslim graves were intended as drinking vessels for birds.

An innovation occurred in the seventeenth century, when horizontal grave plaques were combined with vertical stones. This is possibly as a result of the lengthy co-existence of Ashkenazim and Sephardim. For the

Horizontal gravestone with depressions intended as receptacles for memorial lights.

Mehmet the Conqueror invited the Jews 'to dwell in the best of the land, each beneath his wine and his fig tree'.

most part, it is the graves of prominent rabbis or wealthy merchants that demonstrate such composite arrangements.

Of particular interest are the sarcophagus graves that appear for the first time in Hasköy in around 1610. The most eye-catching stones in this category, alongside the rounded and other variations, are those exhibiting a faceted top and sides. These stones, some of which have up to nine facets, are often asymmetrically tapering mock sarcophagi that are hollow inside and which lie on a table-like marble slab. The facets are adorned with names and sayings as well as floral, Ottoman ornaments in the form of tulips and sunflowers, sometimes in vases. At the head and foot ends, there are often representations of cypress trees, tulips, vases and rosettes, as well as cartouches containing the initials for *Baruch Ha-Gozer* ('Blessed is the maker of this decree'). Such faceted mock sarcophagi are found in many other Jewish cemeteries in the Ottoman Empire, even the old cemetery in Salonica that was destroyed during Nazi occupation.

Rozen was able to demonstrate that this type of grave appeared for the first time in Anatolia at the end of the eleventh century. 'This unique form, unknown in other Mediterranean and Balkan cultures, wended its way from the banks of the Yenisey River to eastern, central and western Anatolia. From there, it penetrated the funerary art of Jewish cemeteries in Istanbul

Prismatic gravestone with floral decorations.

and Rumelia – a path spanning more than a thousand years and crossing not only rivers, mountains and deserts but also cultures and religions.'[18]

The grave pits

A particularly unusual feature in Hasköy are the grave pits created in the seventeenth and eighteenth centuries. Arranged in tight rows and accessed via the network of paths mentioned above, they were planned and built by the burial societies in the various community sections of the cemetery and sold to willing buyers who wanted to be interred there, often along with family members on stone litters. These subterranean grave chambers, which were up to 10m², were built from bricks, an expensive material in Istanbul where the majority of homes were made from wood. Grave markers were then erected on the grave chambers and their vaults covered with soil. Frequently, steps led down to the entrances that were sealed off with a stone or rock.

On these grave markers 'grow' the cypresses, tulips, lotuses, cloves, narcissi, dahlias, anemones, wild strawberries and sunflowers hewn out of stone by Jewish stonemasons. As well as providing the picturesque impression of a blooming meadow, the cypresses and tulips also represent heaven and eternal life, another feature adopted from Ottoman-Muslim culture. It is of note that the rose is almost entirely missing since it is the recognized symbol of the prophet Mohammed. As well as this plant symbolism, there are of course also original Jewish symbols such as baskets of fruit for women, *Cohanim* hands and the Star of David.

The appearance of tulips on the gravestones of Hasköy coincides with the 'Tulip Era' (1718–30), when cultivated tulips which had been exported from Turkey in the middle of the seventeenth century to Holland, were reimported back into the Ottoman Empire and, as had been the case in Holland, triggered 'tulip mania'.

In Hasköy, Judaism and Islam, Sephardim, Ashkenazim and Byzantine Jews form a unique expression of cultural and social exchange, united in joy at the beauty of the present world and in a belief in the world to come.

the Berlin community grew so much that, by 1676, a *chevra kaddisha*, referred to in contemporary sources as the *Judenkirchhofzunft* or 'Jews' churchyard guild', could be founded. By 1693–4, the *chevra kaddisha* had purchased more plots of land, bringing the cemetery's final area to 0.59 hectares, and by 1750, there were 333 Jewish families, some 2,190 Jews, living in Berlin – a considerable number given the city's total population of 113,000.

The cemetery, separated from the surrounding yards by a wall, featured long, even rows of gravestones, 'not necessarily the norm for a cemetery of this age'.[2] The slightly curved rows ran in an east-west direction and the gravestones were aligned to the south east, to the entrance on the Oranienburger Strasse. Between the rows of graves, winding east to west or north to south, were a number of pathways that had been created partly by design and partly by chance. Alongside the original entrance in the south-east corner, was the *Wiener Ecke* or 'Vienna corner', home to the oldest graves in the cemetery, dating from 1672 and marking the burial plots of the 're-founders' of the Berlin community, who had been exiled from Vienna. Next to the *Wiener Ecke*, the first row of graves was dedicated to honoured Jews, or the graves of rabbis; in contrast, the graves of 'dishonourable' people lay along the cemetery wall.

The *chevra kaddisha* had clear stipulations on the design of gravestones: 'In order to avoid unnecessary expenditure and to prevent any fuss, it was announced in the synagogue on the 16 of Tevet 488 (1727) that the gravestones shall be no higher than three feet, no wider than two feet and no thicker than four inches.'[3] While the majority of gravestones were simple grey, elongated rectangular stones made from sandstone with a rounded crown, there were

After Nazi destruction a new entrance area was built in 2007, complete with gate and basin for ritual hand washing.

Following an earlier expulsion, Jews were readmitted to Prussia in 1671. In 1672, Model Riess acquired a plot of land for a new cemetery and gave it to the community, which was still small, comprising just forty families. The cemetery grounds lay beyond the city wall bastion built in 1658. At the time, the area was still open country with scattered houses. The entrance to the cemetery originally lay to the south-east and a passageway in the row of houses led from the Oranienburger Strasse, past the Jewish hospital, into the cemetery. Not far away was a well for ritual hand-washing.[1]

First to be buried in the new cemetery, in 1672, was Gumpericht Jechiel Aschkanasi. Over the ensuing years,

Retaining Tradition

pomegranates. There are gravestones from the neo-classical period that have the shape of Greek gravestones and, with their Greek palmettes, reflect the influence of designs by Karl Friedrich Schinkel, the eminent nineteenth-century German classicist architect. Shortly before the cemetery was closed, a gravestone was laid in the Biedermeier style, with an inverted torch and rosettes. Particularly striking were the cemetery's five large mock sarcophagi. As in Prague, they were built over the graves of particularly outstanding people. The most famous person to be buried in this cemetery is the philosopher Moses Mendelssohn (1729–86). A friend of Lessing, who was also in correspondence for a long time with the philosopher Immanuel Kant, he was the leading figure of the *haskala* or Jewish Enlightenment, through his translation of the Five Books of Moses and the Psalms, and works such as *Phaedon, or on the Immortality of the Soul* and *Jerusalem, or on Religious Power and Judaism*.

In 1824, the cemetery was full and the community acquired a new plot of land on the Allee nach Schönhausen, in the present-day Prenzlauer Berg district. On 24 June 1827, the final burial was carried out in the old cemetery: the gravestone of Sussmann Itzig Gans expressly states that he was the last to be buried here (although this is not quite correct as four more people were buried here in 1827 and 1849).

In 1941, the Gestapo converted the old people's home into a holding centre and more than 50,000 Berlin Jews were herded together here for transportation to the concentration camps. The Gestapo had the cemetery cleared and the gravestones stacked up along the cemetery wall. Afterwards, this expanse was used as a prison yard for those awaiting deportation. Then, during the period before German reunification, the cemetery was converted into a park with a memorial erected to the Jewish victims of the Nazi regime. It is a mark of the Jewish community's resilience that the cemetery was once again demarcated in 2007 and restored to a worthy condition according to *halakhic* rules.[4]

variations on this basic theme, reflecting changing tastes (along with numerous wooden grave markers for the poor). One gravestone, dating from the time of King Friedrich I, has a heavy baroque shape with side pillars wreathed in vine leaves and crowned with

The entrance area redesigned in 2007 with the memorial for Jews deported from this site to the camps.

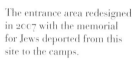

Almost the same view as the photograph of 1925. The gravestones were taken away in Nazi times and the burial field is now empty.

Fürth/Cemetery of Franconia's Jerusalem

HOMINIS VITA BREVE TEMPUS. 18

Fuhrt, Nurmb.

Synagog. Gleithaus.

Quam brē tempus homo vitali vescitur aurā, Mox juvenis mas est, masqz Senex, et obit.

O frommer Christ betracht es ebn, Der Jüngling wächst ist bald ein Mann, Wie sehr kurtz sey des Menschen Leben. Der Mann wirt alt, muß widr von dann.

View of the town of Fürth with its synagogue. Print from Meisnersches Schatzkästlein, 1629.

The Franconian town of Fürth had Jewish residents by the year 1440 but it was not until 1600 that the community had become large enough to be able to organize itself. There is evidence of a rabbi in Fürth by 1607, and a few years later, the Fürth Jews opened a Talmud university, a *yeshiva*, which soon became renowned all over Europe and founded the city's fame as the 'Franconian Jerusalem'.

A cemetery was opened in 1607. Until then, Fürth's Jews from the Bamberg sovereignty were buried in Schnaittach, while 'Ansbacher' Jews from Fürth were buried in Baiersdorf. This assignment of burial sites based on the sovereignty in which the Jews lived was perfectly normal in rural areas during this period. The cemetery was sited at the edge of the city at a distance that complied with the *halakhic* rule of a minimum of fifty ells. However, as a result of the city's growth in the nineteenth century, the cemetery is now found within the city limits.

An engraving in a publication by Johann Alexander Boener of 1705 shows the sloping terrain of the cemetery – by now about 0.6 hectares – in the shape of an elongated, irregular rectangle. In 1653, after expansion, the cemetery had been surrounded by a sandstone wall approximately 1.8 metres high.[1] The entrance lay on

the north side, on the present-day Rosenstrasse. Two inscriptions explain the site's purpose: on the gate was the inscription 'House of the living' and to the right, next to the entrance, 'You are happy that you are getting the grave'.[2] The gate was unusually elaborate and a further inscription to the left of the door proudly announces the year in the Hebrew and Gregorian calendars in which the wall and gate were built: 5413 and 1653 respectively. This year was a very important one for the Jews of Fürth, as the city's first Jewish hospital was also built in 1653 below the gate, on the cemetery grounds. 'The Hebrew word for hospital, *hekdesch*, was given to the cemetery and even today, it is known in the Fürth dialect as *Judenheckisch*.'[3] The close relationship between the hospital and the cemetery was perfectly normal for this period; the old Berlin and Frankfurt hospitals, for example, also stood adjacent to their respective cemeteries.

To the left of the entrance, Boener shows a well that is as elaborate as the gate. Two pillars on opposite sides of the well support the beam on which the drawing mechanism is suspended over the well. The well was used for ritual bodywashing and also for visitors who would wash their hands after leaving the cemetery. In front was a specially-created basin that was fed by a pipe. Next to the well is the half-timbered building of the *tahara* house, which is more moderate in style. The unplastered timber framing is clearly visible and has a double-winged door set into it. The construction, therefore, is similar to the type of simple *tahara* buildings found in rural Germany in the eighteenth century.

In the wall niche behind the well and the *tahara* house is a fenced-in, pen-like area used as a stall for the *bechorim*. Between the wall and the last row of gravestones, to the right of the *tahara* house, Boener shows a horned bull. It appears that the Jews of Fürth were also

keeping first-born male animals in the cemetery, a practice also adopted at around the same time in Frankfurt am Main.

There is evidence of a *chevra kaddisha* in Fürth as far back as the seventeenth century, and its activities were described in 1754: '§10 Before I leave the graveyard, I must remember the burial society with a few words. The members of this society gather at the time of the burial and perform the last rites for their brothers by washing the body, making the coffin and digging the grave. They regard this office as a honorary duty, so the people who want to join the society must donate money. They then use this money to buy food or any tools they need to perform the burial. §11 This burial society has a *memar*, a book of the dead, in which they list all the people, be they great or small, whom they bury.'4

By 1705 the actual graveyard, at least in the area shown, was quite densely packed with gravestones facing east. As was normal for this period, there are no pathways visible and the only planted area is a single, free-standing tree at the upper edge of the graveyard. The gravestones are upright slabs, in the Ashkenazi tradition, of more or less the same height and size; at this time, Jews still followed the commandment of everyone being equal in death.

The gravestones that have survived from the seventeenth to the eighteenth century, made from sandstone, show the conventional symbols such as blessing hands (*Cohanim*), Levite vessels, *shofars* and crowns (the crown of the Torah refers to a rabbi). Below the entrance area, Boener's engraving shows separate gravestones that are either half-standing or leaning against the cemetery wall. These probably signify the graves of children and women who died in childbirth, but may also indicate cases of suicide.

View of the Jewish cemetery with gate, well, *tahara* house and stable for first-born animals. Early eighteenth-century etching by J. A. Boener.

Burial scene at the cemetery of Fürth. From Paul Christian Kirchner: *Jüdisches Ceremoniel, circa* 1730.

The cemetery wall.

Tree grown over
a gravestone.

View into the cemetery
with some gravestones.

The development of shared cemeteries

Following their expulsion from major cities in the late Middle Ages, many Jews in the Holy Roman Empire moved to small surrounding towns and villages. Rural Jewry or *Landjuden*, as they came to be known, were generally not wealthy and earned a living through retail and cattle trading. Since the often small village communities were not allowed to maintain their own cemeteries, shared cemeteries developed in which the dead of numerous communities were interred.

From the sixteenth and seventeenth centuries these were voluntary shared plots, founded sometimes by up to ten rural communities that were independent of larger cities. Despite this sharing of land, the majority of village communities had their own *chevra kaddisha* and generally also had their own *tahara* house. The route from the village to the sometimes very distant cemetery was often beset with difficulties like marauding soldiers, bands of robbers and mobs in the villages.

The *Judenäule* – the cemetery on the island in the Rhine

The Jews of the shire of Aargau in Baden lived on the banks of the Rhine in the towns of Endingen and Lengnau, Thiengen, Stühlingen and Wangen. They had a single, shared rabbi and were very closely interlinked through kinship, so it was understandable that they should acquire a shared burial site. Unusually, however, this burial site was located on an island, one hundred and fifty metres long and forty wide, on the northern bank of the Rhine.

The Jews of Aargau had probably leased part of this small island in 1603,[1] although the earliest lease still in existence with the city of Waldshut, is dated 27 July 1689. Over the following decades, the lease was extended numerous times. These agreements stated that, for a defined sum, the Jews merely had the right to bury their dead on the *Äulein* (dialect for 'little island') – other uses were forbidden – and once the island was full, it was to be returned to the city of

XIII. LAGEPLAN DER VORGEFUNDENEN GRÄBER AUF DER JUDENINSEL BEI KOBLENZ

Zeichenerklärung

- Normalgrab (Erwachsene)
- Kindergrab
- Grab mit Grabsteinresten
- Grab mit Grabstein
- Grabsteinreste ohne Grab

MASSTAB 0 1 2 3 4 5 6 7 8 9 10

Rohrfreileitung der Lonzawerke

ehemaliger Friedhofweg

Fusspfad

← Rhein

Waldshut. The Jews were also obliged to protect the island from flooding. The Rhine at that time had not been tamed by dams and forced to flow along a solid bed. As a wild mountain river, it constantly changed its course, and was separated from the German bank by a tributary thirty metres wide. High tides changed the shape of the island and frequently flooded it, causing graves to be repeatedly destroyed. In fact, only a small part of the island was covered with graves; the Jews leased the majority of the land to the sailors of Koblenz 'with the condition that they would ferry them over to the island when they carried out their annual prayer service there'.[2]

Since the island was regarded as separate from the surrounding terrain, as a result of the water between the two, it did not need any walls to protect it from trespassers or wild animals. Over the course of exhumations carried out during a clearing of the cemetery in 1954–5, valuable information was uncovered about the site. The graveyard was around thirty-six by 18.5 metres in size, which suggests that large parts of the cemetery had been eroded away by high tides. The graves, which were just fifty to eighty centimetres deep, as a result of the high groundwater level, were all built facing east. 'All of the graves contained clay fragments from glazed seventeenth- or eighteenth-century crockery that were placed, in accordance with old Jewish tradition, over the deceased's eyes and mouth.'[3] There were no regular rows of graves, but there are indications of the presence of a gathering space.

The new cemetery

Given the hazards of high tide, which were never fully brought under control, the Jews of Endingen and Lengnau bought another piece of land in 1750 for 340 guilders. This piece of land, to be used as a cemetery, was situated away from the Rhine, between the two villages. Jews had been living in Lengnau since 1622, and from 1678 onwards, there is also mention of a Jewish settlement in Endingen: the two villages, nestling in the *Surbtal* valley, offered the Jews sufficient opportunity to make a living despite the ban

on owning land or carrying out a trade. The cemetery lay around one kilometre outside Lengnau, towards Endingen, almost exactly halfway between the two communities. Situated on a slope, it was located on the road between the two villages and was therefore easily accessible.

An engraving of 1750 is one of the most important pictorial sources for a cemetery owned by European rural Jews in the eighteenth century. The layout was at the time completely new. The view goes from the road (marked *G* in the picture) to the cemetery, which is rectangular with its narrow edges facing east and west and surrounded on all sides by a stone wall as tall as a man. In the south-east and south-west corners there are entrances, one for the Lengnau community (*A*) and one for the Endingen community (*B*). The prevalence of spatial separation continues inside the cemetery: the topmost, most northerly row is occupied by 'men's graves' (*C*). Below this is the row with women's graves (*D*), followed by children's graves (*E*), whose number is relatively high as a result of high infant mortality at the time. The grave of a 'woman in childbed' (*F*), a woman who died in childbirth, lies apart in the cemetery's north-easter corner.

The cemetery of Endingen and Lengnau, with two separate entries for the Jews of the two villages. Etching from J. C. Ulrich's *Sammlung Jüdischer Geschichten*, 1768.

pag. 229.

Friedhoof oder Begräbniß Ohrt der Juden zwischen Langnau und Endingen.
A Eingang auf seyten gegen Langnau. B Eingang auf seyten gegen Endingen. C Begräbniße der Männer. D Begräbniße der Weiber. E Begräbniße der Kinder. F Abgesondertes Begräbniß einer Kindbetherin. G Landstraße von Langnau nach Endingen.

The nineteenth-century
entrance gate.

View into the cemetery with
eighteenth- and nineteenth-
century gravestones.

There are also no signs of the commonly found practice of burying families together, the rows being
populated in strict chronological order. The otherwise
usual east-west orientation of the graves was not
preserved either, as all the graves lie in a north-south
direction. At this point, there was no *tahara* house at
the cemetery, which meant that the funeral proces-

sion from Lengnau, composed of numerous men
(women only accompanied the procession when a
woman was being buried) and the coffin, passed
through its assigned gate and moved immediately to
the prepared male grave.

Today the *beth hachaim* of Endingen and Lengnau
is one of the best preserved cemeteries of its kind.

One of the oldest sections of the cemetery.

A rescued gravestone from Judenäule.

Krakow / Kazimierz: Cemetery of the Jewish City

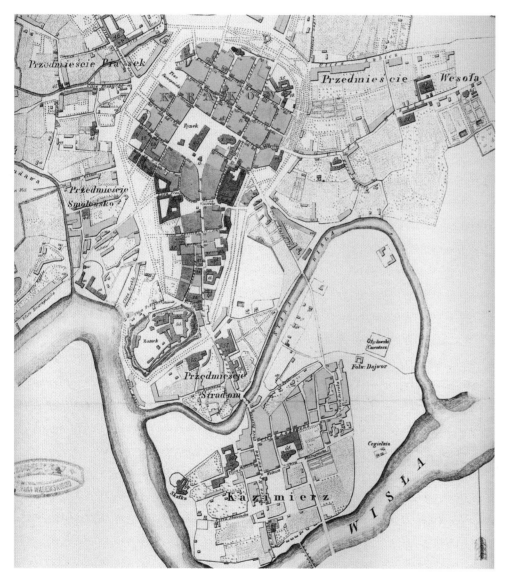

Map of Krakow, 1836. The old town with the Royal castle and the Great market square is seen in the top left side of the map. Kazimierz, still separated from the old capital of Poland by an arm of the Vistula, is clearly visible at the bottom. The Jewish city lies in the top right corner of Kazimierz.

King Kazimir the Great was in constant conflict with Krakow's town council and planned to restrict its influence, along with the power of the local oligarchs, by founding a new city not far from the old one. The course of the Vistula, which flows past Krakow, describes a curve as it passes the city. An island, formed by the Vistula, was linked to Krakow via a road and a bridge. King Kazimir believed the island to be the ideal spot to create the new town, upon which he also conferred market and trading privileges. King Jan Olbracht then determined the north-eastern corner of Kazimierz as the place where Jews had to settle. The city wall separated this settlement (which was rapidly becoming a Jewish city) from the hinterland to the north and east, while on the south and west side, fences were first erected after an expansion in 1553 in order to separate the Jews' living area from that of the Christians. At this time, three gates led into the city of the Jews.

As in Venice, the entire cosmos of Jewish life was brought together, although it was never a ghetto since it enjoyed a considerable degree of autonomy. The religious and administrative power lay with a rabbi and the community council (*kahal*). Between them, they looked after all the necessities of life in the city, with religious and worldly aspects interweaving seamlessly, especially as the two are so closely linked in Jewish community life. The rabbinical elite of the time studied in Kazimierz: Rabbi Moses Iserles (1510–72), known as Remu, the author of the 'Mappa', a summary of the *Schulchan Aruch* by Yosef Karo, created with this work the ultimate codex for pious Ashkenazi Jews right up until the present day. Another of the many scholars of Kazimierz from this period was Nathan Nata Spira (1583–1633), author of the *Megalle Amukkot* and the first teacher of *kabbalah*. Letterpress

From the eleventh century progroms and persecution prompted many Jews to flee from Western Europe further east in order to build a new life. In the twelfth and thirteenth centuries, Jewish settlements in Poland are mentioned for the first time in writing. Since then many Polish rulers like King Kazimir and King Olbracht were sympathetic to the Jews and promoted their settlement, especially in Krakow, at that time the capital city.

printing was also important in Kazimierz and it was here that the first book was printed in Yiddish in 1534.

The Remu cemetery

In 1551–2, the plague raged in Krakow and Kazimierz, causing the death of some 200 Jews. A small, old cemetery in the market square, which had been opened in 1533, was filled to the brim and Krakow's administrators had to agree to build a new one. The new burial place did not lie in the heart of the city, like the previous one, but still – against the rules – within the city walls. The reason for this was the fear of flooding affecting land outside the city walls: the Vistula often breached its banks, as it does today, and graves were being destroyed as a result.

The new cemetery was therefore contained by the city wall to the northern side and a border fence to the west of the Jewish city. The fence was soon replaced by a wall and additional walls followed on the other sides in order to separate the cemetery from the surrounding homes. The former 'city gate' on the present-day Ulitsa Jakuba was thus no longer available for use as such, since daily and in particular *shabbat* traffic into the Jewish settlement could not be directed across the cemetery: a cemetery cannot be entered on the *shabbat*, which is a day of joy. The entrance was therefore moved next to the Remu synagogue, built in 1553, where it is still located today. In the seventeenth century, the former city gate was reopened for reasons unknown. A plaque was attached to the entrance gate (now bricked up), marked with a semi-circle, which stated that this 'is an old cemetery, the resting place of *geonim*, built with community funds in [5]311.'[1] In the nineteenth century, the cemetery entrance from Ulitsa. Jakuba was moved again to the forecourt of the Remu synagogue and the plaque can still be seen there.

After numerous extensions, the cemetery finally reached a size of 4.5 hectares. The large grounds now demonstrate striking differences in height, partly due to natural topography, but also to the fact that, in certain places, particularly in the southern half, burials were performed one on top of another in several layers, as in the old cemetery in Prague.

As was the norm up until the nineteenth century, the cemetery is not accessed by pathways. Instead, visitors walk through the rows of gravestones, not all of which are laid facing east. The gravestones now stand in neat rows, but this was not originally the case. Until German occupation, they stood in the seemingly random disarray characteristic of cemeteries of this period – a disarray that nevertheless took great care to ensure that no grave was damaged by the creation of a

The old cemetery on the market square. Photograph, late nineteenth century.

The old gate at Ulita Jakuba. This was once a city gate.

new one. The Germans 'used' the cemetery as a place for storing rubbish, and many gravestones were cleared and destroyed in the process. There are reports that community members were able to cover large parts of the cemetery with a protective layer of earth just beforehand, thereby saving many gravestones as they were no longer visible. During restoration of the cemetery after 1945, however, this fact was not known. When the overturned gravestones were re-erected, most of them could not be assigned to their original grave plots; many of the gravestones in the cemetery today do not lie above their original graves. Then, during later restorations in the 1950s, it was found that many gravestones were indeed hidden under a protective layer of earth. Numbering more than 700, these too were re-erected. Gravestones of leading rabbis were also found that had originally been believed lost and for whom replacement gravestones had been made, so some gravestones appear in the cemetery twice. Individual fragments of gravestones were collected at the cemetery's eastern wall and inset into it. The result was the 'Krakow wailing wall'.

The first people to be buried in the cemetery in 1552 were victims of the plague. Over the ensuing centuries up until 1800, the cemetery became the final resting place for the dead of the city of the Jews, situated at the heart of the city of the living surrounding it with its roads, houses and market square, and the Remu synagogue that gave the cemetery its name.

The graves of the most famous rabbis are concentrated to the west, very close to the synagogue. This is also the location of the only gravestone not to have

View into Remu cemetery.

been damaged and cleared during the Nazi period: the *matzevah* of Moses Iserles, known as Remu (1525–72), whose name was given to the synagogue founded by his father in 1553. According to legend, the worker who wanted to break up the gravestone for the Germans was struck by lightning. The importance of Moses Iserles, not only as an exceptional scholar but also as a rabbi, leader of the *beth din* (court) and rector of the local rabbinical university, is patently clear. Even today, his grave is visited annually by many Jews from all over the world, especially on the anniversary of his death, the 18 of Iyar.

As well as the typical Ashkenazi *matzevot* – an upright gravestone at the head of the grave – there are also a number of sarcophagi. In some cases, these are graves of Sephardim, for whom such grave monuments are typical. One good example of this is the grave of Mordechai Saba ben Jakub who, as the leading kabbalist and successor of Moses Iserles, ran the local rabbinical university and died in 1576. That of the merchant Juda Leib Landau, who died in 1632, is also a sarcophagus grave, marked as the resting-place of a Levite with a Levite vessel. A further sarcophagus grave is that of Isaak Jakubowicz (d. 1653), a merchant and successful banker who had the splendid synagogue that bears his name built at his own expense between 1638 and 1644. Often, married couples who died at different times are buried next to each other, which supports the conclusion that places were reserved and kept free. Next to the already mentioned Nathan Nata Spira, who died in 1633, is his wife Rosa, who died in 1642. The women's *matzevot* generally bear symbols of the two *shabbat* candlesticks. The men's, on the other hand, exhibit traditional symbols such as the crown (learning), vessel (Levites) and blessing hands (*Cohanim*).

Some of the most famous rabbis and *tzadikim* of the seventeenth century, such as Gershon Saul Yom Tov Lipman Heller, Joel Sirkes, Joshua ben Joseph or Joshua Heshel, are surprisingly not buried near the synagogue, where Moses Iserles and other leading scholars are interred, but rather lie in the present-day rear section, at the now bricked-up gate on the Ulitsa Jakuba.

Detail of a gravestone with *Cohanim* blessing hands.

The old cemetery gate at Ulitsa Jakuba.

This may be due to the fact that it was here, as described above, that the entrance to the cemetery was located for a time. One legend, however, provides another reason why Lipman Heller is buried here. In Kazimierz there lived a rich man who publicly refused to give alms to the poor – a dreadful sin when one bears in mind the importance of *tsedaka*, or charity, in Judaism. Because of his avarice, he was regarded as a bad person and known as the 'miser of Krakow', so that after his death, he was buried in the cemetery's rearmost — worst — row. On the first Friday after the alleged miser's death, the poor of Kazimierz, who were used to receiving money on this day from an unknown benefactor, received nothing. It turned out, to everyone's surprise, that the miser had in fact been a great *tzadik*, but had given his money anonymously, one of the most important virtues as decreed by the *halakha*. And so it was for this reason that Rabbi Heller was buried next to him.

The 'Wailing Wall' of Krakow.

For almost 250 years, the Remu cemetery was the burial place for the Jews of Krakow – in the centre of their city, immediately next to their homes and synagogues. In 1800, the cemetery was closed by the Austrians. Cemeteries within cities were no longer permitted and shortly afterwards, a new cemetery was built on the Ulitsa Miodowa.

Krakow and Plaszow – an epilogue of Nazi infamy

On 6 September 1939, the Germans occupied Krakow. The governor general of the German-occupied territories, Hans Frank, who was executed in 1946, lived in the old royal castle on Wawel Hill and it was from here that he organized his campaign of terror against Krakow's Jews and resisiting Poles. From 1941 onwards, the Jews of Krakow were deported to the Podgorze district, on the opposite bank of the Vistula,

and thousands were herded into a ghetto until it was abolished in 1943 and the surviving Jews taken to concentration camps. The Germans had it surrounded with a wall two to three metres high, its design 'inspired' by that of the gravestones in the Remu cemetery, and the long row of seemingly consecutive *matzevot* can still be seen in certain places. The wall thus broadcast its function in unflinchingly clear terms: it represented the forecourt to death for thousands.

At the end of 1942, the Nazis started building an eighty-hectare concentration camp in Plaszow, memorialized in Thomas Keneally's book and filmed by Steven Spielberg as *Schindler's List*. Plaszow was a suburb of Krakow situated not far from the ghetto, and the Nazis placed as officer in charge Amon Leopold Goeth, who shot many prisoners personally. They chose two adjacent Jewish cemeteries as the location for the camp. One of them was the Krakow community's newest cemetery, which had only been built in 1932. When the camp was set up in 1942–3, the Germans destroyed the monumental cemetery buildings and took away the remnants, along with the graves. Apart from mere ruins, the only

gravestone to remain was that of Chaim Jakub Abrahamer, son of Isaak Meir, who had died in 1932. In the camp, 25,000 prisoners were forced to work like slaves in the workshops, breaking rocks and working in factories. The Nazi aim was to create 'destruction through work' so that thousands died as a result of their labours in indescribable conditions.

Plaszow became a threefold place of death: it was built on desecrated Jewish cemeteries; it was planned with the intention of murdering Jews and Poles; and the victims were piled into mass graves. Only a few survived – the ones whom Oskar Schindler saved in his factory.

The site of Plaszow concentration camp with the ruins of the mortuary hall of the destroyed new Jewish cemetery.

Remaining section of the Nazi ghetto wall.

Rome/Under Papal Rule: Cemeteries on the Aventine

View of the square in the ghetto with the five synagogues. Watercolour by Lenghi. 1832.

With Paul IV's accession to the throne in 1555, Roman Jews began a life in the ghetto that was to last until 1870 and the fall of the church state. Paul IV persecuted the Jews more than any other Pope, and in a bull issued in 1555, had them herded into a tiny district next to the Tiber. The quarter was surrounded by a wall and could only be reached by two (later five) gates. Above the main gate on the Ponte Quattro Capi was a plaque with a Hebrew inscription quoting Isaiah (65: 2-3): 'I have stretched out my hands all day to a rebellious people who walk in an evil way, following their own thoughts; to a people who continually provoke me to wrath.' The constant presence of this – deliberately misunderstood – verse by the Catholic leaders, who thus put themselves in the place of God, represented a serious provocation to the Jews.

After being forced into the ghetto, the Jews continued to use the cemetery at the Porta Portese, even though it soon became almost full. In 1645, it was finally closed and under Pope Innocent X, the Jews were given a new burial site. The *Ghemilut Chassadim*, the *chevra kaddisha* that was based on the Prague model and that had received its own licence from the Pope, was in charge of the new cemetery.[1]

The new, later to become known as the *Vecchio*, or 'old', cemetery, lay on the Aventine, one of the seven hills of Rome, above a valley that stretched to the foot of the Palatine, the hill on which emperors had built their palaces since the time of Augustus. In the valley was the Circus Maximus, an elongated hippodrome, where horse and chariot races were held from the fourth century BCE until 549 CE, and large enough for some 300,000 spectators. On the Palatine side, below the ruler's palace, was the imperial box. It was directly opposite this that, 1,100 years after the last chariot race, Rome's first post-medieval Jewish cemetery was built,

PIAZZA DELLE
SCVOLE

easily accessible from the ghetto. Like the cemetery at the Porta Portese, it was surrounded by vineyards.

The irregularly shaped plot of land was accessed from the Via di San Prisca and surrounded on three sides by other streets. The entrance, with a large building, was enclosed on the cemetery side by a yard that was separated from the cemetery proper by a wall, with a further gate leading from the forecourt to the cemetery. This building was probably used as the *tahara* house and by the superintendent, while the forecourt had a ritual function for the *Cohanim* who were not allowed to enter the cemetery itself. The cemetery was surrounded on all sides by a wall, of which, even today, large stretches remain and in which the remnants of the building can be seen.

By 1728, the old burial ground was full and had to be extended. When this extension became full, the community purchased a neighbouring piece of ground in 1775, separated by a street, to be used as a new cemetery. In 1895, Hermann Vogelstein described the cemetery in a typically sensitive way: 'These cemeteries, so beautifully located and surrounded by vineyards, offered a ray of hope following the strict edicts of 1625 and 1775.'[2] These edicts had stipulated that only the Inquisition had the right to permit gravestones and that even the erection of gravestones without inscriptions was forbidden. Shortly afterwards, the community did succeed in securing gravestones without inscriptions at least for rabbis, and later for certain other people; but after the reappearance of plaques with inscriptions a short time later, the Inquisition commanded the removal of the stones and the community was punished. To circumvent this victimization, even during Antonio Bosio's[3] time (1575–1629), many graves were marked with a seven-branched *menorah* hewn into the stone. Often, the Jews rescued these gravestones from destruction by placing them in their own homes, and a number of which came to light when the ghetto was destroyed from 1886 onwards.

In around 1890, the new cemetery was also full. Since it was not possible, given the increasing size of the population, to create a further cemetery on the

Aventine, it was decided to build a new burial site on the large communal cemetery to the south east of the city, on the Campo Verano.

Under Fascist rule from 1922 onwards the cemetery was divided by a street, gravestones were taken to Campo Verano and after the war, a rose garden was planted on both sides. As a result of the papal edicts, many of the graves did not have headstones, and it is assumed that the areas that now house the rose gardens still contain graves. 'That older part of the original cemetery seems to have been made up of unnamed graves – and in all probability the earliest layer of tombs still lies undisturbed beneath the roses, thus respecting the Jewish prescription for perpetual burial.'[4]

OPPOSITE PAGE: Remaining building of the ghetto with Roman and medieval stonework and a *tsedaka* box.

ABOVE LEFT: View of the cemetery before demolition. Photograph, *circa* 1920.

BELOW: The rose garden on the site of the cemetery.

View over the cemetery
towards the dome of the
New Synagogue.

View into the main burial field.

In 1780, Emperor Joseph II succeeded Maria Theresa to the Habsburg throne. During his reign, the Josephian reforms were enacted that were ultimately, over the course of the nineteenth century, to lead to the equality and emancipation of the Jews in the Habsburg empire. Since 1796, more and more Jews had settled outside the ghetto (66 in 1796, 243 in 1846), resulting in marked changes for the old Jewish city. At the same time, tensions grew between the traditionalist groups around the rabbis and the mostly younger Jews who urged emancipation, enlightenment and ultimately assimilation. It was in the middle of this tremendous intra-Jewish upheaval that the old Olsany plague cemetery was reopened and its use changed.

The year 1784 was decisive. For hygiene reasons, Emperor Joseph II forbade the continued burial of the dead in cemeteries that lay within the town centre, and indeed laws to this effect were being passed across Europe around the turn of the century. This spelled an end for the graveyards situated around inner-city churches just as much as it did for the old cemetery of Prague's Jewish city. The community therefore remembered an old plague cemetery in Olsany which had been in use since 1680, and decided from that point forward to use it as a regular burial ground. A former hospital on the site became a cemetery building and a dwelling for the cemetery superintendent. However, due to the proximity of the homes in the Jewish city, the *tahara* continued to be carried out in the burial society's ceremonial building at the old cemetery. The cemetery, which by this point had stood for 56 years, is depicted in two paintings commissioned by the *chevra kaddisha* in 1840, which were intended as additions to the picture cycle from 1772 (discussed in the introduction to this book).

The first painting shows the entrance. A double-winged, highly segmented, wrought iron entrance gate set into the wall stands adjacent to the former

hospital building, whose façade has been rebuilt in the neo-Gothic style that was in vogue at the time. Ogive doors and windows give the low building an almost picturesque quality. A stepped tympanum above the fascia in the centre of the façade bears an inscription, probably a psalm. Attached to the building is a lectern-like construction, and behind an ornate front is a set of steps leading to a platform from where eulogies for the dead were given. The orator speaks from a double-winged window and can be clearly seen by the male mourners below, wearing frock coats and top hats, and standing around the coffin, which will soon be carried from the cemetery forecourt to the prepared grave.

Next to the orator's pulpit, although separate from it, is a tall, white-plastered sheer wall, with a niche set into it containing a stone basin; water falls from a pipe set into the wall. This is intended for the ritual hand washing required when leaving the cemetery, and still remains today. A plaque on the front of the fountain, above the stone lintel over the niche, recounts the *tsedaka* of the leader of the *chevra kaddisha*, Wolf Gadels Zappert (1731–1810), who had the fountain built at his own expense.

The entrance gate, cemetery building, orator's pulpit and fountain should be seen in the context of a representation of the forecourt, with the intention of not representing the cemetery as a place of sadness, but rather as a scenic, friendly, almost serene 'park'. Tall trees and bushes surround the buildings and courtyard. Several benches invite people to linger, while an ornamental trellis frames a planted area with a decorative flowerbed. The wall also features a dazzlingly white, neo-Gothic, elaborate wall grave, surrounded by greenery. This was an extremely modern design, with almost unheard-of elaborateness compared to the modest headstones of the old cemetery.

The cemetery was extended in 1855 and a lane of poplars planted that led from a newly created entrance to the centre of the cemetery. Since Rousseau Island in Ermenonville, the poplar had been regarded as a 'worthy' tree and thus seemed particularly suitable for planting in cemeteries, so it is no surprise that several

OPPOSITE PAGE, TOP: The entrance area with the old hospital building and the fountain. Painting, 1840.

OPPOSITE PAGE, BOTTOM: Burial field in the northern, oldest section of the cemetery. Painting, 1840.

ABOVE: The redesigned entrance area with the old hospital building. Photograph, early twentieth century.

LEFT: The 1792 fountain. Photograph, early twentieth century.

mature poplars are already evident in the second painting from 1840. The picture shows the embracing of contemporary landscape design and the late eighteenth-century gardening theories of Christian Hirschfeld, with leanings towards the sentimental, almost melancholic-landscaped garden.

From the traditional *matzevah* to the Doric temple: changes in sepulchral culture

The second painting shows the cemetery in a serene mood, with graves, trees, shrubs and grassy areas. The rows of the oldest graves can be seen on a bank in the north-western part of the cemetery. Alongside traditional, low gravestones are the taller, more elaborate and 'modern' headstones in neo-Gothic or classical, ancient-style shapes (obelisks). This clearly illustrates the change in sepulchral culture at the time, as Jews were now allowed to live outside the ghetto and were increasingly aligning their customs with those of their Christian fellow citizens and drawing on the models of antiquity for inspiration. The earlier gravestones, such as those of chief rabbi Ezechiel Landau (d. 1793), his wife Liba (d. 1789) and their son Samuel (d. 1834) are still preserved in their entirety, exhibiting traditional shapes with Hebrew inscriptions and semi-circular pediments. By contrast, the grave of the 'Father of the Prague Enlightenment', physician Jonas Jeiteles (1735–1806) and his son Isaac (1779–1852), with its Latin and German inscriptions in oval configurations and neo-Gothic tympana, already show evidence of the new spirit. The headstone of entrepreneur Joachim Popper (1721–95) is particularly interesting in its traditional design, but reaching the extraordinary height of more than two metres. Here, the traditional Jewish headstone as an expression of bourgeois self-portrayal touches the boundaries of its formal possibilities. The graves of the Jerusalem family of industrialists (visible in the painting) depart completely from the traditional Jewish canon of designs, with their obelisks almost three metres high. The zenith of this development is the family crypt of the entrepreneur and representative of the Prague Jewish community Friedrich Efraim Ritter von Kubinsky (1814–88). The family vault is designed in the shape of a classical Doric temple, plainly showing the status of a Jew who had completely integrated into the society of the imperial and royal monarchy and risen to the ranks of the nobility, yet

The gravestone of Prague's head rabbi Ezechiel Landau (d. 1793).

who actively represented the needs of his 'fellow believers' and did not, like many later assimilated Jews, abandon Judaism.

The Olsany cemetery, therefore, offers a fascinating portrayal of the history of the Prague Jews in the period between the late eighteenth century and the early nineteenth. The route out of the ghetto led to widespread integration into surrounding society, thanks to the ability of many to choose their professions and enjoy commercial and social success. Traditional forms of Jewish faith and customs were increasingly abandoned, and the path was taken from the traditional *matzevah* to the Doric temple. The old cemetery in the ghetto is still completely characterised by a time of unquestioned tradition. The new one in Zizkov on the other hand (see page 132), opened in 1890, definitely belongs to a new era, with the cemetery in Olsany forming the linchpin between the two.

This is shown by a few further elements in the second painting from 1840. In the centre, a man is walking with his children towards the headstones at the back of the picture – an allegory of the importance that the cemetery, as a place of remembrance, still occupied in the education of Jewish children and which the *chevra kaddisha* wanted to continue in the face of growing assimilation. And suddenly, for the first time in a painting of a cemetery commissioned by a burial society, a woman appears: in the right-hand half of the picture is a stylishly-dressed woman, standing next to a man, contemplating a gravestone. The cemetery is presented as a place visited not just by men, but by women and children too. On the left-hand side of the picture, another unusual feature catches the eye: two grave plots are planted with colourful flowers, contrary to Jewish tradition and clearly demonstrating the adoption of Christian burial customs. Whether the *chevra kaddisha* wanted to encourage such practices is not known, although we may presume that this was not the case. In any event, the two paintings illustrate Jewish understanding of the cemetery in an age that wanted to preserve *halakhic* traditions while at the same time move with the spirit of the *haskala* and surrounding society. The pictures take us from the traditional burial with an exclusively male group of mourners to a park-like, serene forecourt with traditional *matzevot* and classical obelisks.

Huge obelisks marking the graves of members of the Jerusalem family.

The gravestone of the industrialist Joachim Popper (d. 1795).

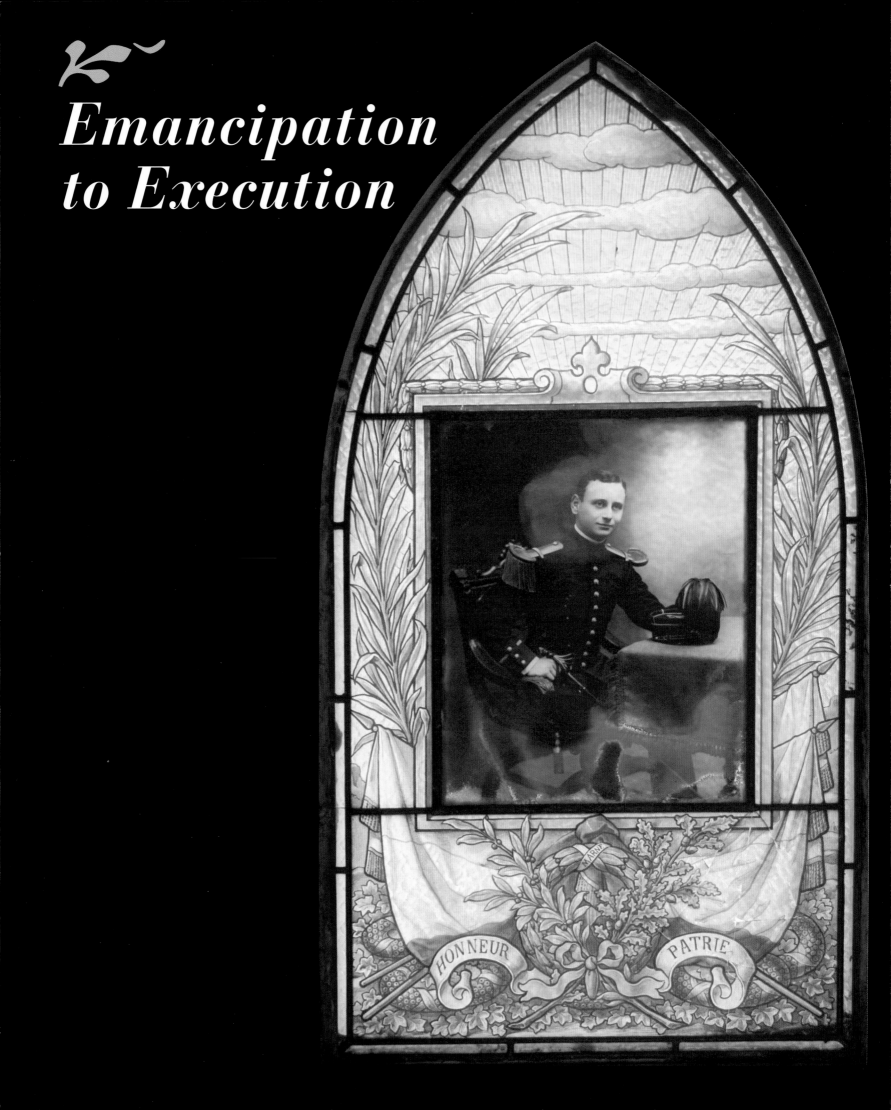

Emancipation to Execution

The Triad of Enlightenment, Emancipation and Assimilation

The process of emancipation for the Jews of Europe, based on the ideas of the Enlightenment, first led to legal consequences in revolutionary France and continued gradually and with varying degrees of success in the other countries of Europe. After the end of the First World War, and as a result of the collapse of the late-feudal regimes in Germany, Austro-Hungary and Russia, the Jews of Europe were regarded almost everywhere as equal citizens. The Jewish cemeteries of the nineteenth century reflect emancipation and Jewish integration into surrounding societies in an impressive way. The adoption of building and grave constructions and of mourning customs from Christian compatriots shows assimilation and the abandonment of Jewish tradition.

New, multi-faith cemeteries

The nature of the generally (but not always) walled-in Jewish cemetery lying outside the gates of residential areas remained unchanged until the end of the eighteenth century when, during the Enlightenment and the French Revolution, rulers – like the Roman emperors of their day – decreed that for hygiene reasons cemeteries had to be moved out of the cities. Many old Jewish cemeteries, swallowed up by the cities' growth and situated within the extended fortifications of city walls, fell victim to this revived regulation and had to be closed, even though they were full anyway. The spatial separation between Jewish and Christian burial sites, which was complete by the early Middle Ages, was thus undone. Both were once again located, just as in Roman times, outside the city gates, and it became possible to build them next to each other or even create them as jointly functioning units.

The circle that started with the multi-faith cemeteries of the early Middle Ages therefore closed in 1804 in Napoleonic Paris, when once again a multi-faith cemetery was built: the Père-Lachaise. For the first time in Europe, the emancipated, equal Jews were assigned a separate section, initially separated by a wall. This trend for creating Jewish sections within cemeteries, built by state organisations or town councils, continued throughout the nineteenth century and into the twentieth. At the same time, however, there were communities who observed the *halakha* more strictly and who insisted on their own separate cemeteries.

Making the cemetery more beautiful

Virtually all Jewish burial sites created in cities in the nineteenth and twentieth centuries, regardless of whether they form part of a multi-faith cemetery or are separate, share a trend towards making the grounds more pleasant and less forbidding.

Stained glass window from a Jewish family vault at Père-Lachaise cemetery in Paris. The portrait of a proudly posing officer does not show any Jewish symbols – only the motto 'Honneur et Patrie'. Emancipation and integration seem to be complete here, shortly before the catastrophic Dreyfus affair.

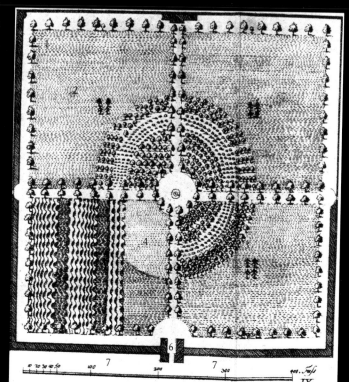

Plan of the new cemetery at Dessau. Rode, published 1795.

The ceremonial building of the Jewish cemetery at Wörlitz, designed by Wilhelm von Erdmannsdorf (1736–1800)

The early example of Prague's Olsany park cemetery was continued throughout the nineteenth century, although its landscaped designs were rarely found until later years, the Rat-Beil-Strasse in Frankfurt being a rare example of such a landscaped cemetery from the early nineteenth century.

In Dessau in 1787, a burial site was created that was to be 'pioneering for cemetery design in the next few decades.'[1] The square cemetery, with its crossroads, central circular flower bed and enclosure of the grave areas with rows of trees became the model for new cemeteries built outside city gates. It foreshadowed the cemeteries of the second half of the nineteenth century with their avenues, large squares, crossroads and spatial segregation of the classes of grave, representing a faithful depiction of the world of the living. The living conditions of the Jews, whether in palaces or villas, or in unhealthy, overcrowded tenements, and the inherently strict social hierarchy, were all reflected in the cemetery. The maxim of equality in death, increasingly brought into question since the start of the nineteenth century, was now completely abandoned. The rich built grave monuments whose size, style and material revealed a desire for an eternal presence this side

an eroded belief in *olam haba*, the world of the future following the arrival of the Messiah. At the same time, many Jews left Judaism, converting to Christianity or leaving their communities, and were thus never interred in the 'houses of life'. In contrast to this, orthodox groups left the main communities and created their own ones, building synagogues without organs and separate traditional cemeteries with modest *matzevot*.

The development of simple *tahara* houses into complex cemetery buildings

In parallel to the design-related and functional restructuring of cemetery grounds, increasingly complex developments were taking place in cemetery buildings. Initially, there are the early simple *tahara* houses of the late seventeenth and eighteenth centuries, such as those in Worms, Amsterdam, London or Georgensgmünd. However, in the second half of the eighteenth century, concerns over the burial of people who were comatose became widespread, along with it criticism of the Jews' practice of a quick burial. As a consequence, the cemetery buildings that appeared around the end of the eighteenth century were intended increasingly for the purpose of watching the bodies to make sure that victims were not comatose. Such a building was requested by the 'Society of Friends', set up in 1792 by inhabitants of Berlin. The society was made up of *maskilim*, Jewish Enlightenists, who urged that the dead should only be interred three days after the first signs of decomposition started to appear. They published a 'Plan for an ... institute for the dead and resuscitated'.[2] The text contained a draft by Salomo Sachs, Prussia's first Jewish architect.[3] Sachs's cemetery building, to be built in the neo-classical style, therefore featured a room for observing the bodies,[4] but no *tahara*.

The first Jewish cemetery buildings also started to make their mark on the city skyline around this the Prince of Anhalt-Dessau, for example, had his architect Friedrich Wilhelm von Erdmannsdorff (1736–1800) build a synagogue and a cemetery at Wörlitz, complete with neo-Palladian ceremonial building, for the local Jewry. This ceremonial building no longer stood hidden behind walls, but instead took a strong position, like later synagogues in Europe, within the town's streets. Design then progressed from an 'inspector's house', complete with mourning room and *tahara* at the Schönhauser Allee in Berlin, plus an elaborate, neo-classical gatehouse with similar rooms in Frankfurt, to the architecturally complete, complex cemetery buildings of Weissensee in Berlin, St Petersburg and Kaliningrad. These buildings contained all the requisite functional facilities, such as a mourning room, waiting room, *tahara*, cool rooms, toilets, offices, archives, workshops and even horticultural nurseries. The process of Jewish *embourgeoisement* is plainly evident from these buildings, as is the increasing bureaucracy of surrounding society. Town-based Jewish cemeteries now had a physical centre from where they were maintained, cared for and administered. Furthermore, the mourning room, which was a new development of the nineteenth century, became the focus of the cemetery as a whole. Eulogies were no longer held outdoors from an orator's pulpit, as was still the case in Prague, or even directly at the grave, but instead were delivered in the warmth of the often heated mourning rooms. Their elaborate décor and furnishings reflected the communities' wealth, and the cemetery overall, together with the graves themselves, became a representation of the Jewish bourgeoisie.

Styles of the surrounding society were adopted everywhere, although the heated discussions that surrounded construction of synagogues in the nineteenth century over the correct, ideally 'Jewish' style, is barely detectable in cemetery buildings, probably due to the fact that they were less in the public eye. Only a few architects, such as Béla Lajta in Budapest, tried to maintain a symbiosis of the country's national style and formal echoes of the Jews' – in this case – Mesopotamian origins. And in 1929 Erich Mendelsohn finally came up with a deliberate, classic modern design for the construction of a Jewish cemetery in Königsberg (Kaliningrad).

However, a different world existed outside the large cities and towns of Europe in the grip of the First World War. In the villages and small towns of western Europe and the *shtetls* of eastern Europe, the old cemetery forms – narrow rows of graves, uniform headstones and strict separation from Christian cemeteries – were preserved.

Design for a cemetery building on a Jewish cemetery. Salomo Sachs, 1798.

Paris / Père-Lachaise:
First Site in the Age of Emancipation

112

Wide avenues are lined
with grand Jewish family
mausoleums in one of the
new sections of Père-Lachaise,
like the grand houses of the
living in the rich quarters of
the French capital.

In the middle of the French Revolution, on 28 January 1790, a decree was issued that gave full citizens' rights to Spanish and Portuguese Jews, thus marking the dawn of a new era for the Jews of France. Along with the Ashkenazim, who were given the same rights a short time later, they were the first Jews in Europe to become emancipated, so that they stood on an equal legal footing with France's other citizens. Many decades would pass before they enjoyed complete equality, particularly in social terms, but they now – at least on paper – had the same legal status as their fellow countrymen.

In 1807 Emperor Napoleon instituted an assembly of French Jews called *Le Grand Sanhédrin* which decided not only on their organisational structure but also on their cemeteries, the creation and mainte-nance of which had always been one of the local communities' most basic duties. The local burial soci-eties took autonomous decisions and the cemeteries they cared for were largely separate from the influence of the local state or feudal authorities. This now changed fundamentally: from now on all French cemeteries were subject to the suzerainty of state administration. New cemeteries were built and main-tained by local authority administrative committees on behalf of central headquarters in Paris, and only existing Christian or Jewish cemeteries remained under the control of local religious authorities. But because these lay mostly within towns or close by, they were closed as the result of a new decree: for hygiene reasons, cemeteries now had to be built outside the city walls or inhabited areas.

Design by Brongniart for the Père-Lachaise cemetery, 1812–13. The separate walled Jewish section lies next to a side entry in the bottom-right corner. Clearly visible are the gatehouse and the tree-lined avenues framing the burial fields.

New, large cemeteries soon sprang up all over France, built and maintained by local councils. The Jews were assigned areas within these cemeteries, known as *sections juives*, that were no longer maintained by the local *chevra kaddisha* but instead administered by local government. This marked the end of the autonomy of Jewish cemetery maintenance, which had lasted centuries and had until this point been central to the way that Jews viewed themselves. It was only with considerable reservations that this break with tradition – and ultimately the *halakha* – was accepted as the price that had to be paid for legal equality. With increasing integration and assimilation, however, this was regarded less and less as a problem. As French among French, the Jews no longer wanted to assume a special role, and the majority of French Jews were soon glad not to be buried among their fellow Jews, but rather among their fellow citizens. For this reason, new legislation of 1881 was also accepted without resistance; it abandoned the segregation of individual parts of the cemetery for members of special faith communities such as Jews, Protestants or Muslims. This precisely reflected the lifestyles of the majority of French Jews: they lived everywhere and, apart from a few specifically Jewish quarters such as the Rue de Rosière in Paris, in close proximity to their fellow citizens

General view of the cemetery. Engraving. *circa* 1835.

Père-Lachaise's Jewish section

The largest of the cemeteries built in Napoleonic times and shortly afterwards are the cemeteries of Montmartre (1798 onwards), Père-Lachaise (1804) and Montparnasse (1825). Each of these has its own Jewish section, with the section in Père-Lachaise being the first of its kind.

Père-Lachaise was built on a park area and the site of a small palace, Mont Louis, which had served as a country seat to the Jesuits in their role as father confessors to the king. It was one of these, Père François de la Chaise, confessor to Louis XIV, who gave his name to the cemetery. Until their expulsion in 1762, the Jesuits built up Mont Louis to become a lavish complex, with parterres, wooded groves and an orangery. Much of this remained until 1804, despite a change of ownership, and shaped the basic structure of the new cemetery. So it was that the Jewish section of Père-Lachaise was built close to the orangery, on the land of a Jesuit vegetable garden.

The design for the cemetery came from the architect Alexandre-Théodore Brongniart, inspector general for the office of public works under prefect Frochot. Brongniart's project planned for a large, park-like cemetery at whose centre would be a mourning room in the shape of a giant pyramid, an idea most probably stimulated by Napoleon's campaign in Egypt. As with

so many projects of the time, however, it did not come to fruition, and it was not until 1820 that the castle was replaced with a chapel. Brongniart planned to site the monumental main entrance on the Boulevard de Ménilmontant, and it was from here that the main axis would have led to the elevated pyramid. The cemetery land rose from the Boulevard in an easterly direction, with individual sections culminating in almost picturesque, steeply sloped areas. Access was via wide, street-like, tree-lined avenues that ran in either straight lines or followed curved routes, and the graves themselves were reached by paths designed in the style of the English landscaped garden.[1] Over the course of the nineteenth century, the countless grave monuments that still so characteristically shape the image of this unique cemetery, were built here.

View into the avenue of the old Jewish section.

Mausoleum in the old Jewish section.

Brongniart planned the Jewish section in the southwestern corner of the new cemetery. The existing perimeter, marked by walls, formed a corner here so that the Jewish section, also known as 'Le Petit Cimetière', was self-contained on the western and southern sides and clearly demarcated from the rest of the cemetery. It was therefore enclosed on the northern and eastern sides by a wall, built in 1809 by Godde, the later builder of the chapel mentioned above, with the entrance being situated on the northern side, towards a forecourt. In 1838, a notable from the *Consistoire* criticized the gate for being too small and narrow, making the entrance to the Jewish section look elongated and undignified.[2] The wall is clearly visible in contemporary illustrations. To the Père-Lachaise watchmen this enclosed area seemed ideal as a kennel for dogs that guarded the cemetery at night, but the *Consistoire* protested strongly against this desecration of the Jewish section and a new kennel was found.[3] The Jewish section, with a side gate from the Rue Saint André, thus has its own entrance, which meant that Jews did not need to enter the cemetery through the main entrance, which was crowned by a cross.

Brongniart had issued strict specifications in his draft of the design. As well as an elaborate gateway with entrance and side rooms, he also wanted to split the section precisely in two using a tree-lined avenue. At the outer edges, along the wall, he envisaged the

A new section with Jewish and
Christian gravestones standing
closely together.

erection of identically shaped family graves, following the interior perimeter of the cemetery, which was surrounded on all sides by trees. Brongniart's design is the first one to be drawn up for a Jewish cemetery by a non-Jew, and could not be more different from the Jews' traditional cemeteries. This draft is clearly an attempt to combine the use of forms from contemporary revolutionist architecture with the model from the Campo Santo in Pisa, a Christian cemetery. The fact that the requirements of the *halakha*, such as the laying of graves facing east, could only be met with difficulty, was overlooked. This may have been the reason why Brongniart's design was never implemented. No family graves were built along the external walls, the elaborate gatehouse was reduced in 1820 to Godde's modest gate and only the central axis appeared in maps dating from the second half of the nineteenth century as the Avenue Rachel, which still exists today, lined with chestnut trees. In this form, the Jewish section built in 1820 satisfied the requirements of the *halakha* thanks to its clearly demarcated position and nature. No new *tahara* house was built; instead, an existing building, probably the small house to the left of the entrance gate to the Jewish section, was converted for this use in 1856.

The new legislation of 1881 marked the beginning of the end for a self-contained Jewish cemetery, a fate that also befell the Muslim and Protestant sections of Père-Lachaise. Shortly afterwards, the gate and the internal wall facing the cemetery were torn down. Today, only the base of the wall remains, creating an offset to the famous grave of Héloise and Abélard further up. Although the regulations of 1881 stipulated that Jewish graves were not to be levelled or reused after expiry of the normal 'period of rest', but instead could expressly be left untouched 'forever', as time went by graves in the former Jewish section were dug up and replaced with the graves of non-Jews. The end for the Jewish section became evident with the building of massive Christian family plots which, following the destruction of the gate and wall to the forecourt, were built behind the side gate on the Rue Saint André. Adorned with huge crosses, they now flank the access to the *ancien enclos juif historique* and its avenue of chestnut trees, which leads to the grave of the first *Grand Rabbin* of France, David Sintzheim. Although his grave still exhibits traditional inscriptions, its pyramid shape is less traditional and more typical of the time. A few other graves from the first quarter of the nineteenth century also demonstrate traditional forms and inscriptions, but this canon soon came to be replaced by 'modern' forms such as cast-iron pillars, chapels such as that of the actress Rachel, picture portraits such as that of Jacob Roblés, or large mausoleums like that of the Rothschilds. The grave of the artist Camille Pissarro, however, is simple and modest.

From 1881 onwards, Jewish graves were laid in the large cemetery extension of 1850. Situated on a plateau to the east of the old part, these extended areas had, unlike the old section, been created in line with a schematic plan, but were nonetheless accessed via wide avenues. The new Jewish graves, for the most part with several grouped together, were laid in sections 94 to 96. Despite this group arrangement, these sections gave rise to a situation where Jews and Christians, Muslims and Buddhists were interred together, next to each other or head to head.

Stained glass window from
a mausoleum, which depicts
Moses holding the tablets
with the Ten Commandments.
He is shown with two horns,
which derives from
Michelangelo's Moses in
San Pietro in Vincoli, Rome.

Berlin/Schönhauser Allee: a Step beyond Tradition

The New Synagogue on Oranienburger Strasse. Oil painting by Emile de Cauwer. 1865.

In 1812, King Friedrich Wilhelm III issued a decree that ended the hundred-year position the Jews enjoyed as 'protected Jews', with all the restrictions and special taxes that went with this. The Jews of Prussia were thus declared 'natives' and 'citizens of the state' and they believed that an end had come to all social and national discrimination. In the decades that followed civil emancipation, up until the founding of the *Reich* in 1871, far-reaching changes took place. A process of adaptation began, aimed at assimilating with German culture and the standards of German society; in many areas, this led to assimilation up to the point of conversion. At the same time, efforts were also made to adapt the religious lives of the Jews to this process of change. There were wide-ranging reforms to services and liturgy which led to the famous German-Jewish version of Liberal services with choir and organ, as in the New Synagogue in Oranienburger Strasse. No longer hidden away in a courtyard, this synagogue, constructed by Eduard Knoblauch and Friedrich August Stüler, rose high above the rooftops and stood proudly on the skyline; was the expression of a new self-awareness among the Jews of Berlin. Behind its eastern-style façade, what was then Europe's largest synagogue concealed a much-admired, modern steel construction and a sophisticated lighting system.

Germany remained different to France where, despite the Dreyfus affair, the social equality of the Jews was more advanced than in conservative Prussia where, up until 1918, the maxim of the unity of the (Protestant) church and throne still existed. This difference is also reflected in the cemeteries of Père-Lachaise and Schönhauser Allee. Berlin's Jews were less at the 'centre of society' than their brothers in Paris, and thus created their own, separate cemetery that was, however, built in accordance with the aesthetic design principles of contemporary society, again reflecting the new spirit of the times.

The new cemetery

The plot of land measuring five hectares, acquired in October 1824, lay on the old road to Pankow. Once the road had been cobbled, it was first called the Pankower Chaussee but was renamed in 1841 as the Schönhauser Allee. Although the old cemetery on the Grosse Hamburger Strasse was simply an enclosed structure with rows of graves arranged in a more or less regular fashion, the community decided some 150 or so years later to have the new cemetery planned by an architect in line with *halakhic* and aesthetic principles. While the government building officer of Berlin, Friedrich Wilhelm Langerhans (1780–1851), commissioned to undertake the project, was a Christian, he was supported by the Jewish community and almost certainly advised by Moritz Normann of the Communal Land Administrative Committee and Jacob Moses Burg, the community's leader. Langerhans, an architect and local politician, had been promoted to his position in 1805 by King Friedrich Wilhelm III. In his period of office, he was responsible for the erection of numerous schools, the conversion of churches and the creation of several Christian cemeteries, along with the construction of the Friedrichshain communal park.

By accepting a non-Jew to create the new cemetery, based also on aesthetic principles, the Jewish community in Berlin abandoned the tradition of building their own cemeteries, simply observing the rules of *halakha* such as walls, the west-east position and the minimum distance between graves. The idea that places of the dead should also be designed to look beautiful, had

Plan of the cemetery, 1882. The entrance area with the superintendent's house is visible in the bottom left corner. The Jew's walk is not shown, but it follows the long border on the top of the map.

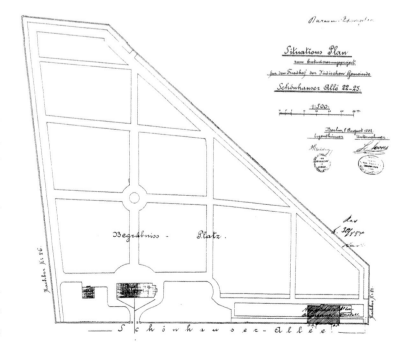

Design for the superintendent's house showing its *tahara* and mourning room, 1854.

already been expressed in the Père-Lachaise cemetery in Paris and the Olsany cemetery in Prague. The Berlin community was thus following, as in so many other areas of life, bourgeois Christian society, which

likewise only began building its cemeteries in line with aesthetic criteria from the end of the eighteenth century. The Schönhauser Allee cemetery reflected the ever-growing assimilation of the Berlin Jews, although the autonomy of the Jewish cemetery was preserved in Prussia and most other German states.

Given this autonomy, but also in the light of a conflict with the *chevra kaddisha* which led to its final abolition, the two influences on the cemetery on the Schönhauser Allee become clear: meeting the requirements of the *halakha*, while at the same time ensuring that the cemetery remained 'beautiful' and 'orderly', in sympathy with the expectations of bourgeois society. The community leaders thus followed neither radical reform nor orthodoxy, instead choosing a course of cautious balance whose principal mission of integration into the surrounding society through partial reforms, was never called into question. The new cemetery thus became the true expression of a reform-driven Prussian Jewry.

Langerhans' design

Langerhans planned for the cemetery to have a dominant east-west avenue, running from one main entrance on the Schönhauser Allee and dividing the cemetery into two halves. The strict east-west layout followed the traditional orientation of the graves towards the east. At the end of the east-west avenue was the eastern gate, which led to a burial path known as the *Judengang* or 'Jews' path'. The eastern gate, with its opening facing Jerusalem, the place from which the Messiah and Redemption would come, is thus charged with symbolic meaning, the cemetery being one of the few to have such a gate. Surprisingly in Berlin, this happened at a time when many reformers began to believe they had found the New Jerusalem on the banks of Berlin's River Spree and abandoned the prayer for the return to Zion. But on the other side, the *Judengang* also shows a more traditional element: 500 metres long, it runs parallel to the cemetery wall and was used as a side entry for funeral processions and for giving *Cohanim* easier access to graves close to the gate.

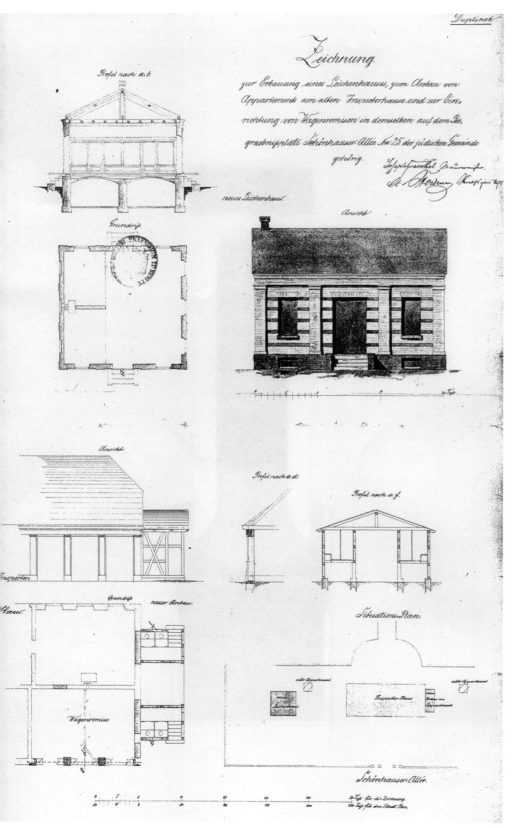

At the main entrance, in the centre of the axis of the east-west avenue, was the superintendent's house, which provided an office and living quarters as well as rooms for the laying-out and washing of bodies. In the centre of the avenue's axis, on the east side of the building, is a large room, looking onto the alley, marked by two pillars set back. This is probably the first mourning room in the German-speaking region.[1] Until that point, eulogies and addresses were made in open spaces close to the entrances, as was the case in Prague. Around the superintendent's house, the walkways were enlarged to form almost square-like areas. To the north, a small, separate house was built for the bodies in 1860.

Cross cuts leading off from the main path divided the cemetery grounds into six grave areas. The points at which these side paths intersect with the main path were emphasized by a round plot. Later, the cemetery was extended to the south, with the new area linking up to Langerhans' path and area system. Along the outer limits of the cemetery, a wall was gradually built that featured ornamented bricks on the side facing the Schönhauser Allee. The cobbled cemetery paths were planted with trees such as limes, chestnuts and sycamores, but the graves themselves were not planted, in accordance with *halakhic* rules. All of the grave areas were marked with cast-iron plaques on which the plot designation and grave row were listed, while the graves themselves were numbered throughout, the aim being to ensure chronological occupation, although this was not strictly observed. Near the entrance, a row of honorary graves was laid in which rabbis and other individuals who led lifestyles in accordance with the *halakha* were buried. The allocation of such honorary grave plots became a source of friction, as was shown in 1860 when the radical reformer Rabbi Samuel Holdheim was interred there, despite the burial institution's resistance.

The cemetery opened on 29 June 1827 as a classical 'avenue-quarter cemetery', in other words, the grave areas, or quarters, were framed by avenues. In this respect, it is similar to Christian cemeteries built at the time. The design, however, also attempts to take into

Intersection of two avenues.

The memorial to Sophie Loewe (d. 1876), one of only four in this graveyard with a picture of the deceased.

account the rules of the *halakha*, by positioning the graves facing west to east and keeping the grave areas clear of foliage. But it went one step further: Langerhans imbued the cemetery with a further symbolic layer, one not found in previous Jewish cemeteries. The entire grounds of the cemetery were laid out to face east and a dominant east-west avenue originated at a mourning room, together with the creation of an eastern gate at its end, features that were completely new to Jewish cemeteries until the beginning of the nineteenth century.

A few years after the opening, a small flower room was built that was supplied with flowers from the cemetery's own nursery, complete with greenhouse. It is here that the changes of the latter half of the century become clearest: the customs of the Christian majority were adopted in defiance of the Jewish tradition that graves and be marked only with a stone slab and remain unadorned.

The Haberland family
vault (1920).

Family graves versus headstones: differentiation among the grave markers

With time, family burial plots were created along the cemetery walls on the north, east and south sides and in isolated cases in prominent positions along the edges of the grave areas. These could be accessed from a pathway that circumscribed the cemetery on virtually all sides.[2] The majority of these family burial plots were not laid facing east, and there was another new feature: families could now purchase a large grave plot in which several members could be interred as time passed. Elaborate monuments were then erected whose styles of self-representation were used by wealthy families to reflect success within the bourgeois and feudal society of Prussia. Jewish family plots soon came to resemble those found in Berlin's Christian cemeteries. The old maxim of the equality of all in death was visibly abolished. The grave monuments of the rich now contrasted with the modest, small and traditional gravestones of the less well-off and less-important families, a trend seen in Jewish cemeteries right across Europe. By way of balancing this ostentation, it was decided that each grave plot, including those whose descendants did not want to find the money for a gravestone, should be marked with a 'headstone' complete with grave number. Since all of the graves were numbered – some 22,801 numbers had been assigned by 1942 – the poor therefore at least were able to preserve their name in the cemetery index. The loss of this index after the war is thus all the more tragic. The headstones make this cemetery a community cemetery that remembers everyone, not just the successful.

The cemetery on the Schönhauser Allee increasingly became an expression of Prussian, class-driven society and the way it lived: the wealthy were buried just as they had lived — in other words, along the wide main roads or avenues of the cemetery. The less well-off were interred inside the grave areas, just as they had lived within the tenements that were beginning to spread across Berlin. This trend reached its peak in the successor cemetery at Weissensee.

The early gravestones, erected from 1827 onwards, exhibited the forms and materials familiar from the Grosse Hamburger Strasse cemetery – traditional *matzevot* made from sandstone with Hebrew inscriptions. But this soon changed. The family plots, with their array of styles from classical (the grave of Hirschfeld by architect Strack) and neo-Gothic (Joachim Liebermann) to neo-Renaissance (Liebermann by architect Grisebrach) and neo-classical (Simon by architect Breslauer & Salinger), reflect the myriad designs of the nineteenth and twentieth centuries. The family of the composer Giacomo Meyerbeer, who is buried here, had an imposing monument built – more imposing even than that of Gerson von Bleichröder, who had financed Bismarck's war against France that led to the founding of the *Reich* in 1871 and who was elevated to the nobility. His grave was designed by the sculptor Begas.

One particular canon concerns graves with pictures of people on them. In line with the Ten Commandments this had been expressly forbidden by the cemetery rules in force at the Grosse Hamburger Strasse. This ban probably also applied to the new cemetery, as the four violations of the ban appear to confirm the inherited rule. Despite all the reform and adaptation to surrounding society that had taken place, here we also see a marked adherence to the *halakha*. This contrasts completely with Père-Lachaise in Paris and its countless depictions of people right back to Moses.

View through the gate into the Jews' walk.

Berlin/Weissensee:
the Wilhelminian Necropolis

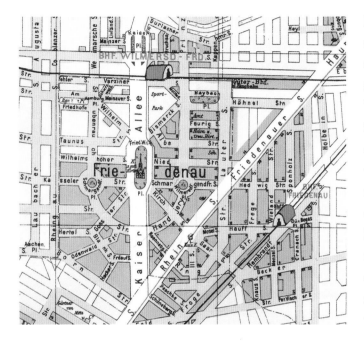

Map of a wealthy district in the Western part of Imperial Berlin, 1902. The avenues and squares are laid out on a grand scale allowing wide vistas and perspectives.

Plan of Weissensee cemetery, 1935. Hugo Licht's design clearly reflects the city of the living with its grand avenues and squares.

In 1871 the coronation of the Prussian King Wilhelm I as Kaiser was greeted by most Germans with much enthusiasm, and the middle classes launched themselves into the adventure of the early boom years of Wilhelminian Germany. Jewish merchants, industrialists and bankers were at the forefront of the new state's economic development, the consequences of which were particularly apparent in the new Berlin. The population of the city was a mere 700,000 in 1871, small by comparison with London, but by 1910 so many people had moved there that the population had reached two million, to the point where it had the largest number of tenement blocks in Europe. As developers strove to minimize costs and maximize building land, the result was tenement blocks of up to seven floors. To make use

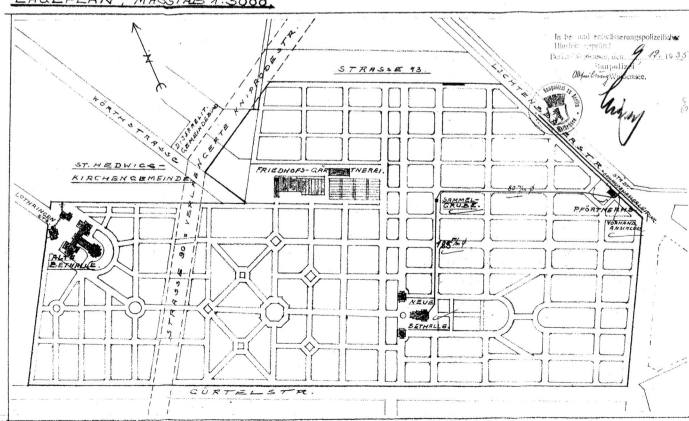

of the depth of the developed areas, the tenements
were simply lined up one after the other. While the
'gentlefolk' lived in the street-facing houses, the workers and lower-ranking white-collar workers lived in
the *Gartenhaus*, a euphemistic term for the tenements
set back from the street. In the courtyards of the proletarian districts meanwhile, utter squalor prevailed.
Dwellings were narrow, dark and damp. Several families often shared a one- or two-roomed flat, one family
living in a single room. The standards of hygiene beg-
gar description and diseases such as typhoid and
tuberculosis became widespread. All this made the
cityscape of imperial Berlin an accurate reflection of
Wilhelminian class society, with its fabulous wealth
and extreme destitution.

In line with the overall explosion in the population
of Berlin, the number of Jews living in the city also
rose. While a mere 36,000 Jews lived there in 1870, or
3.9% of the total population, the figure was 100,000 by
1900; at 172,000 in 1923, Berlin had one of the largest
Jewish communities in the world. Despite its dispro-
portionately high number of independent businessmen
and academics, Berlin Jewry closely mirrored surrounding society. The families of magnates such as the
Rathenaus, Fürstenbergs, Mendelsohns, Ullsteins and
Mosses, for example, lived in palatial properties
around the Tiergarten or in Grunewald. Members of
the Jewish middle class, which was proportionately
larger than the German middle class as a whole and

made up of higher-ranking white-collar workers,
lawyers, doctors and architects, tended to make their
homes in the west of the city around the
Kurfürstendamm, in the Hansa Quarter and the so-
called Bavarian Quarter. A large number of proletarian
Jews also lived in Berlin, particularly in the areas
around Alexanderplatz, in Prenzlauer Berg and in
Friedrichshain.

As a consequence of the pogroms in Poland and
Russia, many more so-called *Ostjuden*, eastern Jews,
moved to Berlin, settling in the Scheunenviertel next
to Alexanderplatz. Many of these Jews were poor
whose faithful adherence to a lifestyle prescribed by
the orthodox *halakha* and by tradition was an obsta-
cle to personal economic advance. It was almost as if
one could remain either pious and poor, or adapt to
surrounding society and have at least a chance of
becoming rich and successful as a bourgeois. Although
most Jews chose the latter, it did not necessarily equate
with assimilation. There were a number of different
ways of becoming a 'German citizen of Jewish faith',
ranging from attempts to develop a modern orthodoxy,
which aimed to harmonize the traditional *halakha*
with a modern lifestyle, to the extremes of the reformers. The diversity of religious orientations within the
Jewish population of the imperial capital found
expression in architecture. The spectrum of sacred
Jewish spaces of this period ranged from the small
Betstibl of the ultra-orthodox eastern European

The neo-Renaissance
cemetery buildings (1880) by
Hugo Licht.

Walkway to the ceremonial
hall.

chassadim in the Scheunenviertel, to the Liberal
Temple, in the German Romanesque style, on
Fasanenstrasse near the Kurfürstendamm.

The cemetery

It was apparent soon after the foundation of the
empire that the cemetery on Schönhauser Allee,
opened in 1827, would be entirely full by around 1900.
As it soon became surrounded by residential buildings,
the community began to look for land for a new cemetery. The suburb of Weissensee provided a suitable site
for the construction of the largest Jewish cemetery
in Europe.

As had become customary with major municipal
projects, a competition was launched for the design of
the cemetery grounds and buildings. It is apparent
here, as with the Schönhauser Allee cemetery in 1827,
that the Jewish community saw the creation of a new
cemetery as a partly aesthetic undertaking. This
applied explicitly not only to buildings like the mourning hall, *tahara* house and administrative building,
but also to the overall design of the cemetery, with its
burial grounds and access paths. The trend towards an
aesthetic conception of a Jewish cemetery, of which the
Schönhauser Allee had already provided a taste, was
continued here. The chief architect of Leipzig,

Professor Hugo Licht, renowned for building the Leipzig town hall and the Grassi Museum, won the competition in 1876 at the second attempt, and building work started in 1879. Because of the plot's location next to a main road, Licht had to site the entrance and associated buildings in the north-western corner. Through lavish, outward-swinging gates, he leads visitors into the cemetery and a forecourt, upon the central axis of which stands the recessed mourning hall. Running in front of this is a colonnaded passageway at either end of which the *tahara* house and the administrative building are located. An eight-sided dome emphasises the central axis of the structure within the colonnade. The mourning hall is in turn connected with the passageway by another colonnade. The entire construction, built of yellow clinkers and decorated with terracotta and sandstone elements, adheres to neo-Renaissance forms.

Its huge size of forty hectares made it vital that the cemetery, which had been extended on several occasions, be developed in systematic and aesthetically pleasing fashion. Because of its size, which made graves hard to locate for visitors, it was undesirable to develop the site more or less at random, as in the case, for example, of the small cemetery on Grosse Hamburger Strasse. It was, moreover, essential to utilize every inch of the expensive land as effectively as possible. This required a complex system of major and minor avenues, squares, and a network of minor paths. Hugo Licht's award-winning design provided for a cemetery featuring all these elements and reflected the avenues, streets and squares of Wilhelminian Berlin created by the city's Chief Architect Hobrecht and his successors. The 'house of life', for millennia a place whose key component was the individual grave, now became the city of the dead, the necropolis, its form a faithful reflection of the city of the living. Just as the rich and prosperous lived on Berlin's great squares and avenues, they installed their family graves in the cemetery in Weissensee on the avenues and squares created by Licht. Over the course of time, these were lined with grave monuments and mausolea which in turn mirrored the houses of the liv-

ing in style and form. The Wilhelminian neo-Baroque, neo-Renaissance, neo-Gothic and neo-Romanesque grave monuments were astonishingly similar to the façades of the great houses on the Kurfürstendamm and the villas in Grunewald. Licht's system of avenues and squares also missed the Schönhauser Allee's symbolic east-west orientation towards an east gate, this erosion of Jewish belief and practice again reflecting a drift from traditional Judaism.

As we have seen, in the past equality in death had been documented by simple, modest gravestones, generally placed in uniform rows. In Weissensee, we see the continuation of the opposite tendency first seen in Schönhauser Allee. The gravestones installed there until around 1850 still adhered to the old simplicity, but the Hirschfeld grave monument, designed by Johann Heinrich Strack in 1860, revealed the shape of things to come. The burial plot, upon which simple gravestones redolent of antiquity still stood, was furnished with a lavish classical architecture featuring columns, entablature and mounted vases – all elements deployed by Strack in the construction of villas. In the same way, behind the family graves in Weissensee, which often grew to monumental proportions, and behind the distinguished street-facing houses of the dead, were buried those who had lived

Streetscene from the Hansa-Viertel a wealthy jewish neighbourhood, *circa* 1920.

The neo-Baroque mausoleum to Rosalie Ernst (d. 1899).

around the first, second, third or fourth courtyard, each further from the street. Here were no broad avenues or squares but merely narrow by-paths. Even at the time, this came in for heavy criticism: 'Enormous wrought-iron back walls featuring nothing less than floral orgies in iron separate the graves of the rich from those of the less well-off.'[1] Yet the graves faithfully reflected Wilhelminian class society, divided into the medium-sized 'optional plots' and the small 'row plots'. Each of the latter type lay close to the next; the gravestones were simple, modest affairs, often of necessity. At times, however, people consciously chose the traditional style of gravestone as a silent protest against the gravestone culture, ultimately an expression of the assimilation of the ruling class of the Berlin Jewry. Wilhelminian notables, dignitaries of the legal, medical and financial authorities, factory and department-store owners, 'Royal and Imperial' court pianists often found few things more embarrassing than the sight of their Eastern European 'comrades in faith' in the Scheunenviertel, and frequently aspired to nothing other than assimilation and upward social mobility.

In 1893, Raphael Löwenfeld for example, called upon fellow Jews 'to swim with the tide of modern thought and sensibility. ... Are we educated Jews closer to the fanatical devotees of Talmudic wisdom than to enlightened Protestants, whose culture and education is also our own? Are we closer to French Jews than German Catholics?'[2] Alongside the lavish architectural arrangement of the graves, it became increasingly common to decorate them with plants, a break with the Jewish tradition of the stone grave. While the Schönhauser Allee cemetery featured nothing more than a small flower pavilion nursery, its Weissensee counterpart evolved into a large-scale enterprise. Plants for ornamental borders were grown in five enormous greenhouses and sold in a shop at the main entrance.

However, as a consequence of growing anti-Semitism from the 1880s on, Jews started to focus on their own traditions again and looked for a way of remaining Jewish. This new attitude was gradually reflected in the design of gravestones. That of the philosopher Hermann Cohen, who died in 1918, marks a return to the traditional form of the mock sarcophagus. Mendel's gravestone, designed by Bauhaus director Walter Gropius in 1923, also featured such a sarcophagus. Without a clear front or back, Gropius sited the travertine coffin asymmetrically on the stone grave site. During the inter-war period the graves' clear forms and avoidance of rich ornamentation reflect the contemporary stylistic trends of Expressionism, Art Deco and Bauhaus modernity, though for the most part the new simplicity reflects traditional forms. We know of no grave monuments from this period featuring portraits of the deceased, either in photographic or sculptural form, which had provoked heated debates in the pre-war period.

A total of 100,000 German Jewish soldiers fought in the First World War. Of those from Berlin, 1,943 died either on the battlefield or later from war injuries. Many of the fallen were laid to rest in individual plots and graves scattered throughout the Weissensee cemetery. Three hundred and sixty-five war victims were, however, buried in a memorial ground built by the

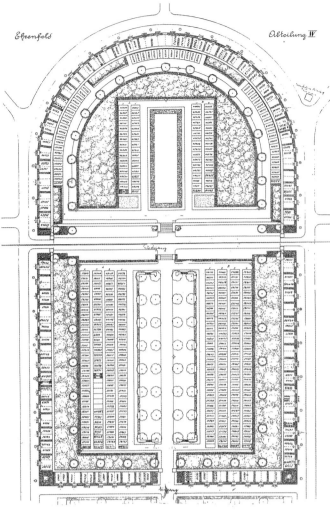

community in 1927. Interred here were those who, as a declaration by the community phrased it, 'have set the seal on Jews' loyalty to the Fatherland by giving their lives'. The memorial ground and monument to the fallen were built according to a design by the Jewish community's architect, Alexander Beer, and consecrated in 1927 in the presence of representatives of government, city, and the Protestant and Catholic churches. The monument has echoes of the altar in the Temple in Jerusalem. Its inscription, which makes no reference to the nation, appears to reflect the sense of resignation in the face of post-war anti-Semitism, in contrast to the war cemetery in Frankfurt, where the community commemorates those 'who sacrificed their lives for the Fatherland in the World War, 1914–1918'. In tragic fashion and under circumstances quite different from those envisaged by the cemetery reformers, the long rows of uniform gravestones realized pre-war demands for uniformity and equality for all in death. The war cemeteries of the First World War are the first military cemeteries in Jewish history.

LEFT Design for the First World War memorial ground for the graves of 365 Jewish soldiers. Alexander Beer, *circa* 1926.

BELOW LEFT The gravestone of the philosopher Hermann Cohen (1842–1918), a revival of the traditional type of sephardic sarcophogus tombstone (compare it with the picture p. 7)

BELOW RIGHT The Mendel memorial, designed by Walter Gropius in 1924.

Meinsdorf/Prussian Village Cemetery

The Jewish cemetery with the chapel of the Christian burial ground behind.

Around eighty kilometres to the south of Berlin is a stretch of land, known as the *Ländchen Bärwalde*, situated some distance from any major roads. Here, in 1848, the cantor Alexander Jablonski and his family, after many difficulties, were given permission to settle in the small village of Meinsdorf, two kilometres from Wiepersdorf. There were, however, two formal conditions. First, Jablonski had to demonstrate that he was a member of a Jewish community, but since there was no such community in the area, he affiliated himself with the Jews of Schönewalde, situated not too far away. Secondly, he had to prove the existence of a burial place that could be no further than four kilometres from his residence. Since there was no such burial place in Schönewalde, Jablonski was forced to create his own cemetery. Together with the merchant Götzel Frank from Schönewalde, he acquired a suitable plot of land on the Schönewalder-Dahmeschen Strasse in Meinsdorf. Father Rindfleisch of Meinsdorf confirmed in writing on the 9 December 1847 that he had no

objection to the project, but the purchase was only entered into the land register on the 2 July 1853: 'Jewish cemetery: a plot of land of approximately [5] square roods in the field near Weissen, separated from Meinsdorf by farm and estate land no. 4. The merchant Alexander Jablonski and the merchant Götzel Frank purchased from local judge Johann Gottlieb Hertel by the agreement of 17 September /5 January 1853 for nine *talers*.'[1] Ironically, Jablonski and Frank bought the land from a village judge who had originally been obliged to deny Jablonski's residency permit.

Meinsdorf cemetery is small, measuring just under 200m², and is situated next to the Christian cemetery on the edge of the village. A wall, 1.2 metres high and made from characteristic bog iron ore, complete with small gate, was built around the rectangular plot of land. Jablonski's family and business prospered. Not long after he arrived in the village, he married Auguste Platzeck, by whom he had four children: Wolff, Ottilie, Otto and Bertha. The children attended the Christian village school in Meinsdorf, but they were taught the Jewish religion by their father. Together with another child, there were seven Jews living in Meinsdorf in 1859, allowing contact with relatives and the community in Schönewald to continue.

Even back in 1850 – long before the entry in the land register – a burial, probably of someone from Schönewalde, had taken place in the cemetery. 'Husband and father Joseph Jonas died aged 72'[2] and was buried in November of that year. In 1857 and 1860, members of the Frank family were buried here. The gravestones, inscribed on both sides in Hebrew and German, were produced in Berlin by the stonemason Zachart. The merchant, Lewin Gerson Lewin, was buried in 1871, and on 6 February 1865 Alexander Jablonski himself was finally laid to rest leaving

בס
איש ישר ונבכך
ילא ב ותחלך הנעים
כה אליקום
בן כה יונה
נולד יד המוז הקהלט
נטר כש בכרו הדרבו
הנצבה
†

Modest and traditional
nineteenth-century
gravestones.

behind a wife and five children. His sons Wolff and Otto went to Berlin to work as salesmen, and their mother soon followed with her daughters. The heirs of the Frank family from Schönewalde also left the *Ländchen Bärwalde* for Berlin, Leipzig and the USA, and all traces of them have since been lost. This was typical of the widespread tendency in the second half of the nineteenth century for people, Jews and non-Jews, to move to large cities.

After the Jablonskis had gone, the cemetery lapsed into obscurity. Overgrown, it even appears to have escaped the Nazis and it survived without disturbance.

People visiting today, after a long journey on country roads, will find a typical example of a small Jewish cemetery, one that offers a faithful impression of the law-abiding nature of German rural Jewry in the nineteenth century. The gravestones, facing east and inscribed with Hebrew and German epitaphs, illustrate the two sides of the coin: Jewish religion and culture as well as integration into German society. This growing integration, perhaps even assimilation, is evidenced by the change of names. While the fathers were still called Alexander, Moses, Isaac and Ascher, the children were given names such as Ottilie, Otto and Bertha.

Grand late nineteenth-century apartment buildings with the 'Jubilee synagogue' (built 1906).

Between 1897 and 1917 Jewish Prague, the former ghetto, was almost completely replaced by a modern grid of streets and appartment blocks. Only some synagogues and the Jewish town hall survived this radical clean-up which made many Jews move into other parts of the city. It was during this period in which the city of the Jews was being destroyed, and with it the traditional Jewish custom of living together in one district,

that the new cemetery was built in Zizkov. In 1884, the Zizkov local authorities had forbidden further burials on the former plague cemetery in Olsany. In 1886, the *chevra kaddisha* therefore purchased a plot of land from the city that was situated not too far from the cemetery in Olsany.

The cemetery grounds, which sloped slightly downwards in a south-easterly direction, were virtually rectangular, and on three sides, with the exception of the side earmarked for extension, the cemetery was hemmed in by a specially designed wall. The entrance, with its customary architectural features, was situated on the north side. The entire grounds were accessed by a regular network of paths, initially encompassing twenty-two square grave areas, the numbered grave areas being labelled with plaques in order to help visitors find their way around. By 1893, the impressive ceremonial hall had been built at the highest point and the road leading to it became the cemetery's principal avenue. The regularity of this avenue-quarter cemetery could not be more different to the old cemetery, with its irregular rows and paths. Here, the same orderly attitude appears to reign that did away with the winding alleys and courtyards of the ghetto – the clean-up project begun at around the same time. Funeral processions now moved in a straight line from the imposing ceremonial hall down the main avenue and branched off at one of the cross-cuts. The grave areas and the graves themselves were given numbers, just like the houses of the living. At the same time, the intense proximity of the ghetto's inhabitants and their attendant solidarity dwindled. So too did the inherent chaos and poverty of their living conditions. In came the new, orderly spirit of bourgeois society, characterized by individualism, social separation and the mastery of bureaucratic structures, common themes running throughout the work of Franz Kafka, who is buried in Zizkov. His grave in area twenty-one, is the most frequently visited.

The main entrance was built in a neo-classical design as a towering, triumphal arch-like construction bearing a quote from the Bible: 'Dust thou art, and unto dust thou shalt return" (Gen. 3:19). The double-winged door of the entrance archway, with rounded edges like that of the Olsany cemetery, effectively provides an open view towards the ceremonial hall, situated about fifty metres away. This building, designed by the architect Bedrich Münzberger in the neo-Renaissance style, was erected between 1891 and 1893.[1] It has a striking cupola, sixteen metres high, which originally made it clearly visible from all the grave areas and paths before trees were planted. It also

represents the hub of the cemetery grounds by marking the change of direction between the main entrance pathway and the main avenue. Behind the hall, completely hidden by it and therefore not visible from the entrance, stands the *beth tahara*, built in around 1891, (before the ceremonial hall).

In the decades after the opening, more than 15,000 people were buried in the new cemetery, which

View through the entrance gate towards the ceremonial hall.

The main avenue looking towards the ceremonial hall.

ultimately covered just over ten hectares after its expansion. Depending on their wealth or their wishes, large and small, elaborate and simple grave markers were erected exhibiting all the styles of the late nineteenth and early twentieth centuries. The graves of Prague's chief and local rabbis, cantors and preachers are mostly simple, although they do not necessarily have the design of a traditional *matzevah*. In contrast, along the eastern wall of the cemetery, elaborate vaults were built for the richest and most influential families of Prague. These graves — of Kubinskys, Elbogens, Thorsches, Sobotkas, Bondys, Waldes and many other families — exhibit the broad spectrum of styles, from the neo-Gothic (around 1890) and neo-Renaissance (around 1900) to Art Nouveau (around 1910) and Modernist (from 1920 onwards). Many of these graves, which often rise up into towering mausoleums, were created by renowned Czech architects such as Kotera, Balsanek, Grotte, Wertmüller, Fanta, Zasch, Mühlstein and others. Particularly striking is the fact that many of the graves, whose inscriptions are mostly written in German, but also in Hebrew, Czech or other languages, frequently feature portraits of the dead in the form of busts, reliefs, medals or photographs.

In November 2001, an unusual, symbolic granite tomb (designed by Kurt Gebauer) was unveiled in the central section of the cemetery (23C). This monument covers some 160 vessels containing mortal remains that had been found previously during construction work at the site of the 'Jews' garden', an early medieval Jewish cemetery and forerunner of the old cemetery next to the ghetto. Thus the circle of Jewish history between the 'Jews' garden' and the newest cemetery in Prague appears to close.

A grand family mausoleum
(late nineteenth century).

A young man's modest
gravestone with his
portrait, *circa* 1920.

In the nineteenth century the three 'patriarchal *kehilot*' of Frankfurt, Mainz and Worms, had new cemeteries built by non-Jewish master builders, all designed as part of large, communal cemetery complexes. Despite their own entranceways and separating walls, the Jewish sections were one part of a communal cemetery, thus documenting, as in Berlin, the process of the emancipation and integration of the Jewish minority into Christian, bourgeois society. The contrast to their medieval predecessors could not be more stark. These new cemeteries, with their classical, Moorish and Art Nouveau buildings, orderly networks of paths and avenues, no longer had anything in common with their dark, densely-packed and often chaotic medieval predecessors, where the rules of *halakha* had presided.

Frankfurt Rat-Beil-Strasse

In 1828 at the northern end of Frankfurt, directly adjacent to the new Christian cemetery that was built around the same time, the Jews of Frankfurt acquired a plot of land which, following several expansions, finally reached a size of 7.4 hectares and served as a burial site until 1929. The architect Friedrich Rumpf used a neo-classical style for the entrance building on the south side of the rectangular cemetery, complete with portal, forecourt, *tahara* and mourning room. Above the temple-like Doric portico, visible from far and wide, stands in Hebrew letters a quote from Isaiah: 'Those who walk uprightly enter into peace; they find rest as they lie in death' (57:2). The construction, reminiscent of a classical Roman house with its function rooms grouped on three sides around the peristyle-like forecourt, stood in stark contrast to the almost concealed entrance to the medieval cemetery next to the hospital on the Judenmarkt. Behind Rumpf's building extend the cemetery grounds designed by the gardener Sebastian Rinz, accessed by a landscaped path lined with sycamores. This path could not be more different from the strict, symmetrical shapes of the entrance building. With this landscaped design, the Frankfurt cemetery is on a par with the Olsany cemetery in Prague.

Mainz Zahlbach

In 1864, shortly before orthodox members split from the main community, Mainz Jewry purchased a plot of 11.3 hectares immediately next to the Christian cemetery

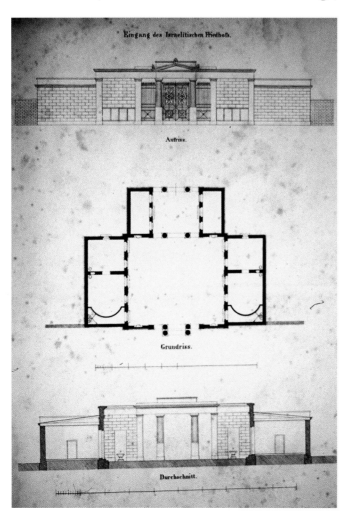

Design for the cemetery building of the Rat-Beil-Strasse in Frankfurt. Friedrich Rumpf, 1829.

that had been built in 1803. The elongated stretch of land rises towards the west and is accessed by an avenue of limes that is divided by a circular square, with the graves lying to the right and left of this avenue. At their foot and axially symmetrical to them lay the mourning room and *tahara*, built in the Moorish style. The cemetery was inaugurated on 2 January 1881. The plans came from the Mainz city government building officer Kreyssig, who had already extended part of the city in Mainz and redesigned the orthodox synagogue. The cost was 30,000 gold marks, a considerable sum for the time. With its Moorish design, the Mainz mourning room is an example of constructional pairing, as it was built in the same style as the community synagogue. The latter, which was inaugurated in 1853, desecrated in 1938 and destroyed in the Second World War, had striking, minaret-like turrets.

Worms Hochheimer Höhe

After the *Judensand* could no longer be extended, the community decided to create a new cemetery next to the main communal cemetery in Worms. As in Mainz, a city master builder, the later mayor Georg Metzler, was commissioned to undertake the work. The land for the new cemetery was an elongated rectangular plot. Towards the street, an elaborate gateway was built with a gatekeeper's house, while a driveway behind led to the mourning room, which was situated on the central axis on a raised area of ground. Unlike the cemetery chapel, the mourning room, inaugurated in 1911, was built in the *Darmstadt Jugendstil* style. By making such a choice, the community demonstrated its openness to the latest art that had been propagated by architects such as Peter Behrens and Joseph Maria Olbrich in 1901 at the industrial exhibition in Darmstadt. Behind the mourning room and extending along the central axis, we find the cemetery paths and grave plots, lined by rows of trees. As in Mainz and Frankfurt, the contrast to the picturesque disarray of the medieval *Judensand* could not be greater.

The Frankfurt cemetery building by Friedrich Rumpf.

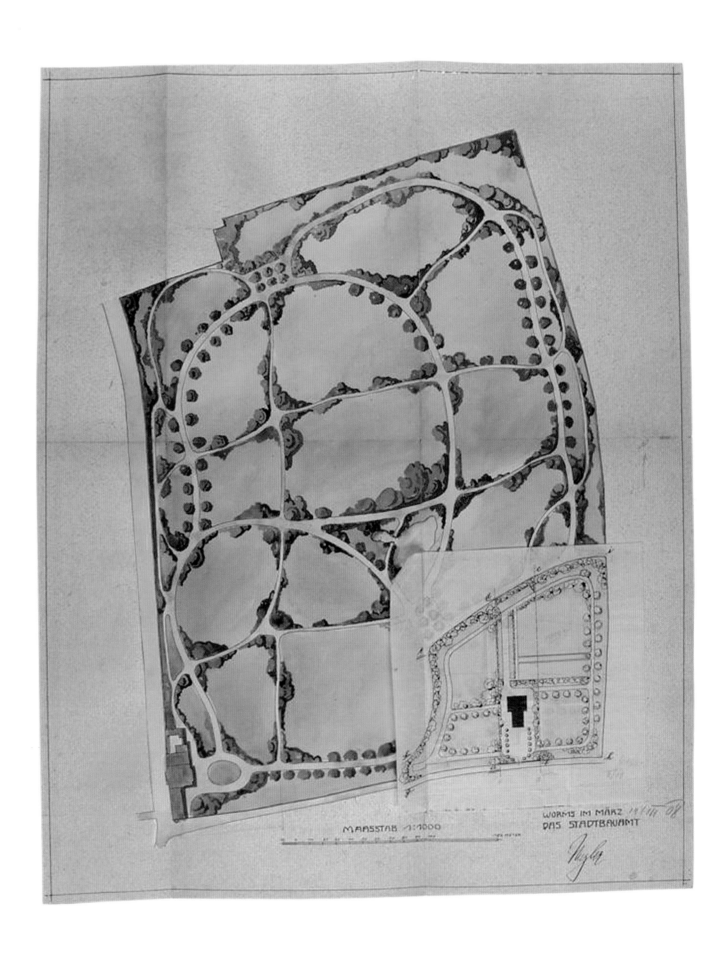

Design for Hochheimer
Höhe cemetery in Worms
with the new Jewish
cemetery in the bottom-
right corner. 1908.

View through the gate
towards the ceremonial
hall of the new cemetery
in Worms, built 1911.

The ceremonial hall of
the new Jewish cemetery
at Zahlbach, Mainz,
built 1881.

Jews had lived in the town of Buda since the thirteenth century, situated high above the Danube in the shadow – and protection – of the royal palace, in return for which they played an important role in the kingdom's finances. From 1526 onwards, the Turks began to conquer the country from the east so that in 1541, Buda finally fell to Ottoman rule. During the fighting, the Jews remained in the city and one legend tells of how they handed the keys of the city to Sultan Suleyman the Magnificent. The period of Ottoman rule, lasting just under 150 years, was a highly prosperous one for the Jews of Buda, for which they showed their gratitude by defending the city in 1686 against the

attacking Austrian and Hungarian troops. Yet their efforts were in vain. 'The end of Turkish rule also meant the end of the Jewish community: at least half of the Jews were massacred by the Austrians, their homes plundered and their Torah scrolls burned.'[1]

The first decades under Austrian rule were extremely difficult, and the situation only improved when in 1783 Emperor Joseph II, following the ideas of enlightened absolutism, gave the Jews the right to stay anywhere in the country, enabling them to take up professions that they had previously been barred from and to farm the land. But Hungarian Jews, as elsewhere at the start of the nineteenth century, began to

The palace of Mór
Wahrmann (1832–92)
on Andrássy Utca.

ask themselves whether they should accept the state's offering and become equal citizens, despite the price of assimilation, or follow traditional orthodoxy and the social isolation that went with it. For the majority, the position was clear: they chose the path that took them to the heart of the dual monarchy constituted in 1867 from Austrian and Hungarian dynasties. In that same year, the Hungarian parliament granted the Jews political equality.

With the 'reconciliation' between Austria and Hungary in 1867 and the founding of Budapest six years later, the city grew to become a metropolis. Large ring and radial roads were created as wide boulevards that were lined with magnificent private and public buildings. Continental Europe's largest parliament was built, based on the model of Westminster, along with banks, department stores, museums, an opera house, a large number of theatres and an unending number of coffee houses that characterised Budapest's *belle époque* in its golden years between 1867 and 1914. Soon afterwards, Budapest became known as the Paris of central Europe, and even today, this comparison remains valid if you wander through the city's boulevards. In this new glamorous metropolis there developed a trend for wealthier Jews to abandon the old Jewish quarter and move to new fashionable parts of the city. Here, they found splendid apartments in the newly-built, large and elegant rental properties along the boulevards, like the magnificent Andrássy Boulevard, which satisfied the demands of bourgeois, often assimilated Jews.

The Salgótarjáni Utca cemetery

In the second half of the nineteenth century, the first two Jewish cemeteries built in Pest were closed because of the city's burgeoning growth and because they had quickly become full. They were later built over. At the same time, the building of cemeteries was increasingly being regarded as a task for the local authority, both in Budapest and in other major cities across Europe, and Pest's city council decided in 1847 to build a large municipal cemetery in the present-day eighth district of Józsefváros, which was at that time still outside the city gates. Some years after this the

Jewish community decided to build a new Jewish cemetery on the outer, eastern edge of the municipal Kerepesi cemetery.

In 1874, this cemetery on Salgótarjáni Utca was opened. The rectangular grounds extending along the street were accessed from the street that gave the cemetery its name. This meant that the entrance, which faced south, was situated well away from the main entrance of the non-Jewish section on the western side, many hundreds of metres away and on a different street. Consequently, while still being part of the large municipal cemetery complex, the Jewish cemetery remained demarcated from the non-Jewish one. A separate wall was also built on the existing cemetery one that specifically served as a *mechitzah* and was intended to satisfy the ritual requirement for the cemetery's structural isolation.

Two historical trends become manifest through the construction: on the one hand, the Jews of Budapest had 'arrived' as equal citizens in the heart of Hungarian society after 1867 and, secondly, they had increasingly integrated into the majority society. Consequently, the new Jewish cemetery was created in

The entrance area with Béla Lajta's *tahara* and gatehouse is visible in the bottom right corner of the Jewish section.

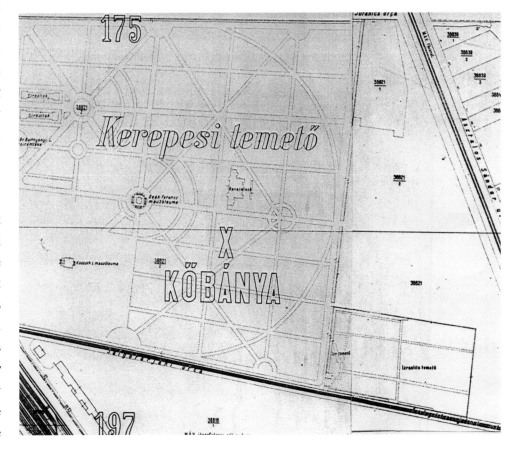

The neo-medieval entrance building by Béla Lajta, built 1908. The domed building next to it is part of the Christian section.

the context of the municipal cemetery. At the same time, however, with its separate entrance and the *mechitzah* wall, the efforts to live by the traditional expectations of a Jewish cemetery are still evident, and with it attempt to retain a level of religious and cultural identity. Nevertheless, and indeed as a result of a failed congress in 1868, orthodox synagogue communities acquired land in 1883 for their own cemetery on the Csörz Utca, where they buried their dead from 1890 onwards.

The rectangle of the new cemetery on Salgótarjáni Utca, which was a cul-de-sac, stretched out in an east-west direction. The entrance was situated in the south west corner, so that visitors needed to turn east to follow the lengthways direction of the grave areas that faced east. Two main paths ran from the entrance area and divided the cemetery into three longitudinal segments, which in turn were divided further by numerous north-south cross-cuts into smaller, individual grave areas. From the longitudinal paths, the individual grave areas were indicated by numbered stones. Along the outer perimeter wall, especially on the west and north sides, were rows of elaborate family burial plots, some of which featured large mausoleums. Parallel to these ran a circumferential

path that intersected with the two longitudinal paths and crosscuts. The two longitudinal paths and crosscuts were originally lined with trees, in an avenue-style design, although some sections of these have now gone. Together with the grid-like system of paths, they formed an avenue-quarter cemetery typical of the nineteenth century whose design was similar to that of the neighbouring non-Jewish section. There were no specially-marked areas for the *Cohanim*, and – unlike the orthodox cemetery from 1890 – there was no special *Cohanim* path (*derech cohanim*) that would separate the graves of men and women. Since the dead lie buried in family groups, it is clear why this cemetery was not acceptable to the orthodox Jews.

From its beginning, the cemetery became the most prominent burial place for the Hungarian capital's Jews. It was here that the rich and famous were buried, in some cases in enormous grave monuments. All of the historic building styles – from the styles of pharaonic Egypt, of Greek and Roman antiquity, of the Gothic period and the Renaissance right through to the Baroque era – are represented here. In some cases, the level of stylistic detail is outstanding, with some wild combinations of styles. The inhabitants of the mansions on Andrássy Utca and the other well-to-do neighbourhoods built a necropolis here which, with its mausoleums, became a faithful illustration of the world of the living. While these mausoleums generally lie near the entrance and in sections of the outer circular path, the level of splendour gradually diminishes as one goes from west to east and towards the inner grave areas. Certainly, the majority of the graves of the less wealthy and traditionalist Jews are marked by simple, almost uniform gravestones made from red natural stone, showing an awareness of Jewish grave culture. The difference between these dignified, ageing but still upright *matzevot* and the slowly-crumbling *belle époque* mausoleums is dramatic, painting a sad picture of a vain attempt to create an eternal life through stone.

Béla Lajta's buildings and graves

In 1908, thirty-four years after the cemetery was opened, the Jewish community decided to have a new entrance building erected, complete with *tahara* and mourning room, and commissioned one of Hungary's foremost architects of the time to carry out this difficult project.

Béla Lajta was born in 1873 to a wealthy Budapest Jewish family. His father, Lipolt Leitersdorfer, who had made his fortune in the construction business, was one of the city's richest men. Lajta did not join his father's company, however, and instead studied architecture at the Budapest Imperial Joseph College under Alajos Hauszmann and Imre Steindl. After his studies, he travelled through Europe for a few years, where he worked as an architect in Berlin with Alfred Messel and Norman Shaw in London. Back in Hungary in around 1900, he went to Transylvania and north of the country. Inspired by his mentor Ödon Lechner (1845–1914), he studied folk art and rural, traditional architecture, and then, together with Lechner, he finally began work in Budapest. As Lajos Hock wrote in 1904: 'He came home with the pledge that he would help to make our architecture

Béla Lajta's *tahara* house. Photograph, *circa* 1910.

Gate of the *tahara* house. Photograph, *circa* 1910.

Ruined late nineteenth-
century family
mausoleums.

Hungarian; that if one comes here, one should find Hungarian-speaking houses, and from these one should learn to speak Hungarian.'[2] Lajta clearly identified himself, as a 'Hungarian of Mosaic faith', so strongly with his homeland that he set himself, a Jew, the daunting task of creating a Hungarian national style. At the same time, however, he reshaped the canon of Hungarian tradition and thus developed his own variation of Art Nouveau as an 'organic unity of Middle-Eastern elements, Hungarian folk art motifs and luxurious modernism'.[2] At the same time, Lajta tried to allow his Jewish roots expression alongside the Hungarian element of his work. This was clearly recognized by his contemporaries. As Pál Nádai said in 1925: 'He was passionate about the Hungarian ideal, he was in possession of the wisdom of those who travelled extensively, and his motto was return to the solemn tranquillity of Judaism.'[3] Up until his early death in 1920 in Budapest, Lajta managed to build a number of residential buildings, commercial premises and municipal buildings. One of his most famous is the Parisiana theatre.

The first thing that modern-day visitors notice when arriving at the cemetery, which now has its own tram stop, is Lajta's gateway. The solid, towering construction looks like a medieval Hungarian castle with its

Gothic arch that reaches up to the first floor, and the smaller passageway gate, again in the Gothic style. The south-west corner of the building is also picturesquely 'fortified' by a laterally adjoined, crenellated round tower. A mock portcullis in the gate's passageway, decorated with features typical of Lajta, continues the castle theme. The gateway building houses the home of the superintendent.

TOP LEFT: The Divine Name shining through a ruined Eternal Light.

TOP RIGHT: A memory of Athens on the Danube.

ABOVE: Modest grave markers in a side walk.

While Lajta's entrance building faces the street, once visitors go through the gate and a walled forecourt, they step into a different world. Positioned axially to the passageway is the solid *tahara* house, for which Lajta chose a style based on ancient Mesopotamian buildings. Both on the north and south sides, the structure returns into view between two mock pylons, where the entrance and exit gates are situated. Above the gates are Hebrew inscriptions (Pss. 90:3 and 36:8). The building was crowned with a flat, 'eastern-style' cupola that collapsed in 1970. While the eastern side, which faces the cemetery, appears to be solidly walled-in and the western side forms the wall to the non-Jewish section, the gate sides of the *tahara* clearly exhibit motifs from Mesopotamian city gates, thus making reference to the patriarch Abraham's origin from Mesopotamia. The thousand-year-old ritual of preparing the body was so crucial for Lajta that he chose a style for the building that referred back to the homeland of the first Hebrews. The exterior of the cemetery, the gateway building on the other hand, is characterized by references to the Hungarian home of Budapest's Jews. Lajta appears here to express a self-understanding based on a strong inner Jewish core and an outwardly Hungarian existence. The building soon became well-known and attracted much praise. In 1925, Béla Málnay wrote: 'The atmosphere of the entrance and the domed mortuary of the old Jewish cemetery is unforgettable. Looking at the Hebrew inscriptions on the huge pylons, the enormous iron gates, the glittering-white Eastern dome above the golden-black interior of the mortuary, we are overcome by a solemn, religious mood. This is art beyond architecture … this is painting, which compels the visitor of the cemetery to feel pathos and anxious reverence.'[4]

As well as his cemetery buildings, Lajta also created numerous grave monuments in Salgótarjáni Utca and in the Kozma Utca cemetery, which was opened later. These illustrate his efforts to reform contemporary sepulchral culture and give it new impetus. The emphasis here was no longer on an eclectic recourse to past styles, but rather on the influence of clear forms and materials combined with contemporary art. The most famous is the Schmidl vault (1904).

The Schmidl family vault designed by Béla Lajta, built 1904.

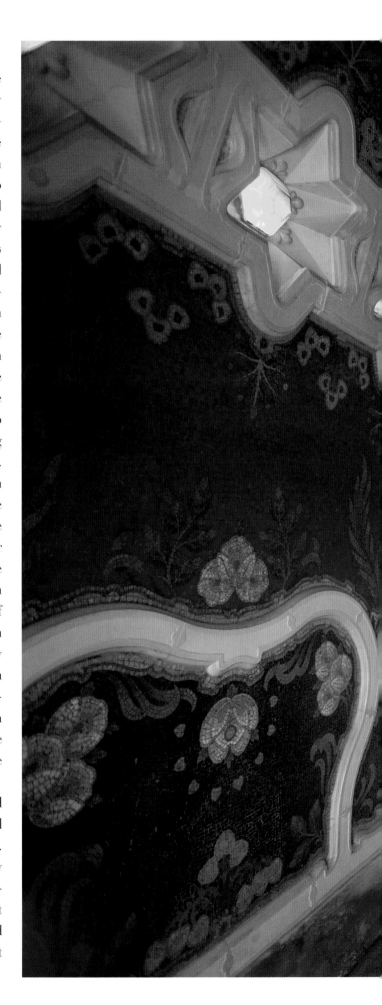

St Petersburg/Moorish-style Cemetery on the Neva

From the foundation of St Petersburg in 1703, Jews lived in this new capital of tsardom. Several of them held lofty positions at court, and they were important figures in society with professions such as physicians and bankers. The most important Jewish entrepreneurs, bankers, intellectuals, artists and scientists were drawn to the capital. The Barons Günzburg, for example, were regarded as the spokesmen and representatives of

St. Petersburg: a city of canals and bridges built into the watery marchland by tens of thousands of soldiers, prisoners and serfs.

all the Jews of Russia. It was not until 1860, however, that a Jewish community was able to form in the city (reaching a population of 35,000 by 1914). Certain government laws permitted only the rich members, the Günzburgs, Polyakovs, Varshavskis, Friedlands and Rosenthals to have a vote in community matters. Just as they ran much of the country's industry and banking system they also ruled the Jewish community and even chose the eastern style for St Petersburg's synagogue, which was built between 1879 and 1883 by Ivan I. Schaposchnikov.

In 1802, a group of Jews, led by Nota Notkin,[1] a successful merchant, leased part of the Lutheran Volkov cemetery to the south of the city. The creation of a separate cemetery, long before the synagogue was built, marked the formal beginnings of a permanent Jewish community in St Petersburg. Lutherans, like Roman Catholics and Jews, were outsiders in a state dominated by the Russian Orthodox Church. It thus became obvious that, if no cemetery of their own was permitted, the Jewish burial site would have to be created in the Protestant cemetery, and for each burial, the Jews had to pay the Lutherans ten silver roubles. In 1859, the graveyard was full and a further plot of land was acquired. A few of the gravestones from the cemetery, with the oldest dating from 1867, remain today.

The cemetery

In 1874, the community leaders succeeded in signing an agreement with the city council on the purchase of land for a cemetery, situated about eleven kilometres to the south near a railway line, now surrounded by industrial plants and run-down housing developments from the Khrushchev era. It was part of a larger, explicitly Christian cemetery complex named after the

The St Petersburg
Synagogue, built 1879-83.

Mount of Transfiguration with sections for non-Russian orthodox groups as well. Unlike in other European cities during the nineteenth century (such as Paris or Rome), the Jewish cemetery in St Petersburg was not part of a dedicated multi-faith community cemetery. After the revolution, the cemetery, apart from the Jewish section, was renamed to remember the victims of Bloody Sunday, 22 January 1905, when tsarist troops massacred almost one hundred peaceful demonstrators outside the Winter Palace. As a result, the paradox arose in St Petersburg that '*preobrazhensky* (transfiguration) is firmly associated in the minds of the inhabitants of Leningrad [St Petersburg] with the Jewish graves.'[2]

The community bore the costs of purchasing the land, partly enclosing it with a fence and constructing a neo-Gothic building for performing the *tahara* and burial ceremonies. The rectangular cemetery grounds, which extend in an east-west direction, were accessed from the present-day Prospekt Aleksandrovskoy Fermy, being surrounded on all sides by a path that ran parallel to the perimeter fence. The internal area of the cemetery was in turn accessed by five longitudinal paths and five cross-cuts, and later expansions followed this system but created bigger grave areas. The mourning room stood at the highest point of the cemetery, while the graves lay lower down so that in some places the terrain was almost marshy, making grave-digging difficult. To mitigate this, drainage ditches were dug parallel to the paths, which still exist today, creating a system of small canals. Here and there, small bridges stretch from the paths to the grave areas, reflecting the layout of the city itself.

Unlike in Berlin there seems to have been hardly any attempt to enhance this rational network of paths from a design perspective, for example through the creation of circular squares. Only the middle one of the original longitudinal paths, which now leads to a corner of the mortuary hall built in 1912, was designed a little wider than the others and probably served as a central axis, leading to the mourning room built in 1873.

Gevirtz's buildings

In 1907, a committee was set up to oversee the planning of new buildings in the cemetery, as the old one from 1873 had fallen derelict. After a competition between ten architects the committee chose a design by the young Yaacov Gevirtz (1879–1942), who as a Jewish architect erected a wealth of buildings for Jewish communities in Russia. On 15 September 1908, amid great ceremony, the community's leaders laid the foundation stone for the new buildings that were built in roughly the same areas as the mortuary hall of 1873. In 1909, the roof of the shell was completed and the building was declared as kosher by Rabbi Katznelbogen. In 1910, the exteriors of the *tahara* and of the mourning room were completed, the cupola was covered with red copper and heating was installed in the cellar. Work then began on the interior design, and the finished buildings were handed over in the summer of 1912, being officially inaugurated on 23 September. Two commemorative plaques on either side of the entrance to the mourning room remember the laying of the foundation stone and those who financed the building.

To mark the inauguration ceremony, a Russian-Hebrew programme was printed that describes the entire procedure in detail. There was a ceremonial handing-over of keys by the chairman of the building commission to the chairman of the construction

Plan of the cemetery, the original grounds with the buildings by Gevirtz on the left.

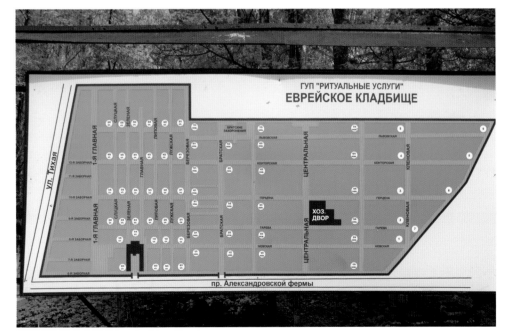

committee, who opened the door of the mourning room. A choir sang and – quite unexpectedly, since normally these are only carried to the cemetery when no longer kosher and are ritually buried there – Torah scrolls were carried into the building as part of the procession that followed. The rabbi preached and there was the obligatory prayer for the welfare of the tsar, his family and the government. Following further speeches, the ceremony ended with the *kaddish*. The programme illustrates how greatly this ceremony was shaped by similar contemporary, non-Jewish events from surrounding society. The carrying of the scrolls of the Torah resulted in the programme referring to the mourning room as a synagogue.

Gevirtz framed the cemetery entrance with two monumental pylons and pillars, reminiscent of Mesopotamian ziggurats, through which the view continued to a forecourt and the mourning hall, which lay with axial symmetry beyond. Between the pillars, grilles and a double-winged gate between the pylons closed off the forecourt from the street. The impression created by this monumental entry was overwhelming, and displayed a strong self-awareness on the part of the St Petersburg community.

The forecourt was framed on both sides by arcade-like walkways, closed off from the grave areas. They featured free-standing pillars with elaborate 'Moorish' capitals and pointed arches on top, also in the Moorish style. The arcade walkways, together with the

View from the street towards the Moorish mortuary hall through Gevirtz's monumental gate of pylons and pillars, reminiscent of Mesopotamian ziggurats.

The forecourt with the Moorish-style arcades.

View through the arcaded walkway.

adjoining mourning room, were reminiscent of the forecourts of the large, classic Ottoman mosques, such as the Blue Mosque and the Suleyman Mosque in Istanbul. These walkways were connected to the mourning room through shorter adjoining wings with no arcades. The building, which featured a showpiece front, was again designed to create a monumental impression. Picking up the motif of the pylon-like pillars of the gateway, two towering walls, clad with coarse, bossed granite squares, formed the framework for the entrance gate, designed as a Moorish arch. The mourning room was crowned by a flat, copper-covered green cupola, again inspired by the Moors and the east.

The interior was designed as a central space over which the cupola, resting on four Moorish arches, sat. There was an *exedra* with two windows and a cabinet between them which would contain the Torah scrolls. This *exedra*, in the axis of this entrance, in the frontal wallis strongly reminiscent of the prayer niches, or *mihrabs*, that indicate the direction of Mecca in mosques. In the centre, under the dome, stood a catafalque-like table on which the coffin would be laid. Fascias displaying quotes from the Psalms in Hebrew extended along the walls of this room which, given its many ogives used in the windows, walls and doors, looks considerably more Moorish than the exterior. One is almost reminded of a synagogue from the Iberian Peninsula before the expulsion of the Jews.

Gevirtz's mourning room was designed to maximize the construction volume and the contrasts of light and texture. The undivided, large, roughly square walls can be interpreted either as a surprising example of early Modernism or as a throwback to ziggurat architecture. In this context, the Moorish elements such as arches, capitals and cupolas, symbolize the continuation of an architectural tradition of two cultures in which Judaism had developed. A similar combination of historical throwback and Modernist forms was also seen in Lajta's contemporary Budapest buildings, whose *tahara* building exhibited many similar features to the larger one by

Gevirtz. Strikingly, there is a complete lack of the traditional Russian architecture in fashion at the time. Strong colours and onion domes are eschewed, with reference being deliberately made to other cultures. Such a Russian-Orthodox style might have been seen as too assimilated.

In this context, it is interesting to note that the new, grand mosque situated not far from the banks of the Neva opposite the Winter Palace, was inaugurated at the same time. This building, visible from afar and significantly more imposing than the synagogue can, along with Gevirtz's cemetery buildings, be regarded as a symbol of the growing self-awareness of these two populations outside the tsarist-orthodox establishment. In St Petersburg, this self-awareness on the part of the Jews was particularly evident among families of magnates who ruled the community almost as oligarchs, and whose grave monuments are grouped together around the mortuary hall. As usual for this period, they are designed in all the familiar 'neostyles', starting with Romanesque graves and large,

perfect Gothic 'chapels' to monuments featuring Renaissance and Baroque styles. However, the revival of national Russian architecture is also found quite frequently, and a few family graves exhibit Art Deco-like shapes.

The graves of the less well-off, with their broken pillars and tree trunks, urns and traditional gravestones, exhibit the entire spectrum of the sepulchral culture that was popular in European cemeteries before 1914. Of note are graves designed with traditional Russian features such as onion domes and other typically Russian objects; particularly striking is the fact that almost all the gravestones feature photographs of the dead. This completely normal practice in the non-Jewish cemeteries of St Petersburg is in direct violation of the *halakha* and it is very rare to see it on such a large scale in a Jewish cemetery of this period, even compared with Rome's Campo Verano. Only a few gravestones can be regarded as truly traditional: the grave of the community rabbi Katznelbogen being one.

The interior of the mortuary hall. Photograph, 1912.

Avenue lined by
modern graves.

A walkway with a street
sign, lined on both sides
by little canals.

A mausoleum designed in a
mix of Moorish and Russian
styles. *circa* 1900.

Emancipation
to Execution

Bridges leading over the
canals to the burial fields.

A Ottoman-style
gravestone.

A seemingly stranded grave
next to a canal.

A variety of gravestone
designs from the late
nineteenth to the
twentieth century.

The cemetery of Bobo, former Galicia, Poland.

Since the beginning of the sixteenth century, the Jewish population in Eastern Europe grew constantly and Galicia in particular became one of the most important centres of Eastern Jewish life, with the Jews developing the role of mediators between city and country. But fortunes changed following the massacres under Bogdan Khmelnitsky (1595–1657) when 125,000 Jews where killed. The Jews, whose social and religious lives were thus unsettled, sought retreat in Kabbalistic teachings, the promises of the 'False Messiah' Sabbatai Zvi and then the mass movement of Hasidism founded by Rabbi Israel ben Eliezer.

Up until the second half of the nineteenth century most Eastern European Jews lived in small towns, known as *shtetls*, a Yiddish term derived from *shtot*, a diminutive form of 'town'. *Shtetls* were Jewish centres in a non-Jewish, mostly farm-based community. In

some of these villages and small towns, such as Vitebsk, the Jews even represented the majority of the population. The economic situation was difficult, and the lives of most Jews in the *shtetl* were characterized by terrible poverty, but also by strong religiousness. They were poor, but they were proud of their Judaism.

Lives were lived in narrow streets, dark, timbered houses and marketplaces. 'In the centre is the marketplace with its stalls, tables and slaughter blocks. Every day, except in winter, the farmers and their wives travel from many miles around into town, bringing their animals and vegetables, their fish and their game, their cartloads full of grain, melons, parsley and garlic. In return, they bought the "town products" that the Jews introduced: hats, shoes, boots, lamps, oil, spades, hoes and shirts. The tumult of the marketplace is a wonder of the world.'[1] The density and closeness of social relationships, and the network of mutual support, along with the intensive practice of their religion and a wealth of artistic production, led to the *shtetl* myth – one that culminated in films such as *Fiddler on the Roof* and *Yentl*.

creatures of the fleeting present could communicate with the eternity of past and future.'[2] More than the Jews of Western Europe, who were becoming increasingly 'enlightened', the Jews of the *shtetl* believed in a close spiritual link between the living and the dead.

Shtetl cemeteries

The *shtetls* illustrated very poignantly the concentration of Jewish life. *Yidishkeyt und Menshlickeyt* were expressed here in countless activities, the intention of which was to live the life of a 'good Jew'. These actions were performed in the synagogue and at home, in the sanctity of the eagerly awaited *shabbat*, and in the worldliness of the marketplace. They were part of the community and family structures. Life was played out between the synagogue, *yeshiva*, home and marketplace. The cemetery too, known generally as the *besoylem* or house of eternity, was inextricably linked to this way of life. 'The cemetery was the permanent home, to which one moved after completing one's brief stay in the *shtetl*. As the place where the dead were buried and the living came to visit, the cemetery provided a bridge between them, where the

'*Shtetl* Jews believed in an ongoing interaction between the living and the dead, with the deceased playing an active role in the *shtetl*'s daily routine, as well as in special events, both joyful and sorrowful.'[3] This often went so far as people believing that the dead gathered in the synagogue at midnight to pray. The road to the cemetery, known as the *besoylem gessl*, was also the object of many superstitions: wherever possible, people should not travel alone lest they meet the spirit of a dead person.

The entire *shtetl* gathered at the *besoylem* for burials, *yahrzeit* ceremonies and stone-laying rituals. It was here that they went for *tisha b'av* and before *Rosh Hashana* to pray for the souls of the dead. But also in times of need, during wars and imminent pogroms, or during periods of collective uncertainty, the *shtetl* would go to the cemetery. 'At night we used to leave

The cemetery of Sakopane, former Galicia, Poland

for the cemetery, which was not too far from the *shul-hoyf* [synagogue yard]. As the battle continued to rage, we lay next to the graves, trembling with fear that a bullet might hit us. ... Friday morning, September 9, 1915, on the eve of Yom Kippur, we returned to the shulhoyf ... Russian soldiers entered the Old Beth Midrash (*the schoolhouse, author's note*) and fired a few shots, one of which hit a young girl who was a refugee from Aran, a *shtetl* not far from Eishyshok. ... Friday evening we again assembled at the cemetery, as the bullets of the "haters of Zion" flew over our heads and bright flashes and gunpowder lit the skies above us. But nobody, thank God, was hit. We survived. At sundown, there among the graves, we recited Kol Nidre.'[4]

Famous scholars and rabbis are buried in many of Eastern Europe's cemeteries. Almost like pilgrimage sites, these cemeteries were visited frequently. Prayers were said beside graves that were often built like small houses, known as *ohalim*. 'The men and the lads went from tombstone to tombstone seeking the graves of the great *zaddikim* [righteous ones], who were buried in Eishyshok. Their tombstones are already sunk in the ground, so everyone took care not to step on the graves. When they reached the row of the *ohalim* [mausoleums] where the great rabbis are interred, they entered the *ohalim* and prostrated themselves in prayer, just as they do in the times of trouble.'[5] Among the most famous of these pilgrimage sites are the Zaretche cemetery in Vilnius, where the Gaon of Vilnius and Count Potocki (a famous convert), are buried, and Radun cemetery where the *ohel* of Hafetz Hayyim is situated.

Marc Chagall

In accordance with the *halakha*, plots of land were chosen outside the gates of the *shtetl*. In larger towns, these plots of land were enclosed by a wall, often with large entrance gates, such as those of the cemetery of his native Vitebsk[6] that Marc Chagall depicts in his 1917 painting entitled 'The Cemetery Gate'. Between the two brick pillars with illegible inscriptions, which were probably blessings to be uttered on entering the

cemetery, a triangular tympanum straddles the wooden gates. A quote from the Prophet Ezekiel (37:12-14) is written in a banner-like form in the triangular capitals of the pillars and in the tympanum. Two dates, 1890 on the left-hand pillar and 1912 on the right, probably record the date of the cemetery's creation and the building of the gate. To either side is a wooden fence that encloses the cemetery. Through the gate, the path leads into the burial ground, whose gravestones, including sarcophagi, are clearly displayed. Between the graves are trees that merge with the sky and together with a larger tree next to the gate form a Cubist division of space.

In many cemeteries for larger *shtetls*, next to the entrance was a house for the *kvoresmann*, the gravedigger and cemetery superintendent, who lived here with his family. A nearby well served a water basin for washing hands after leaving the cemetery. It also supplied the *tahara* room. Here, the bodies of the deceased from surrounding villages that did not have their own cemeteries were ritually cleansed, while in *shtetls* with their own cemeteries, bodies were prepared for burial in their own homes.

The tradition of equality in death was increasingly threatened by growing social differentiation in the cemeteries of bigger *shtetls*, less so in smaller ones. One well-documented and somewhat extreme case is the cemetery of Eishyshok. 'Within the cemetery were three types of soil, the finest being the yellow sand located in the highest part of the cemetery, which was made for excellent drainage. There the *shtetl* buried its most esteemed citizens: the rabbis, scholars, and other notables. ... In the centre of the cemetery, where the soil was a mixture of yellow sand and red clay, the *shtetl* buried its artisans and those among the poor who were known for their good character, their piety, or their learning. Where the cemetery sloped gently down to the public bath, the soil was all red clay, which turned to mud after the thaw and during the rainy season. This was the final resting place for the poor, simple, uneducated Jews, whose humble wooden grave markers sank rapidly into the ground. Within each of these general divisions, of course,

The Cemetery Gate. Oil painting by Marc Chagall, 1917, Musée National d'Art Moderne. Paris.

The Cemetery. Oil painting by Marc Chagall, 1917. Musée National d'Art Moderne, Paris.

The Dead Person. Oil painting by Marc Chagall, 1919. Sammlung Marcus Diener.

were even more finely demarcated burial zones.'[7] There were thus special sections for particular groups, such as *Cohanim*, for women who died in childbirth, for children and for people who had died a violent death. Baptized Jews, people with a bad reputation and suicides were either buried in a 'dark' corner or outside the cemetery walls. Another painting by Chagall, dating from 1917, shows such a *shtetl* cemetery. In the foreground you can see an area of modest graves where the *matzevot* appear to move in frenzied undulations to the sides. In the background and to the left edge of the picture are house-like buildings, the *ohalim* of rabbis and wealthier members of the community. In some places their roofs appear to have fallen in.

Many *shtetls* practised the custom of consecrating the cemetery as part of the wedding celebrations of two poor orphans. The community arranged and paid for the wedding. 'Paying for the marriage of an orphan couple and providing for their living expenses for a number of years to come was an act of charity that was thought to have the power to nullify evil decrees.'[8] The maintenance and upkeep of the cemeteries remained the responsibility of the *chevra kaddisha*, whose annual banquets that preceded a day of fasting became one of the *shtetl*'s social highpoints; there was usually a local women's *chevra* as well. The *chevra* would list the names and grave plots of the dead in large registers (*pinkas*). On the occasion of each burial, a member of the *chevra* would appear in the *shtetl*'s marketplace, in the synagogue and on the main streets and cry out, '*Yidden, geit zu di levaieh*' ('Jews, go to the funeral'), then during the burial, all shops and schools would be closed and all activities ceased. Everyone, with the exception of the *Cohanim*, attended the funeral. If a rabbi or a particularly respected person had died, the coffin was carried to the cemetery; otherwise, the coffin was placed on a funeral cart and driven to the cemetery, accompanied by the *shtetl*'s inhabitants. 'At the head of the funeral procession were the members of the *chevra kaddisha*, who carried huge charity boxes which they rattled ceaselessly, all the while reciting the Hebrew phrase '*Zdakah tazil mi-mavet*' ('Alms from death').'[9] Before the procession reached the cemetery, the coffin was carried into the synagogue, where it was set down at the place of the dead and the rabbi gave the eulogy for the deceased. It was only then that the coffin was carried to the cemetery, where it was lowered into the grave. The *kaddish* prayer would then be recited; if the deceased had no son or other male relative, his daughter would also be allowed to say the *kaddish* for him.

The world of *shtetls*, the world of most of Eastern European Jewry, was wiped out during the German occupation from 1939 onwards. The armed forces and SS murdered the Jews in their millions, and burned the *shtetls* to the ground, their houses, synagogues and schools. Today the cemetery is often the only trace of this lost world. The *shtetls*' destruction is poignantly described in a poem by Mordechai Gebirtig (1877–1942) translated by E.G. Mlotek:

It's burning, brothers, it's burning!
Oy, our poor Schtetl *is burning,*
Raging winds are fanning with wild flames
And furiously tearing,
Destroying and scattering everything.
All around, all is burning
And you stand and look just so, you
With folded hands…!
And you stand and just look so,
While our Schtetl *burns.*

Faro/First Cemetery in the Algarve after the Expulsion
164

In the former Jewish
quarter of Faro

Planta da propriedade dos Israelitas no sitio de São Luiz na qual se acha installado o seu Cemiterio

Escala 1/1000

Propriedade de António do Poço

Terreno da Camara Municipal

RUA LEBO PENEDO

HOSPITAL

Superficie total

Rua projectada

Cemiterio

Propriedade dos Israelitas

ESCOLA

Herdeiro de Luiz Lacerda

Stadium de Manoel Santos

PARQUE DE ESTACIONAMENTE

Estrada para a Penha

ESTRADA DA PENHA

Conceição

Lôra 1925

The small cemetery in Faro, the capital of the Algarve, dating from the early nineteenth century, is the only remaining vestige of the first post-inquisition Jewish presence in Portugal. Since the two other cemeteries in Lisbon and Estrela have been destroyed, it is an important witness to a period when Jews were gradually, some 300 years after their expulsion, re-admitted into the country. In around 1800, Jews began to settle again in Faro, primarily from places such as Morocco and Gibraltar. Even before their expulsion, the region had had a significant Jewish community. There are no longer any traces of the cemetery of this earlier community, apart from one gravestone dating from 1315 that was found during excavations in the Tomar synagogue, located some 150 kilometres to the north of Lisbon, a replica of which now stands in front of Faro's modern cemetery.

The Faro community ultimately comprised sixty families and maintained two synagogues: one since 1820 for wealthy community members, at Rua Castilho 4, and the other in the nearby Rua de Bocage, although both are no longer in existence. As in so many other places in Europe, the town was proudly proclaimed 'Little Jerusalem'. The Jews of Faro lived among their Christian neighbours and the community prospered, achieving its greatest size between 1870 and 1900. After this, many Jews left Faro, while young people in particular moved to the country's major cities, so that in the second half of the twentieth century, there were practically no Jews left and the two synagogues were abandoned. Furniture from the larger of the two synagogues was stored in a private house and in 2006 it was restored in a specially built museum created at the cemetery.

When, in 1838, the community's rabbi, Rabbi Joseph Toledano, descendant of a famous family of scholars, passed away, the community sought out a plot of land suitable for a cemetery at the edge of the town, outside the city's eighteenth-century fortifications, and the rabbi was buried there. On his gravestone is written: 'Burial Gravestone – of a true Scholar, lauded in Israel, risen from Scholars – Rabbi Joseph Toledano. Died on Friday 12th of Adar 5598. May his soul be united to the sheaves of the living.' However, it was not until 1851, that the cantor, Joseph Sicsu, and leaders, Moses Sequerra and Samuel Amram, could acquire cemetery land for the community. Further burials were carried out in that same year, and in 1887 the cemetery was surrounded by a wall; this was enlarged in 1930 to a height of four metres, into which was set a portal with a triangular tympanum and gate with rounded arch. The white portal, so typical of the Algarve, proudly bears the year of its creation: 5638. The wall also enclosed two old trees that had stood on the land before the cemetery was created.

Measuring 1,000m² and hidden from the outside world, the cemetery has a square layout and is oriented in an approximately north-west/south-east direction. In its southern corner is a small building with two rooms for the *tahara* and the warden. There is now a museum here that provides information on the cemetery's history. It was occupied starting from the middle, with men and women being interred in separate areas. The 106 gravestones are all horizontal, in line with Sephardic tradition, and seventy-one of them are made from natural stone. Other graves, including small children's graves, are simply marked with small mounds made from river pebbles. No particular order can be identified: the graves are aligned in all directions, in different rows that often run into one another. Up to 1932, the year of the last burial, some 106 people were interred here, an indicator of how small the community was, even compared to its predecessor community before the expulsion.

Design for a new street plan in the outskirts of Faro, 1925. The plan shows the square Jewish cemetery ('Cemetiero') in the left of the dark lined rectangle.

The outside of the cemetery
by night.

The inside of the cemetery.

Rome / Campo Verano:
from the Aventine to the Pincetto

View from a street below the
Capitol towards the New
Synagogue (built 1901–04).

In September 1870 Rome became the capital of the new
kingdom of Italy. King Victor Emmanuel II emancipated the Jews as equal citizens, who then self-assuredly
took their places within the country's bourgeois yet
patriotic society that had been formed following
unification. The confines of the old ghetto were finally
demolished in 1870, and apart from a few remnants
around the edges, it largely disappeared during the
following decades. In 1901–4, the monumental new synagogue was inaugurated as a deliberate expression of a
new era 'of liberty, equality and love'[1] as was the
Jewish section of the Campo Verano cemetery. By 1900,
around 12,000 Jews lived throughout Rome

The architect, city planner and archaeologist
Giuseppe Valadier (1762–1839) was commissioned in
1807 to 1812 to plan a municipal cemetery to the
south-east of the city on the Campo Verano. Opened
in 1836, the rectangular, central section has a strict,
axially symmetrical architectural design with rectangular grave areas and is typical of Italian cemeteries.
Following the opening of Valadier's section, Virginio
Vespignani (1808–82) erected a gateway with colon-
nades between 1874 and 1878 in a classical style, the
famous *quadriporticus*. The project, which had started out as a municipal cemetery, was continued
despite numerous changes of government. After 1878,
it became apparent that the existing facility was too
small for Italy's rapidly growing new capital and
there began a gradual process of expansion that continued into the twentieth century.

In 1890 the Jewish cemetery on the Aventine was
closed. In the true spirit of the new era in which the
Jews understood themselves to be Italians of the Jewish
faith — similar to the Jews of France, Germany and
England — it was a logical step for the Jews of Rome
not to create their own cemeteries, but to acquire land

adjacent to the new municipal cemetery and create their own, separate section. Just as they lived everywhere in the city, integrated into the majority society, so too were the dead no longer to be buried in isolation. At the northern edge of the Campo Verano, the community found a rectangular plot of land that was accessed from one of the main streets, the Via Tiburtina. This gave them the opportunity to build a separate entrance and to create a monumental gateway with rounded arches and crowning triangular pediment. The gateway, built in brick with structural elements made from travertine like a Renaissance city gate, had a portcullis through which the view led along the main axis of the Jewish section. In a similar manner to Valadier's creation, the new cemetery grounds were divided up with axial symmetry. On both sides of the main avenue, rectangular grave areas of different sizes are laid.

The new mortuary hall is situated in a central axis, which was widened to form an avenue lined with cypress trees and pines. The building, which exhibits an Egyptian style, is fronted by a portico designed to accentuate the distant effect, of the entrance gate on the Via Tiburtina, framed by the cypress trees. The old inscription plaques from the seventeenth and eighteenth centuries, with blessings and ritual instructions, have been transferred from the previous building on the Aventine to the walls of the portico – which widens to become an entrance hall – thus creating a bridge of tradition between the old and new burial sites.

Perimeter walls were built on all four sides with the external wall to the Via Tiburtina being the tallest, at four metres in height. Besides two other entrances, there was a side entrance on the external wall from which one can still access the Protestant section. This section, similar in design to the Jewish one, together with the secular and Muslim ones, confirms the municipal, multi-faith nature of the Campo Verano. The strict surrounding walls, however, ensured that *halakhic* requirements for spatial segregation were satisfied, despite the impression of integration into the Roman necropolis. Undoubtedly the section could be classed as a separate Jewish cemetery.

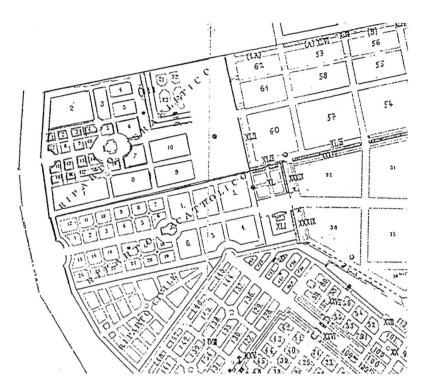

Map of the Campo Verano cemetery with the Jewish section in the top-left corner, *circa* 1920. The entrance to the Jewish section is from the street on the left and the mortuary hall is in the centre. In the top left corner the terraces of the 'Pincetto' area are visible.

The main avenue leading towards the mortuary hall, opened 1895.

View of the Pincetto with its monumental mausoleums.

The cemetery was opened in January 1895. The date, along with the inscription 'Cimetero Israelitico', is recorded in tablets on the arch of the entrance gate. By 1916, the cemetery had to be extended eastwards, doubling in size as a result. The community acquired the land from the city's administrators, '… thus guaranteeing for the first time that its dead could receive perpetual burial.'[2]

There was a hilly area in the south-eastern periphery that had been terraced. As a result of the expansion, other steeply-rising peripheral areas were also incorporated into the Jewish section, offering a welcome opportunity to build up to three-layered terraces with large flights of steps, balustrades and fountains, together with planted areas featuring palms and cypress trees. The Jews of Rome soon began to name this elaborately built section of the cemetery the *Pincetto* or 'little Pincio', after one of the seven hills of Rome. The Pincetto became the preferred part of the cemetery, where the rich families of

Rome built their monumental burial plots, exhibiting every possible style, and some even appearing to reflect the style of the New Synagogue in the previous ghetto. Stylistically distinct creations are also found, including a mausoleum that bears a striking similarity to Belá Lajta's mortuary hall in Budapest.

In 1934, some old gravestones that had been removed during the clearing of the old cemetery on the Aventine were restored to one of the terraces. In their simplicity, they could not have been more different to the grave monuments of the Pincetto. While there were few gravestones on the Aventine until the nineteenth century, as a result of a papal ban, (the few that did exist were extremely small) there was a veritable explosion of sepulchral culture from 1870 onwards. On the Aventine (see p.101), in the years until its closure in 1890, elaborate and in some cases mausoleum-like monuments were built. But it was on the Pincetto that these monuments grew to the size and grandeur already described, similar to the graves found in the Catholic sections of the Campo Verano and in cemeteries all over Italy. The need for representation expressed here is that of the bourgeoisie and the upper middle classes of the new Italy, be they Christian or Jewish. For the Jews this meant assimilation into Catholic society, which had long enjoyed a tradition of monumental family burial plots. As we have seen, the abandonment of the doctrine of equality in death, and with it the use of a simple grave marker, had already occurred in many Jewish cemeteries of the nineteenth century. In Rome, which housed Europe's oldest Jewish community, this led to an expression of individualism in sepulchral culture that was unusual even for the period around 1900. It

seems almost as though, after such a long ban on grave markers, the floodgates had opened and nothing was more desirable than to break free from the uniformity of the cemetery and represent oneself in death, less as a Jew, and more as a civic individual. For example, the ban on imagery was completely ignored, as almost every single grave is adorned with pictures of the dead, ranging from small, medal-like photographs and bas-reliefs to busts and life-sized figures in the form of Rodin's 'Thinker' or even an Egyptian priestess. By contrast, the bourgeois Ashkenazim in Berlin Weissensee, despite their desire for representation, rejected, more or less voluntarily, any display of likenesses in the cemetery.

Family vaults on the Pincetto.

A Rodin-like 'Thinker' and an Egyptian 'Priest' in front of family mausoleums.

London/Willesden: Cemetery of Victorian High Society

A burial field.

For the Jews of the United Kingdom, the nineteenth century was an era of increasing equality and emancipation. With the start of the reign of Queen Victoria in 1837, which lasted until 1901, a process continued that led to Jews gaining seats in the House of Lords, as peers, and being elected as Members of Parliament to the House of Commons. As a consequence of their social success the Jewish upper and middle classes moved away from the East End of London to the west and north of the city. This meant that new cemeteries had to be built close to new residential districts. The task was taken on chiefly by the Ashkenazi United Synagogue's burial society, which had been established in 1870, one of whose first building projects was a new cemetery in the north west of the city, in Willesden. Unlike France, where the Jews were assigned separate sections in the main cemeteries, the autonomy of religious communities not belonging to the state church remained unquestioned in matters relating to burial in Britain.

In 1871 the architect Nathan Salomon Joseph was commissioned to plan the cemetery and its buildings . Joseph (1834–1909) is a particularly good example of a successful Victorian Jew who combined an active life as a self-confident, religious Jew with considerable success in English society, becoming a Fellow of the Royal Institute of British Architects and Chairman of the Russo-Jewish Committee. In 1873, *The Builder* printed an article about the new cemetery which was in those days in the countryside: 'On a pleasant site at Willesden Lane, and plentifully planted with evergreens, the United Synagogues of Metropolitan Jews have formed a cemetery, which they have inaugurated.'[1] Shortly beforehand, on 5 October 1873, the cemetery had been consecrated by the Chief Rabbi during the interment of the 66-year-old Samuel Moses, J.P. whose home address can still be read on his gravestone.

At this time, five acres of the cemetery were enclosed by a wall, while one of several future extensions remained without a boundary. The rectangular

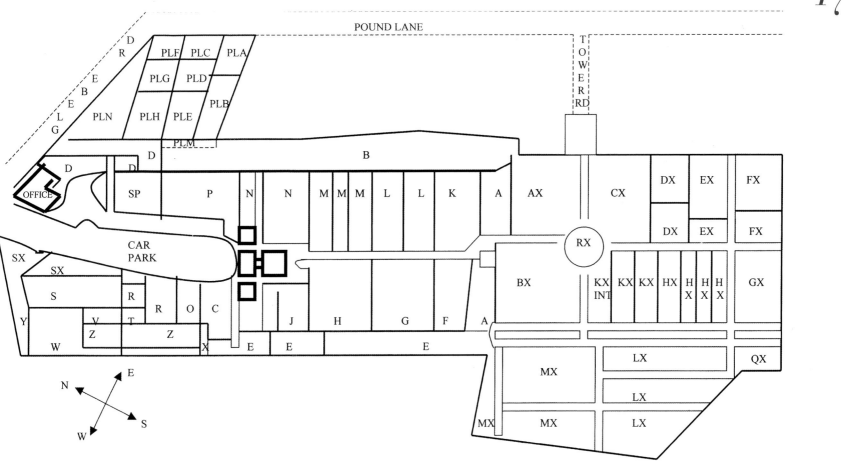

POUND LANE

cemetery area extended in a north-west/south-east direction, making an exact easterly alignment of the graves difficult. From a gate on Glebe Road, an originally arc-shaped, eastward-oriented, tree-lined path led to the slightly elevated main cemetery building. This complex, built in the 'Gothic Style of the Geometric period'[2], from Kentish rag and Bath stone, had been created from three separate, later connected buildings: the mourning hall in the centre, to the east of it a separate building for the *Cohanim*, and to the west of the mourning hall the *tahara* with its adjoining WC. In 1920, in a style adapted to the old construction, an open loggia was built in front of the mourning room. The flat buildings had slate-covered, pointed roofs, with the roof of the mourning room being accentuated by a chimney. The non-axial, curving path and the neo-Gothic building style are typical of landscaped cemeteries of this period. While considered at the time to be fitting for sacred buildings, the Gothic style was also regarded as English and nation-

ally acceptable, and so could be used for Jewish cemetery buildings. For a synagogue on the other hand, mostly Moorish or Romanesque styles were used.

The mourners entered the hall from the north west and exited, together with the coffin, through a door on the opposite side to reach a pathway leading to the grave areas. This main path is now lined with trimmed plane trees, which appear to refer to an elaborate and differentiated planting scheme: 'Considerable care was taken in the planting of evergreens, such as laurel and fir, cedar, yew, holly and cypress, an unusual level of landscaping in a Jewish cemetery to rival the best of the new public cemeteries. Today, the impression is rather bare.'[3] This lack of planting continues after leaving the main path, which leads south east to a circular square and which is intersected by a cross-cut. In the 1920s a neo-Georgian style administrative building was constructed which stands in complete continuity with the other styles.

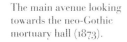

The main avenue looking
towards the neo-Gothic
mortuary hall (1873).

One of the monumental
Victorian graves.

From the cemetery's main axis, which runs in a
north-west-south-east direction, lateral cross-cuts lead
off in all directions and provide access to individual
grave areas. Apart from the circular flower bed, this is
a functional and simple network of paths that by no
means indicates, as is the case in Weissensee, Berlin, a
hierarchical system of squares, main avenues, side
avenues and cross-cuts with commensurate grave
plots. It seems to reflect the often chaotic pragmatism
of London's layout, which has never been characterized by an absolute will for axes and wide avenues, as
in Berlin and Paris. This is also evident from the
arrangement of the graves, as the graves of the rich are
distributed across the cemetery. Often, but not always,
they are in the front rows of both the main and side
paths. To the Victorian Jews, the cemetery is clearly
not the place for displays of status and wealth, as is the
case in Weissensee or the Campo Verano, even though
it is the necropolis of the country's greatest Jewish
families, with many belonging to the 'cousinhood' of
leading families. 'The cemetery is tucked behind the
Rolls-Royce coachworks of Ward Mulliner and is,
appropriately, the Rolls-Royce among London's Jewish
cemeteries. Here are buried members of some of the
most important Jewish families in Britain, including
numerous Rothschilds.'[4]

The entrance of the
mortuary hall with an
imposing clock echoes
Psalm 90:

*'Lord, teach us to count
our days, so that our
hearts grow wise.'*

Model of the cemetery
buildings by Erich
Mendelsohn. 1927.

In 1927 the Jewish community of Königsberg (now Kaliningrad) commissioned Erich Mendelsohn (1887–1953), who was born in Eastern Prussia, to plan its new cemetery. Mendelsohn was already one of Germany's best-known modern architects. He had to plan the entire complex to include all details devised for Jewish cemeteries since the first half of the nineteenth century: a mourning room, rooms for the *tahara*, cold rooms, waiting rooms, WCs, offices, apartments for employees, flower rooms, gatekeeper's rooms and, of course, the burial area itself. And, with the dawning age of the automobile, a car park was also required. The grounds for the new cemetery lay at the edge of the city and were accessed from Steffeckstrasse. 'The cemetery, which has been created in the west of the city in a particularly picturesque setting, encloses a hilly area of land which borders the Steffeckstrasse on one side.'[1] A nearby recreational area was already situated here, into which the cemetery was to be integrated. 'Creating a new cemetery in this new spot in the middle of parkland, surrounded by paths and facilities was no easy task. Yet the new building and design techniques made it possible for this parkland not to be interrupted, but instead for the new cemetery to be inserted into its surroundings to form a self-contained whole.'[2] Mendelsohn positioned the main cemetery building at the edge of a hillside, below which the grave areas were to extend. Standing on a specially built plateau, the mourning room, which towers above the building complex, appears almost to rise up from the ground, like Mendelsohn's Einsteinturm Observatory. At the same time, the harsh buildings form a stark contrast to the landscape and greenery. 'We note the remarkable skill with which the mortuary hall has been integrated into the surroundings through the large infill of earth. The feeling for the desired unity of building and landscape, which has for so long been lost, is finally evident once more.[3]

Mendelsohn placed the main building with the mourning room on a plateau for another reason, too. His intention was to create the longest possible entrance axis from the access road, which runs past the cemetery at a forty-five-degree angle. Here, Mendelsohn built an open, triangular forecourt separated from the cemetery by a wall in which a white-painted iron gate bears inscriptions in Hebrew and German. On the inside of the wall are an alms box, a register of donations and a washbasin for ritual hand washing. On the right-hand side of the forecourt, he built a flat-roofed construction containing the gate-keeper's lodge, offices, flower room and apartments. Cleverly, a semi-lunar projection indicates the change of axis here between the street and the cemetery grounds. Starting from the forecourt, whose left-hand side balances the flat-roofed building with a group of trees, Mendelsohn created a monumental, eastward-facing spatial axis whose zenith is the main building and mortuary hall. From the forecourt, a wide path leads along the central axis to the mourning room, whose plateau is reached via a staircase. On either side of the path, Mendelsohn built corridor-like, tiered, man-height hedges that frame strips of grass elongated in four intervals and intended for honorary graves. The hedges were intended to restrict the view and focus the eye on the only visible central section of the main building, the mortuary hall.

Like the outer buildings, the main building is also designed with complete symmetry and faces east. In the centre, it surrounded the mourning room with a raised, elongated central aisle and two lower, lateral side aisles for the separate-sex *tahara* rooms. Towards the cemetery entrance, the lateral wings adjoining the side aisles enclosed a small inner courtyard. 'Here, the realm of death begins, and the dark stone walls, tempered only by the flowers, prepare those who enter.'[4] The mourning room was entered from the eastern wall of the inner courtyard. A speaker's pulpit stood at the narrow western or entrance side, with the eastern gate opening directly opposite. The dead were carried in facing east. 'By opening the eastern gate, the step into nature, which welcomes the dead in more than just symbolism, is complete.'[5] Although this description echoes an eternal yearning for nature that is not

The mortuary hall seen from the burial fields. Photograph, 1929.

Jewish, it does clarify the stark consequence of Mendelsohn's design. The main building is almost situated over an axis between the world of the living (forecourt) and the world of the dead (grave areas), an axis highlighted at the point where the dead are prepared ritually for burial. The towering block of the mourning room clearly marks this border with the grave area. From the opened eastern gate, one would look down over the grave area,[6] which adjoined the landscaped network of paths like a spacious park.

In Königsberg, Mendelsohn brings the development of the European Jewish cemetery to a high point characterized by superlative spatial and functional consistency. The entire grounds are designed symmetrically around an axis that, just like one hundred years previously in Berlin's Schönhauser Allee, points east to Jerusalem. He creates a dedicated, modern use of form for this task, one characterized by the pure volume of buildings erected in black clinkers and the dynamism and drama of the outdoor space. The complex thus occupies a special position in the context of Mendelsohn's *oeuvre* as it is the only known example of his work as a landscape architect, but it was to be destroyed by the Nazis nine years after the opening in 1929; the entrance building is all that remains. The Königsberg cemetery could thus no longer be adopted as a style. The drawings and photographs of the plans, the architectural model and the buildings that were actually erected, remain as a monument to a high point of German-Jewish sepulchral culture that was extinguished by the *Shoah* and the war.

The entrance building
in 2006.

The remains of the
mortuary hall in 2006.

A Dead Child Speaks

My mother held me by my hand.
Then someone raised the knife of parting:
So that it should not strike me,
My mother loosed her hand from mine.
But she lightly touched my thighs once more
And her hand was bleeding –

After that the knife of parting
Cut in two each bite I swallowed –
It rose before me with the sun at dawn
And began to sharpen itself in my eyes –
Wind and water ground in my ear
And every voice of comfort pierced my heart –

As I was led to death
I still felt in the last moment
The unsheathing of the great knife of parting.

Nelly Sachs
(translated by Ruth and Matthew Mead)

One of the ash ponds
at Auschwitz

After the Shoah

The Auschwitz concentration camp, in which one and a half million Jewish men, women and children were murdered by the Nazis, was finally liberated on 27 January 1945. In all, six million Jews were murdered in Europe. Almost none was accorded a place in a 'house of life': instead, their bodies were burned in the ovens of the camps and their ashes dumped in ponds and on fields.

After spring 1945 the few Jews who had survived tried to leave Europe as quickly as possible, opting to go chiefly either to the USA or Erez Israel, where the State of Israel was declared on the 14 May 1948. On the other hand, those who returned to the places that had once been their homes found nothing but ruins. Destroyed synagogues and community buildings, plundered houses and apartments that were now occupied by non-Jews — often Nazis — were the places in which returning Jews were received by the non-Jews who had remained – a welcome that was anything but friendly.

Everywhere in previously Occupied Europe, the Jewish communities, which were slowly re-establishing themselves in spite of everything, remained extremely small. Since the majority of synagogues had been destroyed, cemeteries often provided the only architectural witness to the Jewish lives that had existed in the villages, towns and cities, but in many cases they had been desecrated, although the Nazis frequently put off finally destroying them until after 'ultimate victory'. Thus many of the small, post-war communities found large cemeteries that had been planned for pre-war ones. Created in the expectation that they would be filled over the course of a few centuries, they now appeared to offer space for an inestimable amount of time. There was therefore simply no need to create new cemeteries: Berlin and Salonica are among the few exceptions. It is only since the collapse of the Soviet Union that the Jewish communities of Europe have begun to grow again and more new cemeteries are being built.

A remaining stretch of the Berlin Wall with an artist's combination of the Israeli and German flags, 2005.

Survivors from Salonica,
photograph taken by
Frederic Brenner in 1992.

'*Lecha dodi* - Come, my friend, to meet the bride; let us welcome the presence of the Sabbath. "Observe" and "Remember the Sabbath day", the only God caused us to hear in a single utterance: the Lord is One, and His name is One to His renown and His glory and praise.'

Shelomo Halevi Alkabez

(first half of sixteenth century)

'I feel Thessaloniki. I was born here. I have people in the old cemetery, where I used to go before I left. I went to cry on their graves, I am from Salonica. To whom Salonica belongs is another thing. What I am, I am. You see?'[1]

Lilly M. in an interview (around 1990)

All over the world, Jews welcome the start of *shabbat* on Friday evening with the *Lecha dodi*, whose first line introduces this chapter. The Kabbalist Shelomo Alkabez composed this song in the then Ottoman Salonica which, due to its large and educated Jewish community, was known as the 'mother of cities amongst the people of Israel'. From Salonica, the *Lecha dodi* spread across the rest of the world, and indeed nothing could epitomise the historical significance of this 'Jewish' city better. Under Ottoman rule the city became a model of a cosmopolitan, multi-faith and multi-cultural city where the dominant Sephardim 'tried to keep their Iberian culture alive, creating the illusion of Spain'.[2] This is one side of the coin of the Jewish history of Salonica.

The other side takes the form of Lilly M., who escaped the terror and almost total destruction of the Jews of Salonica during German occupation. Only a few survived and returned to their homeland, but in a city whose population had once been mostly Jewish, they now represented a small and ever-dwindling minority. Nevertheless, they found the strength to reset-tle here and once again rebuild their community.

The old cemetery

The old cemetery lay immediately beyond the south-east city wall. Being one of the largest Jewish cemeteries in Europe, its appearance resembled in many ways that of the Hasköy cemetery in Istanbul. After Salonica was taken over by the Greeks in 1912 the city continued to grow and the cemetery moved from its peripheral location to the centre of the expanding metropolis. At the end of the 1920s, it was surrounded by the buildings of the university and numerous poor and temporary homes belonging to new inhabitants, which meant that from 1929 there were repeated attempts to seize the cemetery. The Jewish community defended itself fiercely, and the city was often urged by the central government in Athens not to touch the cemetery.[3] The actual 'solution' only came about in April 1941, when the Germans occupied Salonica. In 1942, following the wish of the Greek authorities and

by German force, the cemetery was completely destroyed. The gravestones were reused for the building of roads, a swimming pool and even as gravestones for German soldiers so that after 1945 the construction of the university and other municipal buildings could go ahead. The Germans had helped make the old dream come true. The cemetery was never restored to the Jews and the university still refuses to commemorate the fact that it is built on top of Jewish graves, on top of Jewish bones.

The new cemetery

In May 1943, the Germans began the deportation of around 50,000 Salonican Jews to Auschwitz and Bergen-Belsen, and in the end only three per cent of the city's pre-war Jewish population survived. Following the German retreat in October 1944, the first Jews returned to Salonica, back from the hell of Auschwitz to the place that had been their home, back to all they had remembered, full of longing and doubt, during the seemingly unending years and horrors of the concentration camps. But the majority of those who returned felt that the city was no longer theirs. Salonica became a 'city of ghosts' for those returning, a city in which every step reminded them of the

View over the Old Cemetery towards the city walls. Photograph, 1912.

Since many of the couples had no relatives, group weddings were held. 'These group weddings embody the situation of many Jews in the post-war years in Salonica. The couples married together because they had no relatives to celebrate with, they had only each other for help and support. The weddings are seen both as a means to cope with the feeling of loss and loneliness, and as a sign of a new beginning.'⁵ These people laid the foundation stone for the present-day Jewish community of Salonica, which their president David Saltiel recently described as follows: 'The community of what used to be the vast majority of the city continues to live as if by miracle and assert its dynamic presence, in spite of the fact that in numbers it constitutes a negligible part of the total population of Thessaloniki [Salonica]. Its undying spirit, its organisation and its contributions to society testify to

Burial field of the Old Cemetery. Photograph. 1920.

The sight of the same burial field in 2007.

Gravestone from the Old Cemetery 're-used' as a gravestone for a German soldier.

people who had been taken from them. Yet those who had returned did want to build new lives for themselves. They met to create a joint force for a new future, and soon after came the first weddings: 'It was not an easy time, but at the same time it was a kind of "a new life is beginning". Everyone started having babies. There were many weddings and births.'⁴

a community whose vibrant dynamism outweighs its numbers. A strong community council, social care, school, youth camps, home for the aged, synagogues, museum, choir, youth centres, publication of books, and a variety of cultural activities, compose a picture of a community which, despite its small number, has nothing to envy from its glorious past.'[6]

Saltiel's list makes no mention of the new cemetery in Stavropoli. By 1937, in order to increase the pressure to dissolve the old cemetery, the city administrators transferred to the Jewish community a piece of land in this former district south west of the city, with the condition that the required new cemetery be built there. In the same year, the community was forced to hand over the 1.3-hectare section of the old cemetery to the university, but new burials continued to be performed in it. During the period when the total destruction of the old cemetery began in the autumn of 1942, the community's leaders were able to transport a few exhumed graves and gravestones to Stavropoli. It was only after the war, however, in the 1950s, that the community began to create a regular cemetery on the ground it was forced to occupy. This new cemetery no longer lies, like the old one, idyllically in front of the old city walls, relatively close to the Jewish quarter in the port, but rather far outside the city in an industrial area that only in recent years has become residential as a result of Salonica's rapid growth. Bounded today on two sides by wide arterial roads, it is only accessible with difficulty from the centre of the city by bus or taxi. At the same time, the location of the new cemetery reflects the fact that the Jews of Salonica are today less resident in the old quarter, by the port, and more scattered across the entire city and its suburbs.

It was not until the 1960s that the rectangular area of land, measuring 210 by 76 metres, was enclosed by a wall approximately 2.3 metres high. The cemetery grounds, which extend in a north-east to south-west direction, are accessed via Dimitriou Karaoli Street. In the centre of the wall, a gatehouse with wide central gate and two side entrances was built in the 1960s in a conservative, neo-classical style. Between the gates

and the attica are marble slabs on which the purpose of the land behind them is explained in Hebrew, Greek and Latin. The slab also lists the monuments located in the cemetery. After walking through a heavy iron gate, one enters an open hall of pillars from which the view leads down into the lower cemetery. Tablets featuring the usual blessings, a *tsedaka* box and a basin for hand washing are all features of the building.

The main axis, 210 metres long, stretches from the pillar-lined hall to the end of the cemetery. The grave areas are aligned around this axis, within which, as the focus at the end of an elongated forecourt, is a towering monument to the victims of the Salonican *Shoah*. Built in 1962 it dominates the entire cemetery by its size, for decades this was the only such monument in the city, crowned as it is with a stylized menorah and with a dedication inscribed on the plinth. The grave areas are grouped around it so that the dead symbolically

Street scene in a Jewish neighbourhood in 2007.

surround the memorial to the tens of thousands who
were killed and never laid to rest in their homeland.
The entire cemetery is thus focused on the symbol of
the *Shoah*, the event that also shaped in a terrible way
the lives of those buried here. Next to the prayers and
personal memories, the memorial becomes a way of
giving those who were murdered in the death camps a
place in the hearts and minds of the Jews of Salonica,
in a desperate attempt to return them to their home, at
least symbolically. The new cemetery is thus one of the
cemeteries created after 1945 that is most consistently
designed as a monument to *Shoah* victims, reflecting
the absolute centrality of this event for the post-war
community. The graves are arranged virtually concen-
trically around the monument, with gravestones that it
was possible to save from the old cemetery forming the
outer edge; next to a central area behind the monument, they are lined up along the outer wall, providing
an historical framework for later graves.

The axial design is accentuated by long rows of
cypress trees, which frame the central axis and grave
areas, and cross-cuts that emanate from it. The cemetery is occupied chronologically, starting at the
entrance, next to which the building for *tahara* is

The entrance building to the
New Cemetery.

Plan of the New Cemetery. The
entrance at the top with a fleet
of steps leading to a long
square with the monument
to the victims of the *Shoa*.

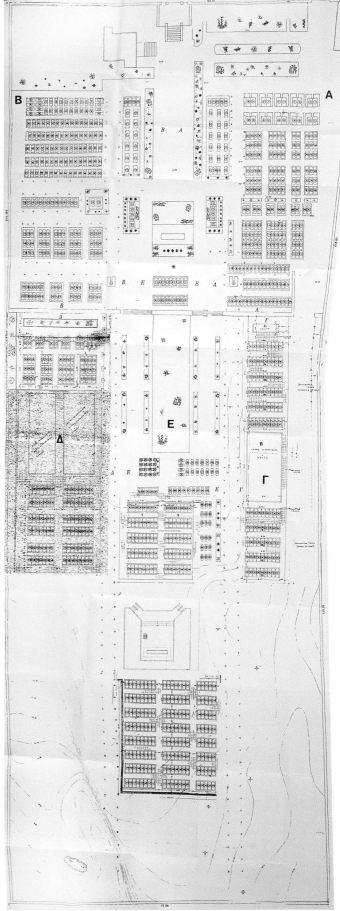

located with a mourning room (this is the old guards' house, which was converted for the purposes of *tahara* only in the 1960s). Close to the monument are honorary graves for rabbis and other important figures in the community, some of whom succeeded in rescuing remains of their relatives during and after the war and bringing them here, where they were interred in new graves, also located close to the entrance. Behind the monument, the ground falls away by about one metre over walls and two wide sets of steps. In the central axis are the areas already mentioned, where gravestones rescued from the old cemetery have been resurrected.

Between the twin rows of cypress that frame the central axis, a memorial was erected in 2003 to the 7,000 Jewish soldiers of Salonica who fell at the Albanian front in the Greco-Italian War (1940–1) fighting Fascist Italy. The graves which are laid facing north-east are built in the traditional style, as in the old cemetery: simple clinker brick plinths with mostly rectangular headstones resting on top, although unlike those graves, the level of ornamentation is markedly reduced. The headstones are in Greek and Hebrew, and there are no pictorial representations of

the dead. The graves laid in the last few decades are all designed in a similar way with only the inscriptions varying. The equality of all in death is thus resurrected and continued in Salonica. And another tradition that used to be observed in the old cemetery is again being continued: women do not traditionally accompany the coffin to the grave. On Yom Hashoa, between Passover and Yom Hazmaut, Israel's Independence Day, however, everyone gathers at the cemetery to remember the 50,000 dead.

The centre of the cemetery: the memorial to Salonica's *Shoah* victims.

View over a burial field.

Berlin / A Cemetery for a Divided Community

A remaining stretch of the Berlin Wall with an artist's combination of the Israeli and German flags, 2005.

After the *Shoah*, only 6,000 people were left of the once blossoming Jewish community in Berlin: in 1933, 160,000 Jews had lived there. The growing confrontation between East and West led to a need for the Jews of West Berlin to create a new cemetery on West Berlin soil, as the Weissensee cemetery in East Berlin could only be visited with difficulty, not to mention risk. In 1953, the year in which Berlin was divided into East and West, an area of forest measuring some 1.5 hectares was acquired in Grunewald, close to one of the main arterial roads in the eastern sector of Berlin. Following the design of the architect Curt Leschnitzer, a simple mourning room, a *tahara* building and various functional buildings were erected around a forecourt. From here, one passed through a gate to reach a square and the burial grounds themselves. The marked simplicity of these buildings also reflected the reticence that many German Jews of the time felt as they were unsure whether they should display themselves and their religion in such clear architectural terms in the 'land of the murderers'.

The plans for the irregular cemetery grounds, also designed by Leschnitzer and landscape architect Bernhard Kynast, divided them by a main avenue emanating from the entrance square, lined with birch trees and running in an approximately east-west direction, ended in a seating circle at the western end. Between the grid of graves, Kynast planned the irregular planting of trees which, coupled with the birches of the main avenue and the hedges, gave the site the air of a wooded cemetery. Some years later, the cemetery was extended.

In the 1980s, and in particular as a result of the growth of the community to around 11,000 members – caused by an influx of Jews from the states of the former Soviet Union – it became clear that the

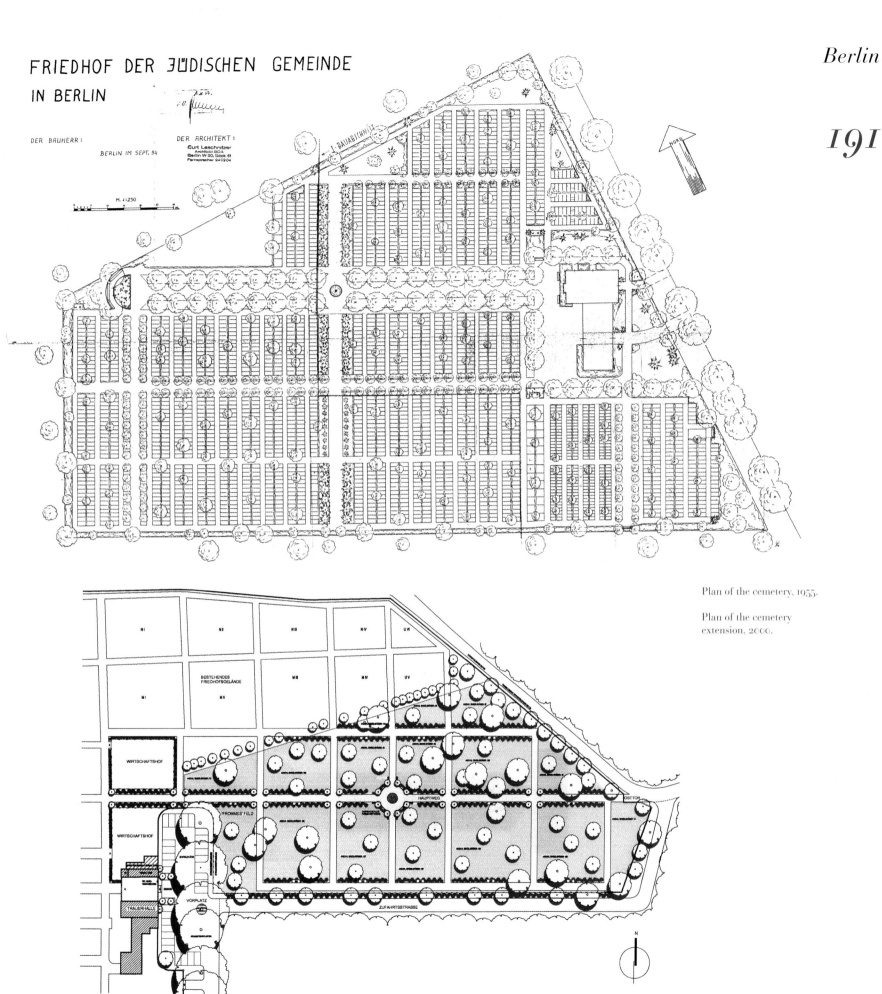

FRIEDHOF DER JÜDISCHEN GEMEINDE
IN BERLIN

DER BAUHERR:

BERLIN IM SEPT. 54

DER ARCHITEKT:

Curt Leschnitzer
Architekt BDA
Berlin W 30, Linie 62
Fernsprecher 240204

M. 1:250

Plan of the cemetery, 1955.

Plan of the cemetery
extension, 2000.

PLANUNG: DR. JACOBS & HÜBINGER, BERLIN, BÜRO FÜR GARTENDENKMALPFLEGE
UND LANDSCHAFTSARCHITEKTUR, ZEICHNUNG: F. KOLBE

The main axis of the extension.

The central square of the new burial fields.

cemetery would once again require expansion. Despite the efforts of his predecessor, it was only the then leader of the community, Andreas Nachama, who managed to acquire a further plot measuring one hectare in 1999 for the extension. This area was covered by a plantation of pine trees, most of which were felled, although some older ones were left standing and integrated into the new cemetery grounds.

The plans for the extension[1] created conflict from the beginning. On one hand there was the aim of finding a design that was true to the *halakha*, symbolizing a bridge to the historic cemeteries of the Jewish community, and on the other the desire of the environmental authorities to create the cemetery in the form of a wooded space, as they insisted on a smooth transition with the surrounding wooded areas: the community had to pay a high sum of money in compensation for fallen trees. The new grounds were to accommodate as many trees as possible; new trees were to be planted in lines that looked natural. Thus the model of the wooded cemetery was resurrected, this time with an ecological twist. Even the cemetery's new access road was planned in accordance with ecological criteria. The wooded character was to be balanced by the deliberately traditional design of the paths and grave areas, which would borrow from the historic cemeteries of Schönhauser Allee and Weissensee. The result was a traditional, ecological cemetery that was faithful to the *halakha*.

The basic structure of the field system for the extension was determined by the existing cemetery's path system. A route forms the central axis, travelling from west to east and passes through the new part of the cemetery. From a point immediately adjacent to the mourning room, this main route leads to the eastern tip of the extension area and ends at the eastern gate which, perpetually closed, symbolizes the direction of the cemetery and graves towards the east, to Jerusalem. This creates a symbolic link to the cemetery on the Schönhauser Allee, with its own eastern gate. Side paths lead off from this main route, while the spatial centre and design focus of the cemetery is a

circular area, which lies in the approximate middle. Just like all of the cross-cuts of the main route, marked by maple trees in all four corners, the area is also enclosed by benches and hornbeam hedges, and in the centre is a decorative flowerbed planted with roses and lavender. The design of the square is a deliberate reference to the cemeteries of Schönhauser Allee and Weissensee. The individual grave areas are marked with specially designed demarcating stones hewn from granite, and fourteen new areas accommodate around 1,500 double and single graves. The paths are made of pale-coloured concrete and paths that are not overshadowed by trees are marked with blue paving stones at intervals of one meter. These signify routes that are ritually accessible for the *Cohanim* as they are considered to be outside the cemetery. Some years ago, several medieval gravestones from the Spandau *Judenkiewer*, which had been uncovered during the restoration of the citadel there, were erected on the circle on the cemetery's main avenue. A historic link between the medieval community and that of the twenty-first century is thus clearly achieved.

A scene during the inauguration in 2000.

Amsterdam/Amstelveen's Garden of Peace

Plan of the cemetery.

In 1938, the Liberal Jewish community of Amsterdam had opened a cemetery in Schiphol, which in the 1990s ran into conflict with the international airport that was expanding in the area. A new runway was to be built one hundred metres from the cemetery, which would have prevented it from being used or visited. The city's authorities therefore offered the community a plot of land for a new cemetery in the nearby town of Amstelveen, the costs of which were paid for largely by the Dutch state. It was situated in a part of the city of Amstelveen, which had been built after the war, as a dedicated recreational and nature conservation area. Criss-crossed by canals, it had originally been part of a polder, an area reclaimed from the sea, and the cemetery was to integrate itself as unobtrusively as possible into this natural landscape – a demand that the community accepted when it finally signed the purchase agreement. For the majority of the

community members living in Amstelveen, a prosperous suburb of Amsterdam, the new cemetery was easily accessible, and in 1997, the architect Jaap Walvisch began work on planning and building it.

The plot was rectangular, 51 metres wide and 362 metres long, and as with a typical polder, it was initially surrounded on all sides by a ditch that, as part of a larger system of canals, helped drain the low-lying land. When the ground was marked out, care was taken to ensure that it lay in a strictly east-west direction. Walvisch therefore arranged for eight grave areas, all facing eastwards, and at the western end of the cemetery he planned to build a mourning room with *tahara* and superintendent's apartment. The linking element was to be a transitional zone in the form of a memorial square. Situated between the grave areas and the mourning room, a cenotaph was to be built to remember Amsterdam's victims of the

View over a canal towards
the cemetery island building
with the mourning room and
tahara.

Shoah, including Anne Frank and Walvisch's father.

On the 18 October 2000, after a lengthy planning and approval process, permission was given to start the project, and building began in January 2001. Initially, a layer of sand 2.5 metres thick was spread over all the future burial areas, to ensure that graves would be laid above the level of the groundwater. Building of the mourning room and *tahara* commenced that April, and the cemetery finally went into service in January 2003.

From Saskia van Uylenburg Street, visitors enter the cemetery over a bridge; the ditch beneath surrounds the entire cemetery, almost making it an island. Relatives of the deceased are given a chip card, which they can use to open the door electronically; others must report first to the administrator. The gate is programmed so that it opens only at certain times of day and not on *shabbat* and holidays.

The cemetery buildings

A forecourt leads to the mourning room, known as the *aula*, for which Walvisch drew his inspiration from the *Kabbalah*; the three-dimensional triangle is a key element in the spatial division, direction and, for the enclosure, framework of the basic elements of his creation. The two-dimensional triangle, on the other hand, with the letters S-*Sijen*, M-*Mem* and A-*Alef*, represents parts of the human body, basic elements and seasons: head-fire-summer, stomach-water-winter and breast-light-autumn. The basic triangular shape of the *aula* and the administrator's apartment is the structural interpretation of this Kabbalistic concept of the world. Integrated into the dimensions of space and time, the building becomes the translation of the concept of creation, making reference to the day when the dead will reawaken to eternal life. The main triangular section is clearly segregated on the inside: the main

A still empty burial field.

The monument to the victims
of the *Shoah*.

entrance leads into an anteroom. To the left are rooms
for the *tahara* and a waiting room for relatives, and to
the right a larger area where condolences are offered
after the burial and drinks are imbibed to provide
fortification. The axis of the main entrance leads
between these into the mourning room, the *aula*. The
side facing the forecourt is glazed with large windows,
thus opening itself up to the light and view of the
cemetery itself and also provides an exit, through
which the mourners and the coffin leave the building
for the grave.

The southern wall is made of sandstone blocks from
Israel, which symbolically represent the hope of life
and the return to Jerusalem. Next to the *aula* is an
additional side entrance, separate from the rest of the
building, with an antechamber, linked to the *aula*
visually by windows from which *Cohanim* can observe
the funerary events without being in the same room as
the dead.

The memorial square
and burial areas

After leaving the *aula*, the mourners and rabbis pass
the memorial square following the coffin. At the centre
of the square is the monument, created by Appie
Drielsma, to the *Shoah* and on certain days of the
year such as Yom Hashoa, the community holds its

The wall of the mourning room built from stone brought from Israel.

remembrance services here. The forecourt is part of a visual axis, which begins on the south side in the adjoining recreational area and continues along the north side in a park and sports area. Together with a second visual axis, crossing the cemetery further to the east, it attempts to integrate the cemetery into the surroundings of the former polder landscape. i.e. with the world of the living.

Along the southern side of the cemetery island runs the cobbled main path, from which all eight grave areas are accessed. A small rectangular plot at the entrance to each one lets *Cohanim* follow a burial ceremony without getting too close to the grave itself. The strictly eastward-facing graves are accessed through spur paths and cross-cuts filled with white gravel. Each of the eight grave areas is enclosed in almost room-like fashion by native shrubs about 1.5 metres high, and they are screened off from the surrounding graves and the cemetery background by further planting. This both protects visitors from prying eyes, and integrates the cemetery further into its natural and recreational setting. The first area is now populated with graves.

This cemetery, the first of the twenty-first century, shows how the rules of *halakha* are followed by a Liberal community with a strong sense of tradition and it also captures the history of European Jewry, now more than 2000 years long.

Conclusion

Burial chamber with frescoes in the red-green linear style at the Vigna Randanini catacomb, second century.

One of many myths about the Jews says that they are essentially rootless. But this picture of the eternally Wandering Jew is wrong. If free from persecution they are generally happy to stay put. They may be mobile in terms of thinking, travelling, working and trading, but they are not nomads. Thus in rare cases Jewish families can trace their forebears over thousands of years, just as some Roman families know of ancestors brought as slaves by Titus in the year 70. Everywhere Jews settle they do so, hoping not to put up a portable tent but to build a solid house made for future generations to live in. Cemeteries are an expression of this Jewish way of thinking. Building a cemetery is a positive act of belonging, because you wish to visit the graves of your parents, relatives and friends who have passed away. The longer Jews were allowed to stay in one place and the more prosperous, self-confident and even emancipated they became, the more the cemeteries mirrored the surrounding world of the living. These 'Houses of Life', where bodies are laid to rest until the day of resurrection, reflect the good times and the bad

for European Jewry. There are strong similarities between the Jews of Imperial Rome and those of Imperial Berlin, for instance. Both lived in vast and highly developed cities. They lived in societies which thought of themselves as modern, and many of them had almost the same rights as their non-Jewish neighbours. Although they kept their separate burial places – catacomb and necropolis – these become a strong reflection of the metropolises they lived in: villas and *insulae*, mansions and apartment houses, slums and tenements, all find their shadows in the cities of the dead as burial chambers or niches, mausoleums or gravestones. Even the small walkways in the catacombs seem to reflect the uneven streets and alleys of Rome, just as the squares and avenues of the nineteenth-century necropolis correspond with the grand layout of Imperial Berlin. And in both Rome and Berlin the seemingly successful integration into surrounding societies was accompanied by an erosion of Jewish identity and belief in the *olam haba*, the world to come.

Throughout Jewish history periods of freedom and prosperity have been followed by times of persecution. The religiously tolerant world of the *Pax Romana* gave way to centuries of oppression in the name of the new Christian faith. It took more than a millennium to enlighten the Western World and instil ideas of freedom of thought, speech and religion. European Jewry's hope for full emancipation seemed to find fulfilment at the beginning of the twentieth century in many countries. Jewish cemeteries of this period with their bombastic mausoleums look like their beautifully designed Christian counterparts and some are only sections of vast multi-faith burial places. How different from the haphazard cemeteries of earlier, harder times where modest gravestones showed equality in death and obedience to *halakha* rules, giving an overall impression of cramped and meagre waiting rooms for the time of resurrection.

The dream that assimilation would bring emancipation and equality ended in the crematoria of Auschwitz. The ashes and bones of the six million murdered were dumped in ponds and pits, turning Europe not into a cemetery but a 'House of Death'. In 1948, only three years after the Nazi killing machine was stopped, the State of Israel was reborn. Now, more than six decades later, Israel is a strong focus for the Jews of Europe – the Promised Land being a potential haven in case of renewed persecution. And so the 'Israel' stone wall of the Amsterdam *tahara* house of 2003 shows a very long, and ultimately hopeful, journey from medieval Worms and its 'Holy Sand' mythically brought from the Holy Land.

View through the neo-Romanesque arches of a grand family vault on to one of the squares of the Weissensee cemetery, Berlin.

Glossary

Ashkenazim Jews living in Germany, north-east France, Poland and Russia. These territories are also called Ashkenaz.

Bechorim First-born animals which were not killed for religious reasons. Sometimes they lived in cemeteries.

Beth Hachaim House (*beth*) of life (*hachaim*), euphemistic name for Jewish cemeteries.

Beth Kevarot House of caves (*kevarot*), name for Jewish cemeteries.

Beth Olam House of eternity (*olam*), name for Jewish cemeteries.

Beth Tahara Building where the ritual cleansing of bodies takes place.

Bikur Holim Visiting the sick. It is an important commandment in Judaism to visit ill people and give comfort.

Cantor (Hazan) Specially trained person who recites and sings prayers in front of the congregation and who leads them through the service. He is not a priest as from the time of the destruction of the Temple in Jerusalem there has been no priestly service in Judaism.

Chevra Kaddisha Jewish burial society

Chozer Forecourt of a Jewish cemetery

Cohen (pl. **Cohanim**) Members of the tribe of Levy and descendants of the first High Priest Aharon. As priests and as the High Priest they performed the daily services in the Temple in Jerusalem up until the destruction of the Temple. But *Cohanim* still have some special religious rights and obligations (for example ritual cleanness, which is why they normally are not allowed to enter cemeteries).

Conversos Jews who were forced by the Catholic Church on the Iberian Peninsula to became Christians, and subsequently re-embraced Judaism.

Dekalog The Ten Commandments.

Erez Israel The land of Israel during periods when no Jewish state existed.

Etrog Citrus fruit with a pleasant smell which is used during ceremonies on the festival of Sukkot.

Ghemilut Chassadim Acts of loving kindness, also a name for Jewish burial. societies.

Hakafot Circular processing around a coffin.

Halakha (**Halakhic**) Normative Jewish religious law based on the Talmud, encompassing the entire range of human life.

Haskala Jewish Enlightenment of the eighteenth century, very much based on the philosophy of Berlin's Moses Mendelssohn.

Hazan see **Cantor.**

Hekdesch A Jewish hospital, often close by or attached to a Jewish cemetery.

Judengasse Lane in medieval German cities and towns, mainly inhabited by Jews and often locked by gates to separate the Jews from the Christians.

Judensand German for 'Jews' sand', medieval German name for Jewish cemeteries.

Juderia Jewish quarter in a medieval city or town on the Iberian Peninsula.

Kabbalah Tradition. Name of a mystic movement which began in twelfth-century Provence. Central to Kabbalah is the 'Sohar' written in thirteenth-century Spain.

Kaddish Aramaic for 'The Holy One'. The Kaddish is a first- or second-century prayer for the sanctification of God's name.

Karaites A non-rabbinical Jewish sect which goes back to Anan (d. between 830 and 890 CE). He founded a separate school of Jewish thought whose key feature was the rejection of rabbinical teaching and the Talmud. Only the Torah is still followed.

Kiddush Hashem Hebrew for 'sanctification of God's name', often used to describe martyrdom of Jews who refused baptism.

Kvores Name for Jewish cemetery.

Landjuden Jews living in small rural villages of Germany in the late Middle Ages up to the nineteenth century.

Levites Members of the tribe of Levy. who do not derive from Aaron and therefore are not *Cohanim*. But as servants they had to support them during their daily Temple services.

Lulav Palm leaves which are ritually shaken during Sukkot services.

Mahamad The board of directors of Sephardic congregations.

Maranos Spanish for 'pig' meaning baptized Jews, who often secretly went on living as Jews.

Matzevah (pl. **Matzevot**) Gravestone.

Mechitzah Curtain or screen dividing the women's from the men's section in a synagogue. Also used as a term for divisions between holy and profane spaces.

Menorah The seven-branched candelabra in the Temple in Jerusalem. Its design is based on a description given to Moses on Mount Sinai.

Mihrab Ornamented prayer niche in a mosque, indicating the direction towards Mecca.

Mikweh Jewish ritual bath of at least 800 litres of running or 'living' water.

Mishnah The centre of the Talmud or the 'Oral Law', compiled in the second century by Juda Hanassi.

Ohal The term Ohel (lit. "tent") refers to the structure built over the resting place of a Tzaddik, a righteous person.

Olam Haba The after life or 'world to come'.

Piyyut (pl. **Piyyutim**) A Jewish liturgical poem, usually designated to be sung, chanted, or recited during religious services. *Piyyutim* have been written since Temple times and mostly follow some poetic scheme, such as an acrostic in the order of the Hebrew alphabet or spelling out the name of the author.

Rabbi In Judaism a Rabbi is a religious 'teacher', or more literally a 'great one'. The word Rabbi is derived from the Hebrew root word *rav*, which in biblical Hebrew means 'great' or 'distinguished (in knowledge)'. A Rabbi is not a priest as there are no priestly services.

Rosh Hashana 'Head of the year'. The Jewish year begins on Rosh Hashana and the years are counted from the beginning of God's creation of the world. In 2008 this is 5768 years ago.

Sanhedrin Derived from the Greek *synhedrion* for 'council', the Sanhedrin was a Jewish rabbinical court during Hellenistic-Roman times.

Schul German for 'school'; also an Ashkenazi term for synagogues which are meant to be houses of learning as well.

Selicha Forgiveness. A *selicha* is a prayer said before Rosh Hashana and Yom Kippur asking God to forgive sins and evil-doing.

Sephardim (Sepharad) The Sephardim are Jews from the Iberian Peninsula and the south of France, the territories called 'Sepharad'. After the expulsion in 1492 Sephardim moved to the Ottoman Empire, Holland. North Africa and Erez Israel.

Shabbat, Shabbat Hagadol The seventh day of the week on which God commanded mankind to rest. *Shabbat* lasts from Friday night to Saturday night. The Christians moved the day of rest to Sunday to make it different from the Jewish one. *Shabbat hagadol* is the *shabbat* before Pesach (Passover).

Shofar Ram's horn blown shortly before and during Rosh Hashana and on Yom Kippur. The dramatic sound is intended to make people repent and confess their sins.

Shulchan aruch The code of Jewish law attributed to Joseph Karo in 1565, which became authoritative for classical Judaism.

Tahara Ritual cleansing of corpses.

Tallit Shawl worn during prayer. Attached to the four corners are the *zizzit* or fringes. which are taken off if a man is buried in his *tallit*.

Talmud 'Study' or 'Teaching', the encyclopaedic rabbinical work (protocols of discussions) consisting of Mishna and Gemara, the oral law.

Torah The five books of Moses.

Tsedaka Charity. *Tsedaka* is one of the most important commandments a Jew has to follow.

Tzadik (pl. **Tzadikim**) A specially righteous person.

Tzitzit see **Tallit.**

Yeshiva (pl. **Yeshivot**) A Jewish institution for study of the Torah and Talmud. *Yeshivot* are usually Orthodox Jewish institutions, generally catering for boys or men.

Endnotes

Two thousand years of 'Houses of Life' in Europe
Understanding Jewish Cemeteries

1. Pirke De-Rabbi Eli'ezer (Talmudic writing) xxi; cit. from: *Jewish Encyclopedia*. (New York – London 1911, Vol. III), p. 432.

2. See: Künzl, Hannelore: *Jüdische Grabkunst. Von der Antike bis heute* (Darmstadt 1999).

3. Goldberg, Sylvie-Anne: *Crossing the Jabbok* (Berkeley, Los Angeles, London 1996), p. 12.

4. Ibid. p.13.

5. Hüttenmeister, Nathanja; Müller, Christine E.: Umstrittene Räume: *Jüdische Friedhöfe in Berlin* (Berlin 2005), p. 170f.

6. Ibid. p. 173.

7. Ibid.

8. Parik, Arno; Hamackova, Vlastimila; Cabanova, Dana; Kliment, Petr: *Prager Jüdische Friedhöfe* (Prague 2003). p. 15.

Introduction/Beth Shea'rim and the Cemeteries of the Roman Period

1. Künzl, Hannelore: *Jüdische Grabkunst. Von der Antike bis heute.* (Darmstadt 1999). p. 30f.

2. Goldenberg p.25.

3. Geller, Ruth Liliana: *Jewish Rome,* (Rome 1984), p.34.

4. Rutgers, L. V.: *Subterranean Rome. In search of the Roots of Christianity in the Catacombs of the Eternal City* (Leuven 2000), p. 58. He seems to ignore this Jewish background and even takes the Jewish catacomb of Vigna Randanini as an example of a catacomb with 'early Christian wall paintings' (p. 71).

5. *Jewish Encyclopedia,* Vol. III, (New York-London 1902), p. 614.

6. Künzl, Ibid.. p. 45.

Rome/Catacombs of the Vigna Randanini on the Via Appia

1. Toynbee: J. M. C.: *Death and Burial in the Roman World* (London 1971), p. 54.

2. Künzl, Hannelore: *Jüdische Grabkunst. Von der Antike bis heute* (Darmstadt 1999), p. 47.

3. Toynbee, Ibid.. p. 57.

Introduction/The Cemeteries of the Middle Ages

1. Künzl, Hannelore: *Jüdische Grabkunst. Von der Antike bis heute* (Darmstadt 1999), p. 64.

2. Sylvie-Anne, Goldberg: *Crossing the Jabbok,* p.25.

3. There are also isolated Christian cemeteries to be found outside the city walls. These were primarily established as a result of plague epidemics, however. Later, the reformer Martin Luther, also advocated the building of cemeteries outside residential areas.

Rome/Cemeteries of Trastevere

1. *Encyclopaedia Judaica* (Jerusalem 1971), Vol. 14, p. 246.

2. Künzl, Ibid. p. 46 and 64f.

3. Geller, Ruth Liliana: Jewish Rome, Rome 1984, p.34. (Note 4), p. 34.

4. Vogelstein, Hermann; Rieger, Paul: *Die Geschichte der Juden in Rom* (Berlin 1896) 2 Vols. Vol. 1, p. 302f.

5. Migliau, Bice; Procaccia, Micaela et al.: *Lazio Jewish itineraries* (Venice 1997), p. 133.

Worms / 'Holy Sands'

1. Künzl. Ibid.p. 77.

2. Information courtesy of Ulrich Knufinke.

Mainz/Cemetery as Monument

1. Vest, Bernd A.: *Der alte jüdische Friedhof in Mainz* (Mainz 2000), p. 12.

2. Rapp, Eugen Ludwig: *Chronik der Mainzer Juden* (Mainz 1977).

Frankfurt am Main/New Egypt

1. Hermann, Heidrun: *Zur Geschichte des alten jüdischen Friedhofs in Frankfurt am Main.* In: Brocke, Michael: *Der alte jüdische Friedhof zu Frankfurt am Main* (Sigmaringen 1996).

2. Ibid. p. 20.

3. Ibid. p. 23.

4. Lenarz, Michael: *Der alte jüdische Friedhof zu Frankfurt am Main* (Frankfurt am Main 1996), p. 17.

London/A Cemetery for a Country

1. See: Honeybourne, Marjorie B.: *The Pre-Expulsion Cemetery of the Jews of London.* In: *Transactions of the Jewish Historical Society of England.* Volume 20 (Sessions 1959–61). (London 1964), p. 145–59.

2. Roth, Cecil: *A history of the Jews in England* (Oxford 1964), p. 117.

3. Acta sanctorum (Brussels 1853), cit. from: Roth, Cecil: *A history of the Jews in England* (Oxford 1964), p. 13.

4. Lilley, Jane M.; Stroud, G.; et al.: *The Jewish burial ground at Jewbury, The Jewish cemeteries: The archaeology of York 12/3:* (York: The Council of British Archaeology).

5. Grimes, W. F.: *The excavation of Roman and Medieval London* (London 1968), p. 181.

6. Honeybourne, l.c., p. 151.

York/Jewbury: Excavating a Medieval Site

1. Lilley, J. M.; Stroud, G. et al. *The Jewish Burial Ground at Jewbury. The Archaeology of York,* Vol. 12/3, (York 1994), p. 304.

2. Ibid. p. 333. Ibid. p. 151

3. Ibid. p. 341.

Prague/Ghetto Archive in Stone

1. Cit. from: Vilímková, Milada: *Die Prager Judenstadt* (Brno 1990), p. 143.

2. Contemporary source cit. from: Parik, Arno; Hamáckovà, Vlastimila; Cabanová, Dana; Kliment, Petr: *Prague Jewish cemeteries* (Prague 2003), p. 23.

3. Ibid.

4. Ibid.

5. Interestingly, the pogrom is also mentioned in a Christian publication called the *Passio Judaeorum Pragensium secundum Joannem rusticum quadratum* (*Jewish Encyclopedia*).

Sepharad/Cemeteries of Spain and Portugal before the Expulsion

1. *Remembering Sepharad. Jewish Culture in Medieval Spain* (Washington 2003), p. 21.

2. Ibid.p. 22.

3. Ibid.

4. Casanovas, J.: *Nuevas aportaciones . In: Memoria de Sefarad* (Madrid 2002), p. 163.

5. *Remembering Sepharad. Jewish Culture in Medieval Spain* (Washington 2003), p. 108.

6. Ibid.p. 110.

7. Heinen, Eugen: *Sephardische Spuren.* 2 Vols, Vol. II, p. 50.

8. Casanovas, J.: *Nuevas aportaciones . In: Memoria de Sefarad.* (Madrid 2002), p. 163.

9. Trupin, Reevan: *Steine statt Juden.* In: *Jüdische Allgemeine,* 03/07, p. 6.

10. Heinen, Eugen: *Sephardische Spuren.* Vol. 1-2, Vol. II, p. 51.

Venice/Cemetery in the Lagoon

1. Census of 1290

2. An outstanding history of the Jewish cemetery in Venice appeared in 2000: *La Comunita Ebraica di Venezia e il suo Antico Cimitero* (Milano 2000) 2 Vols.

3. Curiel, Roberta & Coopermans, Bernard: *The Ghetto of Venice* (London 1990), p. 155.

Amsterdam/Sephardic Cemetery on the Amstel

1. Nadler, Steven: *Rembrandt's Jews* (Chicago – London 2003), p. 191.

2. Ibid. Note 2, p. 207.

3. Künzl, Hannelore: *Jüdische Grabkunst. Von der Antike bis heute* (Darmstadt 1999), p. 94.

London/East End: the First English Cemetery Since 1290

1. Hyamson, Albert M.: *The Sephardim of England.* (London 1951).

2. Ibid.

3. Laski, Neville: *The Laws and Charities of the Spanish and Portuguese Jews Congregation of London.* (London 1952), p. 47.

4. Holmes, Basil: *The London Burial Grounds.* (London 1916), p. 159f.

Istanbul/Hasköy: Cemetery from the Ottoman Empire

1. *Jewish Encyclopaedia.* (New York – London 1915). Vol. IV, p. 238.

2. Barnai, J.: *On the History of the Jews in the Ottoman Empire* in E. Juhasz (ed.) *Sephardi Jew in the Ottoman Empire: aspects of material culture* (Jerusalem 1990), p. 22.

3. Karmi, Ilan: *Jewish sites of Istanbul* (Istanbul 1992). p. 56f.

4. Karmi, Ilan, *Jewish sites of Istanbul* (Istanbul 1992), p. 57

5. Göncüoglu, Süleyman Frauk: *Tarihte Haskoy* (Istanbul, 2005).

6. Karmi, Ilan, Ibid (note 34) p. 134.

7. Rozen, Minna: *A history of the Jewish community in Istanbul. The formative years 1453–1566.* (Leiden – Boston, 2002), p. 5f.

8. Rozen, Minna, Ibid p.59.

9. Rozen, Minna, *Hasköy cemetery. Typology of stones.* (Tel Aviv 1994), Part I, p. 8.

10. Rozen, Ibid.p. 48.

11. Rozen, Ibid.p. 48.

12. Rozen, Ibid.p. 48.

13. Rozen, Ibid.Part II.

14. Rozen, Ibid.Part I, p. 22.

15. Rozen, Ibid.p. 26.

16. Rozen, Ibid.p. 27.

17. Rozen, Ibid.p. 56.

18. Rozen, Ibid.p. 45.

Berlin/Grosse Hamburger Strasse: Mendelssohn's Cemetery

1. Hüttenmeister, Nathanja; Müller, E. Christine: Umstrittene Räume: *Jüdische Friedhöfe in Berlin.* (Berlin 2005), p. 99.

2. Ibid. p. 93.

3. Statutes of the *Cherra Kaddisha,* cit. from: Note. 1, p. 100.

4. Designed by the firm of Dr Jacobs & Hübinger, Berlin.

Fürth/Cemetery of Franconia's Jerusalem

1. Ohm, Barbara: *Ein ,guter Ort'. Der Alte jüdische Friedhof.* In: *Kleeblatt und Davidstern.* Ed. Von

Heymann, Werner (Fürth 1990), p. 20f.

2. Ibid. p. 22.

3. Ibid. p. 38

4. *Nachricht von der Judengemeinde in dem Hofmarkt Fürth. Teil I und II.* Frankfurt und Prag 1754, p. 38.

Endingen and Lengnau/Island and Hill

1. Grünberg, Florence: *Der Friedhof auf der Judeninsel im Rhein bei Koblenz* (Zürich 1956), p. 4.

2. Ibid. p. 6.

3. Ibid. p. 16.

Cracow/Kazimierz: Cemetery of the Jewish City

1. Duda, Eugeniusz: *Krakowska judaica* (Warszawa 1991), p. 61.

Rome/Under Papal Rule: Cemeteries on the Aventine

1. Migliau, Bice; Procaccia, Micaela et al.: *Lazio Jewish itineraries* (Venice 1997), p. 129.

2. Vogelstein, Hermann; Rieger, Paul: *Die Geschichte der Juden in Rom* (Berlin 1896), 2 Vols, Vol. 2, p. 297f.

3. Bosio, Antonio: *Roma sotteranea.* (Rome 1632) (Reprint 1998). Also by the same author: *Roma subterranea novissima.* (Rome 1651).

4. Migliau, Bice; Procaccia, Micaela et al.: *Lazio Jewish itineraries* (Venice 1997), p. 133.

Introduction/Cemeteries from 1800 to 1945

1. *'O ewich is so lanck'. Die historischen Friedhöfe in Berlin-Kreuzberg.* Christoph Fischer and Renate Stein (Eds.) (Berlin 1987), p. 129.

2. *'Plan zu einer (–) allhier zu errichtenden Leichen– und Rettungs-Anstalt',* (Berlin 1798). National and State Library of Jerusalem Sign. p 63 B 3986. Courtesy of Sebastian Panwitz, Berlin.

3. Information courtesy of Ulrich Knufinke.

4. Knufinke, Ulrich: *Jewish cemeteries in 19th century Germany: between tradition and assimilation* (Unpublished lecture), 2006.

Paris/Père-Lachaise: First Site in the Age of Emancipation

1. Charlet, Christian: *Le Père-Lachaise* (Paris 2003), p. 28.

2. Action Artistique de la Ville de Paris: *Le Père-Lachaise* (Paris 1998), p. 80.

3. Ibid.

Berlin/Schönhauser Allee: a Step Beyond Tradition

1. Information courtesy of Ulrich Knufinke.

2. The exception is the western side towards the Schönhauser Allee, between the cemetery's north-west corner and the present-day main entrance. Here was where the areas known as the 'gardens' had originally been located either side of the former main entrance and, after the main entrance was moved, no family plots were created along the cemetery wall, nor was the circumferential path continued.

Berlin/Weissensee: the Wilhelminian Necropolis

1. Quoted in: Baerwald, Alexander: *Der Friedhof in Weissensee.* In: *Allgemeine Zeitung des Judentums, 1912,* p. 334f.

2. R. Löwenfeld (1893), quoted in: Kinkenberg, Hans Martin: *Zwischen Liberalismus und Nationalismus.* In: *Monumenta Judaica – 2000 Jahre Geschichte und Kultur der Juden am Rhein* (Cologne 1964), p. 322.

Meinsdorf/Prussian Village Cemetery

1. Brandenburg Main Land Archive (BLHA), Pr. Br. Rep. 37 Bärwalde-Wiepersdorf No. 206, cit. from: Langfeldt, Gisela: *Ein jüdischer Kaufmann im Ländlichen Bärwalde.* In: *Mitteilungsblatt der Landesgeschichtlichen Vereinigung für die Mark Brandenburg,* Vol. 105., No.2, May 2004, p.29–38, here p. 30.

2. Ibid. p. 37.

3. Ibid.

Prague/Zizkov: New Cemetery after the Ghetto

1. Parik, Arno; Hamackova, Vlastimila; Cabanova, Dana; Kliment, Petr: *Prague Jewish cemeteries* (Prague 2003).

Budapest/Cemeteries for a New Metropolis

1. *Jüdisches Städtebild Budapest.* Ed. by Peter Haber (Frankfurt am Main 1999), p 11.

2. Lajos Hock, 1904, quoted from: *Jewish Budapest. Monuments, Rites and History* (Budapest 1995), p. 472.

3. *Jewish Budapest,* ed. by: Géza Komoróczy (Budapest 2003), p. 472.

4. Ibid. p. 472.

5. Ibid. p.440

St Petersburg/Moorish-style Cemetery on the Neva

1. Beizer, Mikhail: *The Jews of St. Petersburg,* ed. Martin Gilbert (Philadelphia – London 1989), p. 26.

2. Ibid. p. 175.

Shtetl/Cemeteries of a Lost World

1. Samuel, M.: *The World of Sholem Aleichem* (New York 1943), p. 26.

2. Eliach, Yaffa: *There once was a world. A 900-Year chronicle of the Schtetl of Eishyshok* (Boston, New York, London 1998), p. 230.

3. Ibid.

4. Pessia Moszczenik Skir: *Zikhronot 1910–80.* Cit. from: Eliach, Yaffa: *There once was a world.* p. 242.

5. Wilkanski. Ba-Heder S. 112-13. Cit. from: Eliach, Yaffa: *There once was a world.* p. 239.

6. Harshav, Benjamin: *Marc Chagall and the lost Jewish world* (New York 2006), p. 140.

7. Eliach, Yaffa (1998), p. 233.

8. Ibid., p. 233.

9. Ibid. p. 247

Rome/Campo Verano: from the Aventine to the Pincetto

1. Lazio Jewish Itineraries. *Places, history and art* (Venice 1997), p. 94.

2. Ibid., p. 151.

London/Willesden: Cemetery of Victorian High Society

1. *The Builder* Vol. 31 (1873), p. 832.

2. Ibid.

3. Kadish, Sharman: *Jewish Heritage in England. An architectural guide* (Swindon 2006), p. 50f.

4. H. Meller: *London Cemeteries – an illustrated guide and gazetteer* (Aldershot 1994), p. 184.

Kaliningrad/Erich Mendelsohn's Modernism for Königsberg

1. *Königsberger Hartungsche Zeitung,* 29 September 1929.

2. *Königsberger Allgemeine Zeitung,* 30 September 1929.

3. *Königsberger Hartungsche Zeitung,* 29 September 1929.

4. Ibid.

5. Ibid.

6. *Erich Mendelsohn 1887–1953 Ideen, Bauten, Projekte.* Berlin 1987, p. 75f.

Salonica/A Cemetery for the Few

1. Lewkowicz, Bea: *The Jewish Community of Salonika. History, Memory, Identity* (London — Portland 2006). p. 135.

2. Arouh, Alberto: *Borrekitas de Merendjena and the quest for identity.* In: *Cultural Forum of the Jewish Community of Thessaloniki.* (Saloniki, n.d.), p. 75. Also on the history of Salonika's Jews: Mazower, Mark: *Salonica – City of Ghosts (*London 2004).

3. Salem, Stella: *The Old Jewish Cemetery of Thessaloniki.* In: *Cultural Forum of the Jewish Community of Thessaloniki* (Saloniki, n.d.), p. 55

4. Lewkowicz, Bea: *The Jewish Community of Salonika. History, Memory, Identity* (London — Portland 2006). p. 198.

5. Ibid.

6. Cultural Forum of the Jewish Community of Thessaloniki. (Saloniki, n.d.), p. 7.

Berlin/A Cemetery for a Divided Community

1. Designed by the firm of Dr Jacobs & Hübinger, Berlin.

Selected Bibliography

Action Artistique de la Ville de Paris: *Le Père-Lachaise.* (Paris 1998).

Barnai, Jacob: *On the history of the Jews in The Ottoman Empire.* In: *Sephardi Jews in The Ottoman.Empire. Aspects of Material Culture.* Ed. By Esther Juhasz. (Jerusalem 1990).

Beizer, Mikhail: *The Jews of St. Petersburg* (edited by Martin Gilbert). (Philadelphia – London 1989).

Bosio, Antonio: *Roma sotteranea,* (Rome 1632) (Reprint 1998).

Brocke, Michael: *Der alte jüdische Friedhof zu Frankfurt am Main.* (Sigmaringen 1996).

Brocke, Michael; Hüttenmeister, Christiane E.: *Haus des Lebens. Jüdische Friedhöfe in Deutschland.* (Leipzig 2001).

Casanovas, J.: *Nuevas aportaciones.* In: *Memoria de Sefarad.* (Madrid 2002).

Charlet, Christian: *Le Père-Lachaise.* (Paris 2003).

Curiel, Roberta & Coopermans, Bernard: *The Ghetto of Venice.* (London 1990).

Duda, Eugeniusz: *Krakowska judaica.* (Warszawa 1991).

Eliach, Yaffa: *There once was a world. A 900-Year chronicle of the Schtetl of Eishyshok.* (Boston, New York, London 1998).

'O ewich is so lanck'. Die historischen Friedhöfe in Berlin-Kreuzberg. Christoph Fischer and Renate Stein (Eds.). (Berlin 1987).

Geller, Ruth Liliana: *Jewish Rome.* (Rome 1984).

Goldberg, Sylvie-Anne: *Crossing the Jabbok.* (Berkeley, Los Angeles, London 1996).

Göncüoglu, Süleyman Faruk: *Tarihte Hasköy.* (Istanbul 2005).

Goodenough, Erwin R.: *Jewish symbols in the Greco-Roman Period.* Vol.3. (New York 1953).

Grimes, W. F.: *The excavation of Roman and Medieval London.* (London 1968).

Grünberg, Florence: *Der Friedhof auf der Judeninsel im Rhein bei Koblenz.* (Zürich 1956).

Jüdisches Städtebild Budapest. Ed. by Peter Haber. (Frankfurt am Main 1999).

Harshav, Benjamin: *Marc Chagall and the lost Jewish world.* (New York 2006).

Hermann, Heidrun: *Zur Geschichte des alten jüdischen Friedhofs in Frankfurt am Main.* In: Hüttenmeister, Nathanja; Müller, Christine E.: *Umstrittene Räume: Jüdische Friedhöfe in Berlin.* (Berlin 2005).

Heinen, Eugen: *Sephardische Spuren.* Vol. 1-2, Vol. II, p. 50.

Holmes, Basil: *The London Burial Grounds.* (London 1916).

Honeybourne, Marjorie B.: *The Pre-Expulsion Cemetery of the Jews of London.* In: *Transactions The Jewish Historical Society of England.* Volume 20 (Sessions 1959–61), London 1964.

Hüttenmeister, Nathanja; Müller, Christine E.: *Umstrittene Räume: Jüdische Friedhöfe in Berlin.* (Berlin 2005).

Hyamson, Albert M.: *The Sephardim of England.* (London 1951).

Jewish Encyclopedia. (New York – London 1911).

Kadish, Sharman: *Jewish Heritage in England. An architectural guide.* (Swindon 2006).

Karmi, Ilan: *Jewish sites of Istanbul.* (Istanbul 1992).

Kinkenberg, Hans Martin: *Zwischen Liberalismus und Nationalismus.* In: *Monumenta Judaica – 2000 Jahre Geschichte und Kultur der Juden am Rhein.* (Cologne 1964).

Knufinke, Ulrich: *Jewish cemeteries in 19th century Germany: between tradition and assimilation.* (Unpublished lecture, 2006).

Jewish Budapest. Ed. by: Géza Komoróczy. (Budapest 2003).

Künzl, Hannelore: *Jüdische Grabkunst. Von der Antike bis heute.* (Darmstadt 1999).

Lameira, Francisco: *Faro a arte na história da cidade.* (Faro 1999).

Langfeldt, Gisela: *Ein jüdischer Kaufmann im Ländlichen Bärwalde.* In: *Mitteilungsblatt der Landesgeschichtlichen Vereinigung für die Mark Brandenburg.* Vol. 105., No.2, May 2004.

Lenarz, Michael: *Der alte jüdische Friedhof zu Frankfurt am Main.* (Frankfurt am Main 1996).

Lewkowicz, Bea: *The Jewish Community of Salonika. History, Memory, Identity.* (London-Portland 2006).

Lilley, Jane M.;Stroud, G.; et al. : *The Jewish burial ground at Jewbury, The Jewish cemeteries: The archaeology of York* 12/3; York: The Council of British Archaeology.

Mazower, Mark: *Salonica – City of Ghosts.* (London 2004).

Meller, Hugh: *London Cemeteries – An illustrated guide and gazetteer.* (Aldershot 1994).

Erich Mendelsohn 1887–1953 Ideen, Bauten, Projekte. (Berlin 1987).

Migliau, Bice; Procaccia, Micaela et al.: *Lazio Jewish itineraries.* (Venice 1997).

Nachama, Andreas; Simon, Hermann: *Jüdische Grabstätten und Friedhöfe in Berlin.* (Berlin 1992).

Nachricht von der Judengemeinde in dem Hofmarkt Fürth. Teil I und II. (Frankfurt and Prague 1754)

Nadler, Steven: *Rembrandt's Jews.* (Chicago–London 2003).

Ohm, Barbara: *Ein ‚guter Ort'. Der Alte jüdische Friedhof.* In: *Kleeblatt und Davidstern.* Ed. Von Heymann, Werner. (Fürth 1990).

Panwitz, Sebastian: *Die Gesellschaft der Freunde.1792–1935. Berliner Juden zwischen Aufklärung und Hochfinanz.* (Hildesheim-Zürich-New York 2007).

Parik, Arno: *Prague Ghetto.Prague.* (Prague 2006).

Parik, Arno; Hamackova, Vlastimila; Cabanova, Dana; Kliment, Petr: *Prager Jüdische Friedhöfe.* (Prague 2003).

Rapp, Eugen Ludwig: *Chronik der Mainzer Juden.* (Mainz 1977).

Roth, Cecil: *A history of the Jews in England.* (Oxford 1964).

Rutgers, L. V.: *Subterranean Rome. In search of the Roots of Christianity in the Catacombs of the Eternal City.* (Leuven 2000).

Rozen, Minna: *A history of the Jewish community in Istanbul. The formative years 1453–1566.* (Leiden–Boston, 2002).

Rozen, Minna: *Hasköy cemetery. Typology of stones.* (Tel Aviv 1994).

Samuel, M.: *The World of Sholem Aleichem.* (New York 1943).

Schürer, E.: *Geschichte des Jüdischen Volkes im Zeitalter Jesu.* III. 1-70.

Remembering Sefarad. Jewish Culture in Medieval Spain. (Washington 2003).

Cultural Forum of the Jewish Community of Thessaloniki. Saloniki, no year stated.

Torah, Genesis, (Five Books of Moses)

Toynbee; J. M. C.: *Death and Burial in the Roman World.* (London 1971).

Trupin, Reevan: *Steine statt Juden.* In: *Jüdische Allgemeine,* 03/07, p. 6.

Vega, L. A.: *Het Beth Haim van Ouderkerk.* (Ouderkerk 1994).

La Comunita Ebreica di Venezia e il suo Antico Cimitero. 2. Volume. (Milano 2000).

Vest, Bernd A.: *Der alte jüdische Friedhof in Mainz.* (Mainz 2000). p. 12.

Vogelstein, Hermann; Rieger, Paul: *Die Geschichte der Juden in Rom.* 2 Bde. (Berlin 1896).

Acknowledgements

It has been a great pleasure to work with principal photographer Hans D. Beyer. Many thanks to the Howard Greenberg Gallery, New York, for letting me use the photograph by Frederic Brenner and to the Galicia Museum, Krakow, for the photographs by the late Chris Schwarz.

The poem by Nelly Sachs in chapter 39 is taken from *Holocaust Poetry,* compiled by Hilda Schiff (Fount, London 1995)

Thanks also to Dr. Ulrich Knufinke, Braunschweig, for proof reading and much information and Roddy Tannahill and Eric Meirs .

I thank Tim Cawkwell for his thoughtful and thorough editing.

The following institutions and people have been extremely helpful both in my text and picture research: Jüdische Gemeinde zu Berlin: Rabbiner Dr. Chaim Z. Rozwaski, Beate Musiol, Andreas Greszus, Hendrik Kosche **Jüdische Gemeinde Frankfurt am Main:** Stefan Szajak, Direktor **Jüdische Gemeinde Mainz:** Janusz Kuroszczyk **Jüdisches Museum Franken – Fürth & Schnaittach:** Michaela Fröhlich **Museum Stadt Königsberg, Duisburg:** Lorenz Grimoni **Stiftung Denkmal für die ermordeten Juden Europas, Berlin:** Uwe Neumärker **Historisches Museum der Pfalz:** Dr Werner Transier **Institut für Geschichtliche Landeskunde an der Universität Mainz** Dr Hedwig Brüchert **Spanish and Portuguese Jews' Congregation & Bevis Marks Synagogue, London:** Maurice Bitton **United Synagogue, London:** Charles Tucker **Jewish Community, Istanbul, Quincentennial Foundation – Jewish Museum of Turkey:** Naim Güleryüz, Vice President **Jewish community, Thessaloniki:** Alberto Yomtov **Jewish Museum of Thessaloniki:** Erika Perahia Zemour **Museu Nacional d'Art de Catalunya:** Jordi Casanovas **Jewish Museum, Prague:** Martin Jelinek **Gan Hasjalom, Amsterdam:** Kaki Markus **Stichting Tot Instandhouding En Onderhoud Van Historische Joods Begraafplaatsen In Nederland:** D. Brown **Jewish Heritage UK:** Dr. Sharman Kadish, Director **Congregation Temple Emanuel of the City of New York:** Elka Deitsch **Galicia Jewish Museum:** Ishbel Szatrawska **Jewish cemetery Faro:** Ralf Pinto

Thanks also to: Rabbiner Prof Dr Andreas Nachama, Berlin; Laszlo Pasztor, Budapest and Berlin; Dr Sebastian Panwitz, Berlin; Salma Sieradzki, Custos Jüdischer Friedhof Mainz; Jessica de Grazia, London and Southwold; Paris Papamichos Chronakis, Thessaloniki; Dr Jeremy Schonfield, London; Jaap Walvisch, Haarlem; Catherine Phillips, St Petersburg; Yuri Molodkovets, St Petersburg; Roland Zumbühl, Arlesheim; Prof Gérard Nahon, St Denis.

Index

Picture Credits

Frances Lincoln Limited
4 Torriano Mews
Torriano Avenue
London NW5 2RZ
www.franceslincoln.com

Houses of Life - Jewish Cemeteries of Europe
Copyright © Frances Lincoln Limited 2007
Text copyright © Joachim Jacobs

First Frances Lincoln edition: 2008

British Library Cataloguing in Publication Data. A
catalogue record for this book is available from the British
Library

ISBN: 978-0-7112-2648-7

Printed in China

9 8 7 6 5 4 3 2 1

Title page: The old cemetery in Prague; in the foreground,
the lion from the tombstone of Hendl Barschewi (d. 1628),
the wife of the first Jew ever to be knighted in the
Habsburg Empire.

Introduction opener: *The cemetery*. Oil painting by Marc
Chagall, 1917

This book is for Ian Collins

I want to thank Judy Novak for her loving support and
constant help. Without her, this project could never
have been completed.

Special thanks to Anne Fraser. Our chance meeting
and her wonderful enthusiasm brought *Houses of Life*
to Frances Lincoln.

I am honoured that Robert M. Morgenthau wrote the
foreword to this book.